The WOMAN
WHO WAS
CHESTERTON

The Life of Frances Chesterton,
Wife of English Author G.K. Chesterton

The WOMAN WHO WAS CHESTERTON

The Life of Frances Chesterton,
Wife of English Author G.K. Chesterton

NANCY CARPENTIER BROWN

FOREWORD BY DALE AHLQUIST

ACS BOOKS

Cover Photograph, Frances Blogg,
Courtesy Lilly Library
Indiana University
Bloomington, Indiana

Cover design by Richard Aleman

Cataloging-in-Publication data on file with the Library of Congress.

ISBN 978-1-50510-478-3

ACS Books is an imprint of TAN Books
PO Box 410487
Charlotte, NC 28241
www.TANBooks.com

Printed and bound in the United States of America.

Many who knew her, thought it a pity that so substantive and rare a creature should have been absorbed into the life of another, and be only known in a certain circle as a wife. . . . But the effect of her being on those around her was incalculably diffusive: for the growing good of the world is partly dependent on unhistoric acts; and that things are not so ill with you and me as they might have been, is half owing to the number who lived faithfully a hidden life, and rest in unvisited tombs.

—George Eliot, *Middlemarch*

DEDICATION

To
Mike, Sarah and Robin
and
Barbara Ann & +Kenneth James Carpentier

ACKNOWLEDGEMENTS

Peter J. Floriani, Ph.D., must be thanked first and foremost: he was helpful in all ways on this and many other projects. From research to proofreading, to cheerleading and praying, Peter was involved from start to finish. *Ora et labora.*

I gratefully thank Dale Ahlquist, president of the American Chesterton Society. Over the years, Dale has sent me articles, pictures, papers, and copies of whatever materials I asked for and some I did not know I wanted. His unwavering support for this project has often times kept me going. Thank you for putting up with me, Mr. President.

Thanks as well to: John Peterson, Denis Conlon, Aidan Mackey, Julia Smith, Ann Farmer, Geir Hasnes, Martin Thompson, +Stratford Caldecott, Therese Warmus, Canon John Udris; the librarians at my own library—the Antioch Public Library District; Laura Schmidt, Heidi Truty and the archivists at the Marion E. Wade Center at Wheaton College. Thanks to Carole Gale, part-time librarian at Brooklands College, Surrey, and Duncan Amos, genealogist and historian extraordinaire, of Oatlands Heritage Group, who got sucked into the Blogg family genealogy, all because Frances and Ethel once spent a half-holiday at a home in Oatlands. Thanks to Kevin O'Brien for advice. Thanks to Hannah Korman, intern at the American Chesterton Society for finding the *New Witness* material. Thanks, Rose Korman, Dale Ahlquist, Peter Floriani, Sibyl Niemann and especially Eleanor Nicholson for editing. Thanks to Cameron Duder, Ben Klassen, Felicia de la Perra, Rudi Traichel, and Jacky Lai at the University of British Columbia. Thanks to Hilary Davies at the City of Westminster. Thanks to Rhonda Spencer, David Frasier, Zach Downey, and especially Nathaniel J. Pockras at the

Lilly Library. Thanks to Elizabeth Broekmann at the Notting Hill & Ealing High School. Thanks to Veronica Colin at St. Stephen's College. Thanks to Ann D. Gordon, Editor, Papers of E. C. Stanton & S. B. Anthony, for the George Blogg business card. Thanks to Ann Swabey, military researcher. Thanks to Justine Sundaram and the staff at the Burns Library at Boston College. Thanks to Danielle Robichaud at the Kelly Library at the University of St. Michael's College in Toronto. Thanks to Moira Fitzgerald, Kathryn James, and Diane Ducharme at the Beinecke Rare Book and Manuscript Library at Yale.

I owe a debt of eternal gratitude to the family of Frances Chesterton, her grand-nephews who shared their intimate family memories and photographs with me so generously.

Thanks to Jeremy Oldershaw, grandchild of Lucian and Ethel (Blogg) Oldershaw. Jeremy is the son of Basil Oldershaw, the middle son of Lucian and Ethel.

Thanks to Francis (Frank) Guinness. Francis is the younger son of Catherine Oldershaw Guinness; grandson of Ethel and Lucian Oldershaw, and was named after Frances Chesterton, as his mother planned on him being a girl. Thanks to his brother Geoffrey Guinness, too, the older son of Catherine (Kate) Guinness.

Thanks to Giles, Bob, and Walter Oldershaw, grandsons of Ethel and Lucian Oldershaw. They are the sons of Peter Oldershaw, eldest son of Ethel and Lucian.

Thanks to Nicholas Sheridan Barnett, great-grandnephew of Ada Eliza "Keith" Jones Chesterton, a.k.a., John Keith Prothero.

Thank you to some additional research assistants: Nancy Piccione, Su Morton, Christina Amari, and Marie-Therese Curtin.

Thanks to my Kickstarter team: Debbie Lillig, David Zach, Robin Brown, Tim Canny, Julia Fogassy, Bradley Harvey, Eric Townsend, Home School Connections, Leo Schwartz, Bob Cook, Skyler Neberman, Christopher Ouelette, John Gamble; and those Kickstarter angels who wished to remain anonymous, Emily, John, and Richard. And the Post-Kickstarter: Mary-Eileen Swart. Thanks for believing in this project.

I have no doubt that my trusting prayers to Gilbert, Frances, and Frank and Ann Petta, along with a whole host of the communion of saints also had something to do with the writing of this book.

Although many people helped me with this book, any errors are mine alone. I have tried to be accurate to the best of current knowledge of what is known about Frances Chesterton. I have no doubt more information will be revealed in the future, and will be added to this story.

N.B. Although during her life, Frances's sister-in-law Ada Eliza Jones Chesterton preferred her *nom de plume* John Keith Prothero and insisted that her friends call her "Keith," it is too confusing to use the name Keith when Gilbert's middle name was also Keith. Therefore, for consistency and clarity, she is referred to as Ada in this book.

"This vivid and splendidly researched study of Frances has long been needed, but it is also of major importance for the light it throws on her grateful husband in the warm domestic setting which significantly extended his life."

—AIDAN MACKEY, *Senior Fellow,*
Chesterton Library, Oxford

"A rich and meticulously researched account of the most significant influence in G.K.'s life. Insights abound and important clues uncovered in this warm, compelling portrait of a great woman. Nancy Brown's painstaking detective work is well-deserving of her Chestertonian name!"

—CANON JOHN UDRIS, *Former pastor*
of G.K. Chesterton's home parish,
and investigator of his possible
Cause for Canonisation.

"It is said that behind every great man there is a great woman. G.K. Chesterton alluded to this in his description of William Cobbett's wife as the 'powerful silence' in her husband's life. Admirers of Chesterton have always known that his own wife was a potent presence in his life and it has been a cause of frustration that relatively little is known of her. It is, therefore, a great gift to the world of Chesterton scholarship that Nancy Carpentier Brown has broken the silence in this meticulously researched and wonderfully informative biography of Frances Chesterton, the 'other Chesterton' without whom we would not have the Gilbert whom we know and love."

—JOSEPH PEARCE, *Author of Wisdom and*
Innocence: A Life of G.K. Chesterton

"Nancy Brown has shown us the great woman who was Chesterton, and she is someone you'll find yourself both delighted and intrigued by. Brown introduces us to a woman who's amazing in her own right, but who also played a large part in who G.K. Chesterton was. Thank you, Nancy, for a life well researched. Frances is someone I'm glad to know now!"

—SARAH REINHARD, *Author and blogger,*
SnoringScholar.com, Patheos.com

"This book shows more than anyone before it that Frances didn't happen upon Gilbert by chance and that his story would have been quite different without her."

—GEIR HASNES,
G.K. Chesterton's bibliographer

With *The Woman Who Was Chesterton*, biographer Nancy Brown offers us a compelling new consideration of one of the key ingredients in the genius of G.K. Chesterton: his wife, Frances. A true talent and a steadfast support, Frances—as introduced by Brown—deserves to be known, emulated and admired. Whether or not you're a Chesterton fan, this book will capture your attention and leave you inspired!

—LISA M. HENDEY, *Founder of*
CatholicMom.com and
author of The Grace of Yes

"Since G.K. Chesterton was such a large and lumbering figure, it's easy to miss the small, quiet woman hidden behind his success. But Frances Chesterton, like St. Thérèse, was a small giant, a spiritual force who fired Gilbert's engine and balanced his spinning mind. At long last, thanks to Nancy's excellent book, she has been brought to life. Nancy introduces us to a woman every bit as saintly as her renowned husband. Even more, we glimpse their remarkable devotion and love. The story of the Chestertons is fundamentally a romance, a love tale *par excellence*, and it's one we need in a world desperate for holy marriages. If you want to discover the still, silent voice hidden behind the Chestertonian whirlwind, and find a model for ordinary holiness, read this book."

—BRANDON VOGT, *Content Director at Word on Fire Catholic Ministries*

CONTENTS

Dedication . . . . *vii*

Acknowledgments . . . . *ix*

Foreword . . . . *xix*

Introduction . . . . *xxiii*

CHAPTER ONE
The Girl from Bedford Park (1869–1896) 1

CHAPTER TWO
Forging a Partnership in Wonder (1896–1901) 25

CHAPTER THREE
Wedded to a Rising Star (1901–1908) 51

CHAPTER FOUR
Fame and Fortune (1909–1915) 79

CHAPTER FIVE
Poetry and Plays (1915–1922) 105

CHAPTER SIX
Following Faith (1922–1926) 135

CHAPTER SEVEN
Success and Secretaries (1926–1929) 151

CHAPTER EIGHT
The Inn at the End of the World (1929–1936) 167

CHAPTER NINE

After This Our Exile (1936–1938)....................... 197

CHAPTER TEN

The Fate of Mrs. Chesterton (1938 and Beyond)........ 211

Epilogue... 221

Extras 227

Index.. 261

FOREWORD

THE STRANGE MUSIC
By G.K. Chesterton

Other loves may sink and settle, other loves may loose and slack,
But I wander like a minstrel with a harp upon his back,
Though the harp be on my bosom, though I finger and I fret,
Still, my hope is all before me: for I cannot play it yet.

In your strings is hid a music that no hand hath e'er let fall,
In your soul is sealed a pleasure that you have not known at all;
Pleasure subtle as your spirit, strange and slender as your frame,
Fiercer than the pain that folds you, softer than your sorrow's name.

Not as mine, my soul's anointed, not as mine the rude and light
Easy mirth of many faces, swaggering pride of song and fight;
Something stranger, something sweeter, something waiting you afar,
Secret as your stricken senses, magic as your sorrows are.

But on this, God's harp supernal, stretched but to be stricken once,
Hoary time is a beginner, Life a bungler, Death a dunce.
But I will not fear to match them—no, by God, I will not fear,
I will learn you, I will play you and the stars stand still to hear.

This is a love story. But it is also a detective story. And best of all, it is a true story, told here for the first time. Gilbert Keith Chesterton was a romantic, a writer of detective tales, and a teller of the truth. His own story and the stories he told are becoming better and better known. But what has remained unknown is the story of the most important person in his life: his wife Frances. She has been a mystery. In spite of how much we know about him, we know so very little about her. Part of this was by her own design. Although she accompanied him everywhere, she kept herself under his ample shadow and thus out of the limelight. She even asked him to keep her out of his autobiography, a request which Gilbert of course honored, but it must have been a handicap to write his own story and having to leave out half of it, and what he would have insisted without cliché, the better half.

Nancy Brown has done incredible detective work to uncover the mystery of Frances, tracking a figure who managed to leave very few traces of herself. The project grew out of a love for Gilbert that naturally grew into a deep love for Frances. Nancy Brown's sympathy with her subject is not surprising: she is herself the devoted wife of an artist, an artist in her own right, and a woman of quiet and profound faith. But she pursued Frances with an intensity not unlike that of the poet who wrote "The Strange Music," knowing that there was something hidden in Frances, something profoundly beautiful, too strong for the tragedy which seemed to cling to it, too wise for the trends of times, something that once revealed would make even the angels stand still. She set out to answer the question: Who is this woman well-acquainted with sorrow who became the source of G.K. Chesterton's joy?

It is quite likely that as more is discovered about Frances, more biographies will be written of her, and they will be even more complete. But they will all come back to this one as the point of reference. Nancy Brown is to Frances what Maisie Ward was to Gilbert.

This book will be a grave disappointment to those who are looking for dirt or scandal, especially for those who for some reason think that G.K. Chesterton was anything other than a normal husband. This man loved this woman and she loved him. Chastity, which does not mean prudishness or abstinence, still does mean purity. It means, says Chesterton, "something flaming." And in this story we get a glimpse of chastity. But the veil of the private chamber is not lifted too high. Nancy Brown does not write for the merely curious, but nonetheless corrects some sadly and badly misrepresented facts about the Chesterton's marriage that were spun by a disgruntled sister-in-law. Chesterton's lifelong friend, Edmund Clerihew Bentley called their marriage "a perfect companionship." And it was certainly a companionship that was constant in every way.

It is clear that Gilbert's own goodness was augmented by that of Frances. The great thinker's ideas were influenced by her, his endless creativity inspired by her, and his articulate faith spurred by her. He said she was the first Christian he ever met who was happy. And they began a journey together that ended as all great romances should: happily ever after. But there were dragons to fight along the way. That is what always makes the story interesting.

The portrait of G.K. Chesterton has languished unfinished for too long. Nancy Brown makes the very important point early on in this book: Of all the people in the world, Frances knew Gilbert best.

It is time to get to know Frances.

—*Dale Ahlquist*

INTRODUCTION

How Far Is It To Bethlehem?

How far is it to Bethlehem?
Not very far.
Shall we find the stable room
Lit by a star?

Can we see the little Child?
Is He within?
If we lift the wooden latch
May we go in?

May we stroke the creatures there
Ox, ass, or sheep?
May we peep like them and see
Jesus asleep?

If we touch His tiny hand
Will He awake?
Will He know we've come so far
Just for His sake?

Great kings have precious gifts
And we have naught
Little smiles and little tears
Are all we have brought.

For all weary children
Mary must weep
Here, on His bed of straw
Sleep, children, sleep.

God in His mother's arms
Babes in the byre
Sleep, as they sleep who find
Their heart's desire.

"How Far Is It To Bethlehem?" This simple question presents the poignant pleading and restless desire known to every human heart. This is a quiet poem, and one that has enjoyed a notable provenance: originally written in 1917 towards the end of World War One, the author had it printed on her (and her husband's) Christmas card that year. Since its first appearance in the 1928 *Oxford Book of Carols*, this song has experienced an uninterrupted publication and performance history, including reprints, recordings, and videos of choirs singing it in every language and setting.

What is it within the poem that has allowed it to survive? The meter is more correct than innovative; the sentiment is simple; the language is accessible.

It is within the quiet, simple words of the poem that we find our answer. Truly, "we have naught" but "little smiles and little tears" to offer; but in these we find the entirety of a longing heart—a heart that throbs with each recurrence of the question. *How far is it? Shall we . . . ? Can we . . . ? May we . . . ? May we . . . ? May we . . . ? If we . . . ?* We look from ourselves to Another, and the questioning increases in intensity. *Will He . . . ? Will He . . . ?*

The Christ Child at the ending of the poem is the perfect answer, an answer not yet fully attained. Is the "heart's desire" something that truly can be found? In faith, the poet asserts that it can and will be. Here is eschatology encapsulated: we taste, like the imagined dreamer, that which we will only fully discover after death and in union with the Divine. What we hope for, what we long for, is already realized in our aching, unsatisfied hearts.

This near paradox of the poem, which ends with satisfaction imagined but not yet achieved except in dream, is fitting for Frances, the wife of that master of paradox, Gilbert Keith Chesterton.

The longing and hope she asserts in this little Christmas poem is deeply felt, not simply imagined. Her question—*How far is it to Bethlehem?*—seen in the light of her own life, becomes vibrantly real. How far is she from her own desires? How far is she from Heaven? How far is she from the illusive dream—in her case, the dream of maternity? Frances suffered from infertility, longing for babies of her own to hold. But while the medical world could not offer a cure, she consistently saw hope in the Nativity scene, in the Babe in the manger. *How far is it to Bethlehem?* Frances asks herself, and then she answers beautifully, hopefully, and faithfully, "not very far". In fact, it is as close as the manger itself must be to those who approach it.

Frances's life gives us hope. She experienced sorrows and obstacles; she faced family deaths; she watched as her dream of a large family faded, and her writing career was subsumed by the brighter light of her husband. Yet she remained faithful, hopeful, and loving. While not strictly a forerunner of her husband, she served as his sometime John the Baptist, and might have said: "He must increase, but I must decrease." And in her decrease, she flourished in her selfless love. We find in her an example of steadfastness in the midst of chaos, hope in the midst of fears, a life of unselfish service, humility, and joy in the midst of sickness and death. Bethlehem was not far away, because Frances kept Bethlehem close to her heart.

A BIOGRAPHY OF FRANCES CHESTERTON

There are a number of challenges to be faced in writing a biography, and some special challenges for the biography of Frances Chesterton.

The life of Frances is largely shadowed, but not in the way that ghoulish modern theories might desire: the shadow of her larger-than-life husband; the shadow of gossip and rumor in her own day, most of which were rooted in the antipathy of a jealous sister-in-law, Ada; the shadow of a lack of documentary evidence (Frances tragically lacking the narcissistic impulse to chronicle her own life methodically on behalf of future biographers).

This could lead some to imagine her as a cowering wallflower, overwhelmed by an (unintentionally) tyrannical husband, unappreciated, and excluded from the sunshine by her own timidity and the strength of the personalities around her.

This is a mistaken theory; as the evidence that *does* remain to us clearly shows, Frances chose a quiet position in the background of the impressive figure of her husband and of others. Looking carefully, we shall see, in addition to her many other talents, a woman of profound humility. This particular quality illuminates her life, her marriage, and her relationship with God.

Additionally, it is important to note that this is not a biography of G.K. Chesterton. There are at least ten excellent biographies that present to readers the monumental man who is Frances Chesterton's husband. This work assumes the reader has at least some familiarity with such works and the man himself.

Finally, the biographer comes to the task with talents and limitations. In my own case, I make no pretense of being a scholar. I write as a wife and mother; and as a person deeply interested in all of the facets of Frances: as the wife of a genius, a convert, a nurse, a teacher, an advocate for social reform, a lover of babies, a writer, and a poet.

For nearly a century, Frances's story has been hidden amongst the pages of the poetry Gilbert wrote, Christmas cards sent to friends, letters to priests and relatives stored in library special collections, out-of-print biographies written by literary contemporaries, in boxes in the attics and garages of her grandnephews, and in scattered periodicals and books. Few people are now familiar with the details of Frances's own writing career; few have read her published works.

It is, of course, a story intimately woven with the story of Gilbert. This is, after all, a love story. Frances and Gilbert worked as a team; they were lovers and friends, writing coaches and companions. They worked, ate, laughed, and slept together for thirty-five years, dependent on each other physically, emotionally, and intellectually. The love between them defined her life—and his. She was his first and biggest fan; his most successful marketer, and his most devoted cheerleader. She was the first to laugh at his jokes. She took dictation, dusted his hat, and tied his shoes. She clung to him when her life seemed out of control. She cherished the love poetry he wrote her, treasuring the words tenderly in her heart, never sharing the most intimate specimens with anyone. It is not an exaggeration to say that she was the person who would affect Gilbert's life more profoundly than anyone.[1] He was totally dependent on her for his happiness.[2]

---

[1] Joseph Pearce, *Wisdom and Innocence: A Life of G.K. Chesterton* (San Francisco: Ignatius Press, 2013), 31.

[2] John Sullivan, *G.K. Chesterton: A Centenary Appraisal* (San Francisco: Harper & Row, 1974), 160.

Thus, one can hardly understand Gilbert without under-standing Frances. Up until this biography, in fact, acquaintance with Gilbert has been hampered by the lack of knowledge of his wife. This is not just because of neglectful biographers; Frances herself asked Gilbert to keep her out of his autobiography. With due deference to her modest preference for anonymity, I can only observe: she is not here to stop me now.

Beyond all of this, and beyond even the importance of learn-ing more about Gilbert through Frances, I hope that this humble effort will give readers the opportunity to get to know and respect *her*—as herself, and for herself. I am in good company in this: Gilbert himself clearly thought her well worth knowing. My greater hope is that Frances's life will be an inspiration to all of us, married and unmarried, to live a more faithful, hopeful, and humble life in the midst of good times and bad, for richer, for poorer, in sickness and in health.

Chapter One

THE GIRL FROM BEDFORD
PARK (1869–1896)

*T*he Suburb of Saffron Park," wrote Gilbert Keith Chesterton in *The Man Who Was Thursday,* "lay on the sunset side of London, as red and ragged as a cloud of sunset."

It was built of a bright brick throughout; its sky-line was fantastic, and even its ground plan was wild. It had been the outburst of a speculative builder, faintly tinged with art, who called its architecture sometimes Elizabethan and sometimes Queen Anne, apparently under the impression that the two sovereigns were identical. It was described with some justice as an artistic colony, though it never in any definable way produced any art. But although its pretensions to be an intellectual centre were a little vague, its pretensions to be a pleasant place were quite indisputable.

Here is Bedford Park, fictionally incarnated by an affectionate hand. This extraordinary "first" suburb of London—model for housing communities across Europe and beyond, with its tall three-story homes, cozy red brick angular lines, its quirky tall chimneys, and its sharply gabled roofs—serves as the scene for many a redoubtable protagonist. Little wonder that it must be a critical scene for the presentation of our heroine, Frances Blogg.

As the little corner of the world that would give him Frances, the affection and the detail afforded to this "pleasant place"—which he describes richly in his autobiography as well[1]—is perfectly understandable.

Since its inception in the 1870s, Bedford Park was considered a high point in fashionable London. Home to artists, writers, and intellectuals ("although its pretensions to be an intellectual centre were a little vague"), it could boast an impressive array of talented and well-known residents: the painter Archie Macgregor (in whose studio Gilbert would first hear Hilaire Belloc), the poet William Butler Yeats, the historian Professor Yorke Powell, Celtic scholar Dr. Todhunter, children's author E. Nesbit, playwright Arthur Pinero, the French painter Camille Pissarro, and many other artisans, poets, and radicals, were all to be found here.[2]

Among these, by the late 1890s, we find the Blogg family, who habitually held a Sunday afternoon open house in their Bedford Park home, welcoming friends and neighbors for tea and lively conversation. Topics spanned the very latest in politics, religion, art, and literature. New and old ideas were welcomed, encouraged and debated.

The open house was a product of the "I.D.K. Debating Society" the Bloggs initiated two years earlier. This organization, whose title came from a pithy self-deprecation ("I.D.K." stood for "I Don't Know"), rotated meetings from home to home, and drew members from amongst Blogg friends and neighbors. Most of the artists, writers and intellectuals living in Bedford Park

---

[1] G.K. Chesterton, "The Fantastic Suburb," in *The Autobiography of G.K. Chesterton* (San Francisco: Ignatius Press, 2006).

[2] Tony Evans, "Chesterton Around the World: News from London," *Gilbert* Vol. 1, no. 6 (1998).

participated at one time or another. It was a happy arrangement for the Bloggs; the family loved their neighborhood, thrived on animated discussion, and relished the opportunity to mix and mingle with this literati and bohemian set.

One particular Sunday in the fall of 1896, while the debate society was on hiatus, Lucian Oldershaw, a friend of the Bloggs' second oldest daughter, Ethel, invited a friend to come along to one of the open house gatherings. Oldershaw, who was attracted to the lively blond, Ethel, assured his longtime friend G.K. Chesterton that there were other attractive women in the home.

Twenty-two-year-old Gilbert knew of the Bloggs already; he had heard of them from his friend Mildred Wain. That was the extent of his knowledge (beyond the fact that he thought the name sounded funny); he hadn't yet met the family. He accepted the invitation, little realizing that the gathering would constitute one of the most critical experiences of his life.

Such pending significance would not have been readily apparent to onlookers; Lucian and Gilbert sat in the parlor with the family and a few other friends. While Lucian was comfortable there, and kept his eye on Ethel, Gilbert was nervous and quiet. Then the eldest Blogg daughter, Frances, sat down near him, and struck up a conversation.

Eighteen months later, Gilbert would propose, and Frances would accept.

Who was this woman who would so dramatically impact the life of G.K. Chesterton? Who on earth could be a soulmate to this man, this personality, with all of his wit and eccentricity? To learn this we must first look to the lady herself in her earliest social manifestation—or, rather, (since the infant Frances would have had little to say for herself), to the immediate forbearers of the lady.

❧   ❧   ❧

Frances Alice Blogg[3] was born on June 28, 1869, the firstborn child of twenty-seven-year-old diamond merchant George William Blogg, and his twenty-year-old wife, Blanche.

A Londoner born on February 4, 1842, George was himself the only son of a diamond merchant, George Frederick Blogg (born in 1793), and his wife, Frances Catherine née Ebhart[4] (born in 1814, and the namesake of her granddaughter, Mrs. Chesterton), married October 15, 1839 at St. Luke's Church, Chelsea. The son was followed by two daughters: Rhoda Ellen, born July 10, 1843, and Julia Marsden, born April 28, 1846.

The elder Blogg, George Frederick, worked alongside his brother, James, and eventually founded the family firm. They were jewelers and gold chain-makers. Their father, also George Frederick, had begun his professional life as a weaver in 1785, before becoming a spring maker, a chain-maker, a watchmaker, a silversmith, and, finally, a jeweler. It is in this final family profession that George Frederick and James both followed, eventually partnering with Charles Martin

---

[3] Chesterton biographers frequently claim that Blogg is a derivative of the French/Huguenot "de Blogue", but there is little evidence for this claim. On the contrary, the Blogg family has a long English history. The family thought the name harsh sounding, and informed new acquaintances that it was an anglicized French name (see Dudley Barker, *G.K. Chesterton: A Biography*, page 72). Nevertheless, the only recorded usage of "de Blogue" is associated with Oswald Blogg, Frances Chesterton's third cousin, who legally changed his surname to "de Blogue." Oswald had just one child, a daughter, so the newly restored de Blogue name—if it was a restoration—died out once again.

[4] Frances Catherine Ebhart was the daughter of William and Elizabeth, née Knollis, Ebhart. Elizabeth was the daughter of the Reverend Francis Knollis, the vicar of Buford from 1771 to 1826. The Knollis name comes back as Knollys in Frances's generation, and was also spelled Knowles on occasion. William Ebhart, Frances's great-grandfather, was a major in the British Army.

to establish Blogg & Martin. The younger George Frederick died of typhus in 1846.

The success of the firm was modest, including a showing in "The Great Exhibition of the Works of Industry of All Nations" of 1851 in Hyde Park, London, the spectacular world's fair exhibition sponsored by Prince Albert, consort to Queen Victoria.[5] Since George William was, at this time, only nine years of age, it is likely that either the family partner, Charles Martin, or George's uncle James represented the firm at the "Crystal Palace".

After his father's death, George William matured under the influence of his uncle, James, who lived until 1868.[6] Thus prepared, George moved into the family business. By 1861, when George was nineteen, he appeared in a census report as Head

---

[5] Dr. L. Feuchtwanger, *A Popular Treatise on Gems, In Reference to their Scientific Value; A Guide for the Teacher of Natural Sciences, the Jeweller, and Amateur: together with a description of the elements of mineralogy, and all ornamental and architectural materials* (New York: D. Appleton & Co., 1859), 213-14. In addition to catalogues and other records which note the firm's display at the crystal palace, reports remain chronicling Dr. Feuchtwanger's awestruck examination of "three bags, weighing about five pounds each, of diamonds",

> every diamond of which was of the first water, and weighed from ten to twenty carats. Their value could not have been less than two to four millions of dollars; and they were not in the market for sale.

In his visit to the "treasure vaults . . . of Messrs. BLOGG & MARTIN, the celebrated diamond-brokers", Feuchtwanger concludes: "The sight of so many valuable gems made a lasting impression upon me."

Coincidentally, Frances's maternal grandfather, James Keymer, a silk merchant, was also at the Great Exhibition, displaying his printed handkerchiefs to commemorate the event.

[6] George Frederick's wife was then only thirty-two years old, with three small children, and quite a few business-related challenges on her hands, including the settlement of lawsuits taken out against the Blogg estate by other diamond companies.

of Household at 6 Peterborough Villas, Fulham; occupation, diamond merchant.[7]

In appearance, George William Blogg was thin and wiry, with mutton-chop sideburns and a mustache. He wore his hair parted perfectly down the middle. His most prominent feature in photographs is his intense eyes. Looking back on the limited details available about his life, he combines a hint of romantic daring with the pedestrian reality of mercantile uncertainty.

Frances's mother, Blanche Keymer, was born in Peckham, Surrey, in 1848, the fifth of the six children of James and Mary Margaret Keymer. James Keymer was a successful and celebrated silk merchant, developing new techniques in silk-screen printing. He ran a thriving business that employed ninety workers.

At the time of her marriage, Blanche was a striking woman, with deep-set eyes, thick wiry hair, and an active imagination. She loved to read and sew, and was an avid correspondent. Blanche was also a writer. Later, she would come to write for and edit a periodical called *Home Chat*.[8]

Her temperament was melancholic, with a tendency toward depression that would be manifested in particular as a young

---

[7] He is listed as living with his sister Julia, who was fourteen, three boarders and two servants. His mother may have been out visiting or traveling at the time, and sister Rhoda was working and living as a governess in the home of Clara Kelly, caring for her three daughters ages twelve, five, and three.

[8] Maisie Ward, *Return to Chesterton* (New York: Sheed & Ward, 1952), 36-37; Ian Ker, *G.K. Chesterton: A Biography* (New York: Oxford University Press, 2011), 46. *Home Chat* magazine was published from 1895 until 1956 but has never been indexed or digitized. Copies are available to hand search at the British Library, but authors and poets were rarely given credit; with signatures such as, "Editress" and "Assistant Editress". *Home Chat, A Weekly Magazine for the Home. East, West, Home's Best.* Printed by Harmsworth Brothers Limited and published by B.W. Young, 24, Tudor Street, E.C.

widow.[9] Depression, indeed, was a family malady. Blanche's uncle Laman Blanchard was the most notable case: depressed during his wife's final illness, Laman committed suicide by cutting his own throat. Blanche and her children, especially her son, Knollys, struggled with depression throughout their lives. As she grew older, Frances herself was not immune, suffering from weather-related sadness.[10] Gilbert Chesterton quickly learned that she hated rain; he therefore dubbed all sunny days "Frances's days", heroically claiming the cloudy days for himself.

The maternal heritage was, however, not simply dark; this side of the family tree displays several notable figures. Mary Margaret Blanchard Keymer, mother to Blanche, was the sister of aforementioned journalist Samuel "Laman" Blanchard. Blanchard was the close friend and eventual in-law of Douglas Jerrold's, the famous writer, dramatist, and journalist.[11] Blanchard and Jerrold were both part of Charles Dickens' close circle of

---

[9] Blanche far outlived all of her siblings. Her sisters died at ages thirty-one and forty-six; her brothers both died in their forties. Blanche lived into the twentieth century, till the age of eighty-five—fifty years as a widow. She was known to have had a "complaining temperament" (See Barker, 72). Other biographies indicate a melancholic temperament that tended towards depression. Ada Chesterton stated that she and Cecil could not stand Mrs. Blogg.

[10] "It rained today, so depressing." *Jerusalem Diary*, British Library.

[11] Blanchard suffered from depression and had attempted suicide in his youth. But he recovered, thanks to Jerrold; then married, and became a journalist. Douglas Jerrold founded and edited, with indifferent success, the *Illuminated Magazine, Jerrold's Shilling Magazine*, and *Douglas Jerrold's Weekly Newspaper*; under his editorship, *Lloyd's Weekly Newspaper* rose from almost a nonentity to a circulation of 582,000. When Jerrold died, Charles Dickens, and William Thackeray were the principal pallbearers. He was laid to rest near Samuel Laman Blanchard, "his dearest friend." His daughter Jane was married to dramatist and *Illustrated London News* author Henry Mayhew. He was also a friend of novelist and playwright Wilkie Collins. Collins, coincidentally, wrote a famous story about a yellow diamond that was stolen, *The Moonstone*. Douglas Jerrold died in London on June 8, 1857. Later that June, Charles Dickens offered a public reading to raise money for his widow. And fifty-seven years later, G.K. Chesterton influenced

friends and colleagues.[12] Frances's uncle, Cosmo Monkhouse, was a published poet and well-known art critic.[13] Her aunt, Mary Margaret Heaton,[14] was a well-known art historian and had many works published, the most famous of which was *The History of the Life of Albrecht Dürer of Nürnberg.* Chesterton himself could have studied this book when he went to the Slade School of Art and may have been familiar with her name. In fact, Frances had come from a very artistic and literary family, one that knew well what to do with a writer, poet or art critic, and how to encourage such a person to share his writing with the world.

George and Blanche married in Dartford on July 22, 1868. Frances was born one year later. Six siblings followed: brother Knollys (pronounced *noles,* rhyming with "bowls") in 1871, Ethel in 1872, Helen in 1873, Gertrude four months after Helen's death in 1875 (after a two-week illness), a stillborn son in 1876, and Rachel in 1878. Rachel died in 1881.

The Bloggs were well-to-do; they had a nanny to care for the children and kept a domestic servant for cooking and cleaning.

---

the production of the *Trial of John Jasper for the Murder of Edwin Drood* as a fundraiser for the grandchildren of Charles Dickens.

Mary Margaret's nephew, Sydney Laman Blanchard—Blanche's first cousin—was also an author.

[12] Jerrold achieved popular prestige alongside William Makepeace Thackeray and Charles Dickens as one of the foremost humorists of the age. Jerrold's most famous play, *Black-Eyed Susan*, isn't remembered over a century later, but would have been well-known to G.K. Chesterton.

[13] Monkhouse's judgments were highly valued; he had the rare gift of differing without offending, and he was respected for his honesty. He wrote a book of poetry, which Gilbert illustrated—and his career path was not unlike Gilbert's own. Gilbert wrote a wonderful obituary for the *Daily News* on July 2, 1901, "Cosmo Monkhouse."

[14] Mary Margaret Keymer Heaton is sometimes listed under the author name Mrs. Charles Heaton.

George had a horse and carriage, for which he employed a driver. The family was not notably religious, but, like many at that time and in their circle, espoused a generic, secularized Anglicanism which might as well be called agnosticism.

The family finances waxed and waned, depending on the diamond market. One dramatic tale regarding the business stands out: George claimed that he was robbed while he was traveling in Venice. A thief came into his hotel room in the night and stole the sizable collection of jewels in George's possession. George attempted to catch the thief, but found the man had cleverly greased his body and literally slipped through his hands. The thief then jumped out the window and got away. That night George, in distress over the loss, suffered from heart pain, hinting at the physical susceptibility that would bring about his early death.

In 1873, George was officially named a partner in the Blogg & Martin diamond merchant company, along with a nephew of Martin's named William Jardine; the company was renamed "Blogg, Martin, Jardine and Co."[15] It seemed that stability and serenity had come at last for the Bloggs.

While there is not much in the way of documentary evidence about Frances's childhood, the evidence of the familial context (i.e. middle class Londoners toward the end of the Victorian period) and of her personality and interests later in life, this much seems likely: her childhood included books and flowers, sewing, and gardening. She was a city girl who loved plants and pets and cared avidly for both as opportunity afforded.

Her mother's melancholy must have added somewhat of a shadow to life. Her father's business, the fact that he traveled

---

[15] In 1874, Charles Martin died, leaving a huge estate to his son and nephew, worth £140,000, which is the equivalent of about $4 million today.

frequently, the family's repeated moves to new homes, and that she went to boarding school and was raised by a nanny—these certainly would all have shaped Frances.

When separated, the family kept in close contact with letters. Some of these survive, and occasionally bring more questions than they provide answers about her early life. A letter from her father, for instance, penned on Good Friday, April 19, 1878, reads:

> My darling Frances,
> I hope you will continue to write to me. . . . The regiment to which I belong is to be placed on active service, so I shall have to be quite a real soldier on duty. I went to see the Queen today and she talked to me just like any other lady. But I was very careful not to turn my back upon her but to walk out backwards and to be respectful and polite. I met a friend there at Windsor Castle, one of the Governors of the Bank of England; I rather think that the Queen wanted to borrow a little ready money to send to Malta or to the Fleet to pay her sailors and soldiers, at any rate Mr. Gibbs looked very grave and thoughtful all the way up to town.[16]

The letter illustrates two of the tiny Blogg family mysteries that remain unsolved. First, no record of George's military activity has been found, beyond a single photograph in which he appears to be in a dragoon (or light cavalry unit) uniform. Second, we do not know the circumstances in which George supposedly spoke to Queen Victoria.

Considering how frequently George traveled, it is not surprising that there are other letters. When he traveled to Paris in June 1878, and saw the third Paris World's Fair, he wrote

---

[16] George Blogg, Letter, April 19, 1878, British Library.

Frances a letter in French, in which he told her he saw a doll that could swim and he wanted to buy it for her sister Gertie.

The correspondence was reciprocal; Frances wrote letters to her parents when separated from them, evidencing the different sort of relationship she had with each of them. To Papa she writes:

> Mother is rather mean about our pocket money because she keeps such a lot back for fines and we can't save up enough for a donkey ride. Don't you think you could advance us some? We can't have half such fun with it at home. Good bye, do come down to us,
>
> Frances Blogg

To Mama, in contrast, she writes:

> I am enjoying myself very much here. On Tuesday we went to Hampstead Heath with three of Mary's little cousins where we had a donkey ride. I was going to write yesterday, but we went to Brockley to see Mrs. Leonard Wigg. With lots of love and kisses to Papa and yourself,
>
> I am
>
> Your loving daughter,
>
> Frances Blogg

Such letters grant us a tiny glimpse into the world young Frances inhabited; a child's world of relative happiness, troubled only by everyday sorrows.

All of these changed with the summer of 1883, which brought deep suffering to the family, and a burden of repeated loss that would both change their fortune materially and transform Blanche into a grieving, depressed widow.

On June 1, 1883, Mary Margaret Heaton, art historian and Blanche's eldest sister, died of cancer at age forty-six. The newspaper published a glowing obituary of her literary accomplishments.

She left behind three young daughters, Frances's cousins, one of which (Margaret) would spend all school holidays with the Blogg family from then on.

A month after Mary's death, Frances's paternal grandmother died at age sixty-nine.

That same month, George exhibited an increase in heart trouble symptoms; he complained frequently about his heart, and at times even clutched at his chest in pain. On Monday, July 23, 1883, one day after his fifteenth wedding anniversary, he collapsed and died on a London street. He was on the way to see a doctor, had entered the office, only to find the physician was not in. Blogg left the building, and collapsed on the stairs, dying almost instantly. He was forty-one. Post-mortem analysis was unequivocal: he had suffered a rupture of an aneurism of the heart. He was buried at Highgate Cemetery on July 26 in the family grave, next to his two infant daughters.

Within a short span of time Blanche grieved the deaths of her then-youngest daughter, Rachel, at the age of two-and-a-half, her mother, her oldest sister, her mother-in-law, and, finally, her husband. The young widow fell into depression.

No letters or other documents survive to chronicle the feelings of fourteen-year-old Frances at her father's sudden death. With so much sorrow, and especially with the depression of Blanche, all of the children must have suffered. As the eldest, and as a young woman who displayed deep feeling and sensitivity throughout her life, Frances perhaps understood better than her siblings how much things had changed in the family because of the loss of her papa.

Some biographies reported that the Blogg family fell on hard times after the death of George—that Blanche had to work and the children had to take jobs. Such was not precisely the case. The money left to Blanche in her husband's will provided her with ample means to further the education of all of her children; she did not send them to work, she sent them to school.

Blanche's decision to send the children to school, and the number and quality of schools they attended provide a fascinating insight into both the period (one of significant transition in theories of education, particularly for women) and the value system of the family.

Frances and her sisters had attended the first kindergarten founded in England.[17] For their elementary level education, they boarded at the same school, called, "Ladies' School", run by Rosalie and Minna Praetorius from Germany. This school followed the philosophy of early education propounded in Germany by pioneering pedagogue Friedrich Froebel in the first half of the nineteenth century.[18] His theory, still relatively controversial when the Blogg children were school aged, operated on the assumption that very young children could gain knowledge and skills through play. Simple toys like balls, cubes, and sticks were employed to teach letters and numbers through observation and enjoyment; dances and singing games were encouraged, as were physical activity and culture; cultivating plants in a garden kept the child in harmony with nature, and there was no corporal punishment. This precursor of the Montessori school set the Blogg children apart from most British children at that time.

In the autumn of 1883, after the grievous summer of familial loss, Frances returned to the Ladies' School. She would continue her education there until 1886. While Frances, Ethel, and Gertrude all attended the Ladies' School, Knollys went to

---

[17] This same school the Yeats sisters Lily and Lollie attended. The Yeats sisters also attended the same high school as Frances, Notting Hill. Maisie Ward obituary, *UK Catholic Herald* (December 16, 1938): 9.

[18] *UCL Bloomsbury Project*, accessed January 30, 2014, http://www.ucl.ac.uk/bloomsbury-project/institutions/humanistic_schools.htm.

St. Paul's (where Gilbert Chesterton also attended, though a few years behind Knollys, his future brother-in-law). When the sisters finished at the Ladies' School, they attended high school.

In the fall of 1886, when Frances was seventeen, Blanche enrolled her at Notting Hill High, an all-girls' day school with a college preparatory course of study, where her sisters also attended. Gertrude attained the highest academic achievement of the three sisters, sitting for the Junior Cambridge Exams and passing. This was a particularly impressive achievement, since those exams were only opened to women a few years earlier.

From 1888 to 1891, Frances attended St. Stephen's College, Windsor, the school of an Anglo-Catholic church and convent. The term "college" was a very wide-ranging and oft-used word for almost any establishment offering continuing academic education. St. Stephen's Ladies' College, run by the Clewer Sisters of St. John the Baptist, taught mostly clergymen's daughters, but also the daughters of professional gentlemen.[19] The students at St. Stephen's would also go to Eton and have classes in mathematics and Shakespeare. Unlike most "finishing schools" for girls at this time, St. Stephen's provided girls with a rigorous academic environment. They studied English, mathematics, divinity, French, German, Latin, Greek, science, harmony, drawing, painting, class singing, music, dancing, drilling, and needlework. Deportment and good manners were demanded.

The atmosphere and the ideas in the convent were utterly congenial to Frances, and became the ideas and the atmosphere of her life.[20] Up until this time, the Blogg family had not been particularly religious; in fact, they were described as agnostic by

---

[19] Jenny Balston, *The Story of St. Stephen's College* (Kent: Old St Stephenites' Society, 1994).

[20] Maisie Ward, "Frances, Wife of G.K. Chesterton," *Catholic Herald* (December 16, 1938): 9.

Maisie Ward. Frances's attraction to the faith articulated within the College was both transformative and influential.

St. Genoveva, the school building where Frances lived, housed a small number of older girls, often student teachers or those who were beyond the usual school age. Matriculation to universities (an ambition for some) would be limited, since even limited university degrees would not be granted to women until the 1920s, and full degrees until the 1940s.

Frances's progress followed an expected course: toward teaching. During the Easter holidays in 1891, Frances and Ethel were staying with an old friend of their father's—Mr. William Boore, a silversmith—the day of the census-taking. Census officials listed Frances as both student and teacher.

When her course of study was complete, Frances moved home to Bedford Park. By this time, Frances had matured into a beautiful young lady. A sad handicap developed during her adolescence, however: one of her legs grew faster and longer than the other. She developed a limp and lower back pain, which grew worse over time. This would affect her health all her life.

Frances, as she appeared on the Bedford Park scene, was by this time a dainty little lady ("five foot two" with a slight figure, curly brown hair,[21] and blue eyes), clever and level-headed.[22] There was an air of mystery about her. She was quiet, but she could be fiery, she had a brave face, a wonderful smile, and she was cheerful. Graceful in appearance and possessing great sympathy of manner, Frances had a practical head on her shoulders,

---

[21] Gilbert wrote so much poetry and so many stories about the "red-haired girl" that everyone for years had assumed Frances had red hair. She did not—it was brown. Gilbert's mother Marie Louise, on the other hand, is reported to have had red hair.

[22] Cyril Clemens, *Chesterton As Seen by His Contemporaries* (New York: Gordon Press, 1972), 164.

as well as a good memory.[23] She was very fond of dancing and very fond of the Bible. Her personality was firm—she knew how to assert her authority[24]—yet gentle. She loved pets and gardens, and she adored babies. She had a good sense of humor and enjoyed debate. Her knowledge of literature, poetry and song was considerable.[25] She was concerned for the poor and thus keenly interested in social reform.

Ever since her studies at St. Stephen's, Frances had been a devout Anglo-Catholic, and was now in the habit of attending services each Sunday. In fact, she taught Sunday school to the young children of the parish. This religiosity set Frances apart from the other artistic types living in Bedford Park at the time, who were more inclined towards spiritualism, or to radicalism, socialism, or even communism. William Butler Yeats, for instance, even as he was writing Celtic fairy stories down the street, fostered a strong interest in spiritualism and the occult. Margaret Heaton, Frances's close cousin, was also—as noted in Gilbert's autobiography—drawn towards Yeats and the occult.

On November 8, 1894, Frances, Ethel, Knollys, and several of their friends founded their "I.D.K. Debating Society". They agreed upon a motto: "We feel at least that silence here were sin", a line from Tennyson's rousing patriotic poem (which addressed burning inter-party political debate which would have been well-known at the time, but signifies little now except to historians): "The Third of February, 1852".

The I.D.K. operated with due formality: dues were one shilling per season; members elected Ethel Blogg secretary and

---

[23] British Library folder 73196-55.

[24] Patrick Braybrooke, *I Remember G.K. Chesterton* (London: Dorling & Co., 1938), 21.

[25] *Ibid.*

Ethel Thompson, a friend and neighbor, chairman of the first debate. Arthur Thompson, Ethel's brother, chose the topic for the first debate: "That in the opinion of this House civilization is a failure." His opposer was a Miss Wood. Each made their case regarding the stated opinion before opening the floor. Vote followed general discussion. Eight voted against the proposition and two in favor: the majority ruled civilization a success.

The meetings continued at a rate of about two per month. At each meeting, the I.D.K. drew in one or two new members. They even held a dance at the Blogg home on Saturday, January 12, 1895, inviting all members and their friends.

After eleven meetings, the society concluded their first season. The secretary created an annual report outlining the progress made and new members welcomed, complete with a statement of accounts, presented and audited by Knollys.

During the 1895-96 session, the group continued to grow and expand. Frances took her turn as proposer, opposer, and chairman on various occasions. The society's minutes note her as a frequent contributor to the general discussion that followed the formal portion of the debates. On February 1, 1896, the I.D.K. Society held their second annual dance—this time at Arthur and Ethel Thompson's home.

The meeting of Frances Blogg and Gilbert Keith Chesterton took place during the interim between the second and third sessions.

Perhaps the connection to a literary, artistic, exciting family like the Bloggs was just what Chesterton needed to give direction to his young mind, and hope for his young soul. Gilbert was recently out of art school, and, having wrestled at length with religious ideas, had arisen from the fight believing in God. He read voraciously for work and for pleasure, making his way through a host of celebrated authors, from Walt Whitman to

Charles Dickens to Robert Louis Stevenson. Meanwhile, he was working for the London publisher Redway, wading through the slush pile searching for the gems deserving publication, writing poetry in the evenings, seeing a few of his works anonymously published in major publications, and writing down stories and ideas that would take shape in the future and become *Manalive* and *The Man Who Was Thursday*. He was keeping private notebooks of his own thoughts and dreams. In one notebook, he composed a poem to his future lady shortly before they actually met:

Madonna Mia

About Her whom I have not yet met
I wonder what she is doing
Now, at this sunset hour,
Working perhaps, or playing, worrying or laughing,
Is she making tea, or singing a song, or writing, or praying,
    or reading?
Is she thoughtful, as I am thoughtful?
Is she looking now out of the window
As I am looking out of the window?[26]

The first time Lucian brought Gilbert to Number 8 Bath Road,[27] on a Saturday afternoon, Frances was not there. Gilbert met Blanche, Ethel, Margaret Heaton, a Miss Lepayner, and Ethel Thompson. The second time that he came she was present and, as Gilbert later said, the attraction was keen and immediate. Photographs of the time show she was a beauty, but, even beyond her appearance, Gilbert experienced a sudden, overwhelming insight, later described by him as a voice speaking in his mind "in a flash":

---

[26] Maisie Ward, *Gilbert Keith Chesterton* (New York: Sheed & Ward, 2006), 77.

[27] To see a picture of the Blogg home at 8 Bath Road, please see *Gilbert* Vol. 1, no. 6 (1998).

> If I had anything to do with this girl I should go down on my
> knees to her: if I spoke with her she would never deceive me:
> if I depended on her she would never deny me: if I loved her
> she would never play with me: if I trusted her she would never
> go back on me: if I remembered her she would never forget me.

This description of their meeting, the high point of a lengthy, characteristically romantic letter and frequently humorous from Gilbert to Frances, concludes: "Here ends my previous existence. Take it: it led me to you."

Frances, observant and insightful about others and coming from a literary background, found Gilbert intriguing. His name meant nothing to her, for he had yet to become famous. Nameless though he was, she discovered in Gilbert a budding writer, poet, and art critic, with an interest in the spiritual life. This resonated personally with her on every count.

Gilbert and Frances became friends and had deep talks and discussions. Gilbert visited nearly every Sunday evening. When the I.D.K. Debating Society resumed its session at the end of 1896, Gilbert was its newest member and brought to it his special flair.

The third session of the group began on December 1, 1896. At the inaugural meeting, the proposer, Mr. W. Fox-Bourne, chose as his topic: "That the punishment of crime is unjustifiable." His chosen opposer was new member Gilbert K. Chesterton. Mr. Fox-Bourne attempted to show that the experience of jail is debilitating to a man already morally ill. Instead of going to jail, he suggested, the criminal should go to an asylum and only be released when he is morally better. He should work for his living and continue to support his family. The crime would thus be treated like a disease, and dealt with by a medical prescription.

Chesterton retorted that it was impossible to imagine a society in which crime was not punished. Without punishment, he suggested, our society would not look that different than a society of chimpanzees. In the attitude of the mind that prompts crime, Chesterton stated, there is nothing diseased nor insane. The real object of punishment is not so much remedial as deterrent: fear is a great preventive force. The floor was then opened and members—including Frances—contributed to the discussion. A vote was then taken, and Chesterton won against the proposal.

The debating society continued until the last recorded meeting on March 21, 1899. Gilbert remained a devoted participant, attending all but one meeting. Their membership was fluid, but continued to draw in a range of talented and impressive figures and family members. Lucian Oldershaw only attended two meetings as a visitor. Gertrude Blogg was an occasional visitor, but never elected a member. Her fiancé Reginald "Rex" Brimley Johnson was an active member during the last two years. Gilbert's friends E.C. Bentley, Waldo d'Avigdor, Robert Vernede, and Jack Phillimore, as well as his brother Cecil, all participated in the I.D.K. and had a role in its success. Artists in the neighborhood including Camille Pissarro, Archie Macgregor, Herbert S. Percy, and photographer Adolphe Smith all took part. Douglas Cockerell, the bookbinder, was involved as well. The one notable Bedford Park family that was not involved in the I.D.K. was the Yeats family. (Informally, the I.D.K.'s "Rule Number One" was: "Lollie Yeats must never be allowed to become a member.")[28]

---

[28] William Murphy, *Family Secrets: William Butler Yeats and His Relatives* (New York: Syracuse University Press, 1995), 161. Lollie was an eccentric, with whom few got along.

Meanwhile, Frances continued her professional work. Although she left St. Stephen's College qualified to teach, there is no record of her taking charge of a classroom. Instead, she tutored individual students until she obtained a job at the P.N.E.U.—The Parents' National Educational Union. Hired as the general secretary in 1895, she took handwritten notes at all committee meetings, and wrote them up neatly in the minutes book. When Frances first went to work at the P.N.E.U., the national president asked her if she could write shorthand, to which she answered, "No." Could she type? Frances again answered in the negative. "Then we'll have you," was the unexpected response.[29] In the beginning of their marriage, Frances would hire Gilbert's secretaries in the same way.

Frances served the P.N.E.U. well. She sat in on all monthly council meetings, the executive board meetings, the finance committee meetings, the meeting of local secretaries, the Natural History Club and the conference sub-committee meetings. She was highly involved in all aspects of the union, from ordering supplies to planning the annual conferences. Frances arranged for speakers, took registrations, and helped out-of-town conferees find accommodations. She maintained a lending library for the union, sent out literature to people who requested it, kept the financial ledger, and wrote checks.

By the end of the century, the entire Blogg family was busy. Blanche worked as an editor and a seamstress. These activities were, likely, prompted by her interest and not by financial necessity, since the money left her by her husband was sufficient to support her. She had risen from depression to an enjoyable, busy life, a widow with a "modest income but a smart address."[30] Frances

---

[29] *Return to Chesterton*, 156.

[30] "Frances & Gilbert," *Sacred Heart Messenger*, 17.

was doing well at the P.N.E.U. Knollys worked as a bookkeeper at Lloyds of London in the Merchant Marine department. Ethel was working as a secretary for the London School of Medicine for Women, the first medical school in Britain to train women. Gertrude worked in the home of Rudyard Kipling as his secretary and governess to his young children. Gertrude, the youngest, was the first engaged, plighting her troth to Reginald "Rex" Brimley Johnson, a book editor, who was the eventual publisher of Gilbert's first book, *Greybeards at Play*.[31] Margaret Heaton—Frances's cousin—mentioned by Gilbert in his autobiography as the "cousin on the premises, who was engaged to a German professor, Paul Arndt, and permanently fascinated by the subject of German fairy-tales,"[32] still lived with the Bloggs in Bedford Park. One of her books on fairy tales would by published under her married name Margaret (or Frau) Arndt—*Fairy Tales from the German Forests*; Gilbert provided the illustrations.[33] In addition, Margaret was also involved with the P.N.E.U., and was asked to speak about children's books to their members.[34]

Literature remained very much a family concern. Although Ethel and Knollys were not as directly involved in literary business, they both participated in the I.D.K. club. Knollys, working as a bookkeeper, wrote poetry and essays on the side, some of which were published in the *Parents' Review*, the publication

---

[31] More information about the life of Gertrude can be found in *Gilbert* Vol. 16, nos. 6-7, "Gertrude Colborne Blogg" (2013): 10-11.

[32] *Autobiography*, 95.

[33] See also, *The Meadows of Play*, by Margaret Arndt; with an introduction by G.K. Chesterton, illustrated by Edith Calvert, October 1909. Chesterton was godfather to Margaret Arndt's daughter Barbara, and the introduction is written to her.

[34] P.N.E.U. Notes, *Parents' Review* Vol. 8, no. 1 (1897): 64.

of the P.N.E.U.[35] Two of his essays appeared in *Girl's Realm* magazine: "Mr. Gilbert Chesterton and His Toy Theater" and "A Humorist and His Dolls".[36] The addition of Gilbert to their circle and, eventually, to their family, brought new inspiration. Knollys, who hero-worshipped his future brother-in-law, dedicated his book of poetry and essays, *Ledgers & Literature,*[37] to Gilbert.

Frances's sister Gertrude also participated, if vicariously, in a literary atmosphere. Her life with the Kiplings was full of delight, and her personal library contained several treasures, given to her by her employers: copies of *Jungle Book* (1894) and *The Second Jungle Book* (1895) signed by both Rudyard and Caroline Kipling, and *The Day's Work,*[38] inscribed: "Miss G.C. Blogg from the Author in memory of some proof reading for which he was very grateful: Nov '98."

In addition to the literary activity in the Blogg home, Frances composed essays, reviewed books, and edited articles for two of the publications of the P.N.E.U., a biannual magazine called *L'Umile Pianta* and the monthly *Parents' Review*. She gave speeches and debated at educational meetings and conferences.[39]

The P.N.E.U. was experiencing phenomenal growth as a young organization and there was much enthusiasm for the idea that education could be organized and scientifically based and could be undertaken by the parent or governess in the home. In 1896, there were thirty-one local branches, each

---

[35] "Te Deum," "Christmas 1906," "Demetrius' Coming of Age," and two appeared posthumously, "The Children of Sorrow" and "Ariel's First Christmas" in *Parents' Review*.

[36] *Girl's Realm* Vol. 11, no. 121 (1908): 20-24. Illustrated with nine photographs.

[37] Under the name George Knollys.

[38] Rudyard Kipling, *The Day's Work* (New York: Doubleday & McClure, 1898).

[39] The P.N.E.U. is still in existence today: the Bell Educational Trust in the U.K. and the Charlotte Mason Institute in the U.S. carry on its work.

holding meetings to help parents be better educators of their own children. Fourteen more branches were starting up. New groups were starting in Holland, Japan, Russia, and Australia. It was now international.[40]

It was a time of growth and extraordinary potential, all of which came together to imbue the fledgling courtship of Gilbert and Frances with great hope and enthusiasm. With so many mutual friends, their meeting was veritably inevitable. Their friendship, which began with literature, the spiritual life, art, debate, and poetry, was well situated in every respect: Gilbert, the eccentric and burgeoning genius, needed grounding and a sounding board for his ideas; Frances, the quiet, devoted romantic, needed someone to share a love of poetry, someone to love and of whom she could take care, someone with whom to start a family. The couple seemed ideally suited for battling every fresh challenge life might bring their way—and, as their courtship and engagement would demonstrate, there were many such challenges to be faced.

---

[40] *The Charlotte Mason Digital Collection,* accessed April 04, 2015, http://www.redeemer.ca/charlotte-mason.

Chapter Two

FORGING A PARTNERSHIP
IN WONDER (1896–1901)

There can be no liberal education when the
eyes are closed or the ears sealed.

*T*he thoughts and feelings of G.K. Chesterton in those heady days of early romance are well chronicled in his autobiography[1] and in his correspondence. This hitherto-unpublished letter (most likely written to E.C. Bentley) captures his enthusiasm, his characteristic charm and humor, alongside some fascinating insights into the character of his future bride:

> I wonder how that young lady of mine is getting on. I wonder what she is doing now. Cooking supper, perhaps, or reading Tolstoi [sic], or entertaining Cousin George (aha, I have a rival!) or doing art needlework, or dressing for a party, or wishing she had a vote, or working a telephone, or visiting the sick and keeping herself unspotted from the world, St. James, again. I really feel quite interested in that girl. I assure you that compared with her, Nina[2] is quite inferior. You wait till I find her out. Meanwhile, bother her [for me]. . . .

---

[1] *Autobiography*, 148-49.

[2] Refers to Nina Vivian, see *Collected Poetry* volumes 2 and 3.

... She is good, she is nice, she is polite, she is intelligent. She is sane. These things are scarcely novel, they are among the common objects of a morning walk. If you care to know ordinary conversation, we talked about laughter, and I said how sacred it was, and she said her monosyllable. By the way, not that it matters much, and although she does say "Yes," she is really an acute, if not clever girl, I find. I really didn't know it until I began to throw out a few Christian reflections. She hasn't been broadened enough by reading, but when it comes to interior meanings, she's all there.[3]

Gilbert depicts a young woman well-schooled in all of the domestic arts cultivated by their class ("Cooking", "reading", "entertaining", "doing art needlework", "dressing for a party"). A woman with a social conscience ("visiting the sick"). An intelligent woman and perhaps a bit of a feminist ("wishing she had a vote"—she numbered suffragettes among her close friends, including Isabel De Giberne Sieveking,[4] Charlotte Mason,[5] and Alice Meynell[6]). Her "monosyllable", an asset in the maintenance of polite small talk, throws into sharp relief his perception of her true qualities: "she is really an acute, if not clever girl, I find." The vehicle of his discovery reveals the true foundation of their friendship and eventual love: "I really didn't know it until I began to throw out a few Christian reflections."

---

[3] Transcript letter, with the following written above it: "Letter found among old papers, beginning missing, never posted, probably to Bentley." Excerpt, from G.K. Chesterton undated, G.K. Chesterton Family Correspondence, Folder 317, The Marion E. Wade Center, Wheaton College, Wheaton, IL.

[4] *Notable Sussex Women*, 228. Isabel was the mother of Lance (Lancelot) Sieveking.

[5] *Notable Sussex Women*, 98. Mason was the founder of the Parents' National Educational Union.

[6] *Notable Sussex Women*, 52. Maynell worked on *Samuel Johnson* with GKC.

The depth of her understanding on "interior meanings" (despite the fact that she was not "broadened enough by reading"—a handicap which, incidentally, Gilbert himself worked to correct, supplying her with a reading list)[7] unites with that critical point—"She is sane"—to set her apart from all other women in his mind. She was radically unlike her fellows in that bohemian neighborhood. Even beyond her excellent education and her many crafted skills (such as fluency in French and German, with conversational knowledge of Italian), Frances had natural abilities and a capacity for growth and understanding.[8]

Their age did not seem to be a barrier (Frances was five years older than Gilbert). Over the course of about eighteen months, the two became close, fell in love, and began to look towards a future together. On Thursday, July 21, 1898, at St. James Bridge within St. James Park, standing right in the middle of the span, Gilbert proposed and Frances accepted. Gilbert reports that Frances said "that if the sun had not been shining to her complete satisfaction on that day, the issue might have been quite different".[9] Humor and climate, however, were both in his favor.

Gilbert took an omnibus home, and immediately wrote Frances an effusive letter, speaking of his giddiness, how he did not deserve her, and she should not worry about her mother, because everything would come out right. He never knew what being happy was before that night. He felt so much emotion he almost cried, and he says he had not cried since he was

---

[7] Dudley Barker, *G.K. Chesterton: A Biography* (New York: Stein and Day, 1973), 98.

[8] Though Frances might object to such a suggestion, it is important to note that Gilbert is not infallible on the subject of Frances. In fact, in his autobiography, as he describes his first meeting with Frances, he claims she did not like the moon. Her poetry, however, presents a heart deeply attached to the romantic satellite.

[9] *Autobiography*, 154-55.

seven years old. He said he fell in love with her all over again. He thought St. James must be their patron saint, as St. James Hall, St. James Station, and St. James Park all figured into their courtship. He was ready to dance and sing; at neither of which, he said, he was technically any good.

Shortly after they became engaged, Frances fell ill. This prompted a critical moment of self-revelation: she wrote Gilbert in August, wondering why it was she was frequently sick, why she could not be healthier like other women. Gilbert's response expresses both his devotion to her and his vision of her unique capacity for goodness:

> If there was one touch I should select from all others of its splendor of sincerity, it is the fact that there was none of the canting resignation of the sentimental invalid, but a sort of glorious and boyish impatience which stirs the blood.
>
> There are two broad classes of women a man comes across. The first are the "outdoor" women, people . . . who would remain outdoors if they were locked in the Black Hole of Calcutta. They are made physically as sisters of the Sun and Wind, they develop all the virtues that are the children of Fresh Air; humour, courage, self-reliance, Faith, Hope and Charity. They are very jolly people; for their virtues are easy to them.
>
> The second class are the "delicate" women, who cannot bear loud noises and live behind drawn blinds. They are mostly concerned with their own souls and the people who have not called on them. They are either church people and live in South Kensington or Theosophists and live in West Kensington. They are sometimes very silly people, particularly if they have a little money: their affections, though deep and pathetic, have a tendency to stagnate into bitterness and poison. But a man who should be rude or cold or satiric about them

would be a brute. They have much to bear, pains borne in silence and loneliness, when every day is like the last, pains which real or unreal, organic or nervous, are equally painful. They have physical troubles which I have not, therefore I should be a cur not to respect them. And to their dusty old failures and disappointments, to their fantastic illnesses and needless aversions, —yes, even their microscopic vanities and grievances, I for one would always take off my hat. Lord, as the ancient writer said, count unto them their tears.

And lastly, outside both of these classes a man may happen to come upon another sort of woman—if he does he will probably be higher and a humbler man for ever. A woman who, fated physically to have the virtues of the weaker women, has rebelled and taken the virtues of the stronger—a woman whom Nature, making war, has been unable to defeat, whose body may be in the sickroom but whose soul is in the playground, who has a heart so great that she can hate the privileges of her calamity and the excuses of her depression: who spurns the philosophy that would justify and smooth her down and elects the philosophy that can only knock her about; who would rather conceal her disadvantages and be third in the free race for life, than first in a paradise of poetic egoism; a woman who, to add one last supreme touch, shall have even the faults of a tougher type, and while she suffers inwardly from the collapses and clouding pains that make other women pessimists, shall be challenged and rebuked outwardly for her too dogmatic cheerfulness, her too cloudless philosophy, her too arrogant faith.

If one had ever met it in a hotel that would have been a valiant and splendid figure. To me it is simply you. Even you will, I fancy, admit it is something like your ideal for yourself, isn't it, dearest?

And now you want to spoil it all by having a lot of beastly fat, physical health. And the worst of it is that I am quite inconsistent and want it for you too, for I can't bear you to have three minutes discomfort—which is a mediaeval superstition and a jolly fine thing. But it is perfectly true, as I say, that you could never have been the influence you are, never have given the object lesson you do of the great soul that conceals its wounds that it may serve in the battle, if those wounds did not exist. O you dear, dear discontented saint—don't you see that we do want something to love and adore and go on our knees to, something that really shows that courage is not a bundle of nerves—nor optimism a good breakfast. Won't you be patient on the chilly pedestal, for a little while? We are selfish—but you are not. No, by the sun and moon and all the stars—

—You are not—

All of which I am afraid, doesn't alter the fact that if by taking up the carving knife now lying beside me and cutting off my right hand with my left, I could guarantee you perfect health for life, I would do it and whistle all the time. But then, you see, that is as a man talking about his own dear, true-hearted and beautiful girl whose face gets into his dreams: as a philosopher, speaking of the social influence of a good woman, I am sure the world has reason to bless your bad health.

I do not think, brave heart, that I could praise you better than by writing this odd letter. There are not many women in whose case, when a man has to comfort them in sickness, it would occur to him to point out the good they were doing to the world, as any comfort at all. But to you I *know* it is a comfort.

In addition to the knowledge of the good she did to the world through her suffering, this "odd letter" must have brought its own form of "comfort" to the sufferer. He saw in her something extraordinary, as is shown in his *An Encyclopaedia of Bloggs* (scribbled in his notebook), where Frances is described as

> a harmony in green and brown. There is some gold somewhere in it, but cannot be located on examination. Probably the golden crown. Harp not yet arrived. Physically there is not quite enough of her to carry all that temperament: she looks slight, fiery and wasted, with a face that would be a Burne-Jones if it were not brave: it has the asceticism of cheerfulness, not the easier asceticism of melancholy. Devouring appetite for sensations; very fond of the Bible; very fond of dancing. When she is enjoying herself thoroughly, one has a sense that it would be well for her to go to sleep for a hundred years. It would be jolly fun for some prince too.

Despite the Blogg family struggle with depression, which would resurface at several critical moments in their marriage, we note Gilbert's identification of Frances as tending toward cheerfulness and enjoyment, rather than melancholy. This "asceticism of cheerfulness" would be the *modus operandi* of her life, in the midst of sadness and of joy.

For some time, the latter experience reigned. The engagement was a time of many joys that the couple would weave into the fabric of their marriage: the exchange of love letters; Gilbert's poems; flowers pressed for him by Frances (including pansies and forget-me-nots, which in the language of flowers represent thought and faithful memory); reading books together; long walks; endless conversation. Many mornings, Gilbert would get up early, and, having to pass by the office of the P.N.E.U. at 28 Victoria, would bound up the stairs and slip over to Frances's desk, and write her love notes or draw pictures on her desk blotter for her to see when she arrived at work.

The logistics of their engagement were somewhat challenging. They wanted to keep the engagement secret for a little while, particularly concerned for the support of the two mothers. Gilbert's first meeting with Blanche as his future mother-in-law reflected his anxiety. Blanche, also nervous, asked him what he thought of the new wallpaper. Gilbert strolled over to it, pulled out a piece of chalk, and proceeded to draw a picture of Frances on it. Blanche was not amused.[10] This domestic thoughtlessness did not help redeem her opinion; Gilbert's future mother-in-law considered him impractical, with a disregard for money, and altogether an imprudent match for her eldest daughter. She was not the only one; although they became amicable, Frances's sister Ethel thought Gilbert was not quite right in the head, though (as she wrote in March 1899): "I still think you are the most good-natured soul alive." Blanche did warm to Gilbert, as this early letter indicates:

August 17th

Dear Gilbert,
We are returning home today and I shall be there for a week or ten days. The house will be [fixed] up more or less to [inhabit] but I need be there to look after them—Ethel goes off directly and I hope to get off again with Knollys as soon as he gets his holiday—I have not been well all the time here, but it has been a change though not much of a rest—

   I have sweet happy letters from Frances—come and see me—I want you— yours affectionately,
        Blanche Blogg[11]

---

[10] Ian Ker, *G.K. Chesterton: A Biography* (New York: Oxford University Press, 2012), 45.

[11] Wade Center folder 41.

This eventual support and affection was soothing to the couple, but the challenge of familial resistance was still a marked challenge and, at times, a grief.

The Chestertons were no more supportive. Gilbert's brother Cecil thought Frances was far too artsy. His mother was even more inclined to be prejudiced against Frances. For one thing, Marie Louise Chesterton thought Bedford Park too bohemian for decent people, even though Gilbert had discovered that Frances was different from her neighbors. For another, Marie Louise had already picked out a wife for Gilbert: Annie Fermin. Annie was a childhood friend who got along well with Gilbert when he was a boy, and liked his mother.[12] Gilbert was clearly aware of his mother's predisposition against the match, and was deeply anxious about it (his way of informing her of the seriousness of the relationship was by writing her a letter as he sat across the kitchen table from her).[13]There was some support as well, of course. For instance, Frances's cousin Margaret wrote Gilbert a congratulatory letter, upon hearing of their engagement:

> Dear Mr. Chesterton,
> I cannot tell you how happy and delighted I am to hear the good news. I congratulate you with all my heart. I could not like anyone better for a future relation—may I say brother-in-law—for dear Francesca is almost a sister to me. I need not tell you that I consider you a <u>very</u> lucky fellow; in that Frances is one of the noblest of women; you know even better than I. I wish you both a most perfect union and God's blessings. I have known you pretty intimately for some time now, and I have never heard you say an unkind word to anyone and I

---

[12] *Gilbert Keith Chesterton*, 15.

[13] *Ibid.*, 89-91 for this letter. Note, this points to GKC's lifelong interest in avoiding personal conflicts.

have often observed how you championed the cause of the weak, this makes me feel more confident than anything of my dear Frances's happiness with you . . . I think Francesca needs a great deal of looking after. She is often very foolish and unkind—to <u>herself</u>! —and overworks shockingly. (and underfeeds!). . . . Margaret Heaton[14]

By the time they were engaged, Frances was convinced that Gilbert was a genius with a promising future. She just needed to persuade her family and friends he was the right man for her. This she never fully accomplished. Such was the case with Isabel Sieveking, one of her close friends, whose son later wrote:

Frances . . . was one of my mother's closest friends. One bond between them was the devout Christianity they shared, and another was the fact that each lady thought the other's husband an unsuitable husband for her friend, a point of view which was not altogether without foundation.[15]

This concern may be partly derived from the conception (shared by some) that Frances was subsumed into her husband and somehow lost. Indeed, in later years, it would be said of Frances that she had an amusing habit of saying on the next day what Gilbert had said the day before—not because she had no opinions of her own, but because she seemed to agree with almost every sentiment her husband expressed.[16] The flourishing of talent brought about through the uniting of these two minds and hearts can be seen very early. This is shown in Frances's essay "The Open Road", written for the *Parents' Review* in 1900;

---

[14] Letter from Margaret Heaton to G.K. Chesterton, July 21, 1898. Wade Center folder 160.

[15] Lance Sieveking, *The Eye of the Beholder* (New York: Hulton Press, 1957), 15.

[16] Braybrooke, 21.

a piece in which she explores the notion of the world as a child's blackboard (a metaphor inspired by Robert Louis Stevenson).[17]

By this time, the couple had known each other for four years, and the commingling of ideas, the obvious exchange of thought and experience, led to a striking resemblance between their writings. Several passages are worth note.

> We all know the way in which children give themselves up to the matter in hand and the utter impossibility that grown-up people find of explaining to a child that the charm of jumping off the table into the arms of the patient nurse or sister ceases after the ninth or tenth time. 'Again,' or 'more,' is all the answer one receives.

Compare this to Gilbert's words in the well-known passage from *Orthodoxy:*

> Because children have abounding vitality, because they are in spirit fierce and free, therefore they want things repeated and unchanged. They always say, "Do it again"; and the grown-up person does it again until he is nearly dead. For grown-up people are not strong enough to exult in monotony.[18]

Likewise this passage from Frances:

> There can be no liberal education when the eyes are closed or the ears sealed. In this, as in everything else, the wayfarer must live to the full extent of his being. Pitfalls he must find on that journey, blind paths perhaps, but through it all the philosophy

---

[17] Frances Blogg, "The Open Road," *The Parents' Review* Vol. 11 (1900): 772-74, http://www.amblesideonline.org/PR/PR11p772TheOpenRoad.shtml.

[18] G.K. Chesterton, "The Ethics of Elfland," in *The Collected Works of G.K. Chesterton* Vol. 1 (San Francisco: Ignatius Press, 1987), 264. Originally published in *Orthodoxy* (1908).

of belief in the essential goodness, the actual significance of things created, the state of being, 'in love with life'.

The similarity of ideas is subtler here, finding expression in Gilbert's novel *Manalive,* in which the very essence of Innocent Smith's character is a belief in essential goodness, and a state of being in love with life. Some of the images are virtually identical, as with the following from Frances:

> I fancy we all remember the delightful sensations of childhood produced by the knowledge that a journey was about to be undertaken. The true meaning of packing, or ticket taking, of stations and porters, has perhaps never dawned upon us since, but to the child, there is no doubt of the extraordinary significance of each act in connection with the exciting event.

And this from Gilbert:

> And most of the inconveniences that make men swear or women cry are really sentimental or imaginative inconveniences—things altogether of the mind. For instance, we often hear grown-up people complaining of having to hang about a railway station and wait for a train. Did you ever hear a small boy complain of having to hang about a railway station and wait for a train? No; for to him to be inside a railway station is to be inside a cavern of wonder and a palace of poetical pleasures. Because to him the red light and the green light on the signal are like a new sun and a new moon. Because to him when the wooden arm of the signal falls down suddenly, it is as if a great king had thrown down his staff as a signal and started a shrieking tournament of trains.[19]

---

[19] G.K. Chesterton, *All Things Considered* (New York: John Lane Company, 1909), 25.

Toward the conclusion of her first essay, Frances rejoices in the adventures of the home:

> We must have within ourselves some consciousness of this impelling power that may lead us to travel deliberately through our ages, realizing that the most wonderful adventures are not those which we go forth to seek."

Echoing the same sentiment, Gilbert's chapter "Emancipation of Domesticity" (found in the book *What's Wrong with the World*) passionately argues that the hearth holds more adventure for a thinking woman or man than the dull life of any office or wage-earning position.

This pattern does not indicate a subsuming of one mind into the other, but rather to indicate the unfolding relationship and its powerful inspiration to both parties. This is shown again in Frances's second essay. "P.N.E.U. Natural History Clubs," published in 1901,[20] again demonstrating collaboration and conversation between Gilbert and Frances.

Frances begins with a quote of St. Francis of Assisi. Here we can see the traces of the affection of both Chestertons for the poor man from Assisi. Frances, already a gardener, was enthralled that St. Francis recommended to his austere and practical followers that they plant flowers in their garden for the sake of beauty alone. (Later, Gilbert and Frances had a statue of St. Francis installed in the midst of their flower garden at Top Meadow, their home in Beaconsfield.)

Frances goes on to explain why the P.N.E.U. was interested in Natural History Clubs:

> The sky, the sun, rivers, trees, animals and flowers are to children a subject of ever-increasing wonder and speculation,

---

[20] *Parents' Review* Vol. 12 (1901): 378-81.

and what we desire, who have the question of the right guiding and training of the young eager mind so much at heart, is, above all things, to make this power of wonder, this spirit of enquiry, *a durable and life-long possession*, so that whatever else may face the children in the course of years, the love and healing of Nature may be a priceless treasure to them for ever. (Emphasis added.)

Once again, a glance toward the work of Gilbert shows their shared passion for an idea:

What we are to have inside is the childlike spirit; but the childlike spirit is not entirely concerned about what is inside. It is the first mark of possessing it that one is interested in what is outside. The most childlike thing about a child is his curiosity and his appetite and his *power of wonder* at the world.[21] (Emphasis added.)

Who was the absolute source of this reverence for wonder? What did Frances bring to Chesterton's thought? What did he bring to hers? We will probably never know, and yet we see a fruitful exchange between two minds, a shared growth in that very childlike sense of wonder. The examples, even in these early essays, are innumerable. Frances's statement, "There is a saying that 'nothing succeeds like success,' but though I have no desire to invent a new paradox, yet, in a deep and spiritual sense, 'nothing fails like success' "[22] seems to combine two characteristic "Gilbertisms", that of paradox, and that of turning a phrase upside down. (The phrase that immediately might come to mind: "If a thing is worth doing, it's worth doing badly.")

---

[21] G.K. Chesterton, *"What I Saw in America,"* in *The Collected Works* Vol. 21 (San Francisco: Ignatius Press, 1990), 242.

[22] *L'Umile Pianta: For the Children's Sake* (1900): 9.

Even beyond the readily identifiable points of mutual inspiration with Gilbert, Frances remained busy throughout 1899, working, writing, and, as a letter to Mrs. Sieveking indicates, giving speeches:

> I did not know that there was an account of my speech at Woodford in the Christian Commonwealth. If you happen to have the paper, I would be grateful if you would let me see it. It would help me to prepare an address for Bolton—I am going there next week. Would it bother you to post it to me here? I will duly return it.
>
> Who is your lecturer?
>
> With kind regards and many thanks for your letter. Please give my love to the children.
>
> Yours sincerely,
> Frances Blogg

Life was not all achievement and enjoyment, of course. The words of William Ernest Henley, which resonated in a special way with Frances, express the suffering that came in the midst of joy:

What Is to Come

What is to come we know not. But we know
That what has been was good—was good to show,
Better to hide, and best of all to bear.
We are the masters of the days that were;

We have lived, we have loved, we have suffered . . . even so.
Shall we not take the ebb who had the flow?
Life was our friend? Now, if it be our foe—
Dear, though it spoil and break us! —need we care
What is to come?

Let the great winds their worst and wildest blow,
Or the gold weather round us mellow slow;
We have fulfilled ourselves, and we can dare
And we can conquer, though we may not share
In the rich quiet of the afterglow
What is to come.

Almost one year into their three-year engagement, tragedy struck. On Friday, June 30, 1899, Gertrude Blogg, the youngest at twenty-four years old, bicycled to work as was her wont. Nearby Gunnersbury Station, she was knocked from her bicycle by the shaft of a brougham (a type of horse-drawn carriage)[23] as she tried to pass a van—and one of the wheels rolled over her head. She was taken to a house across the street at 592 Chiswick High-road. She never regained consciousness, and died there on Sunday, July 2.[24] Due to the nature of the accident, there was a coroner's inquest, at which the death was ruled accidental. Gertrude was buried in the family grave at Highgate.

This horrifying accident sent shockwaves through their large circle of friends, as is shown in the letters Gilbert received at this time:

July 5, 1899

Dear Mr. Chesterton,
We were greatly shocked to read of the terribly sad death of Miss Blogg. How the very name of a bicycle is positively becoming a terror, for in our circle the accidents through these

---

[23] A brougham (pronounced "broom" or "brohm") was a light, four-wheeled horse-drawn carriage built in the nineteenth century. It was either invented for Scottish jurist Lord Brougham or simply made fashionable by his example. It had an enclosed body with two doors.

[24] "Lady Cyclist's Death," *Northampton Mercury* (July 7, 1899).

dread machines are multiplying with ghastly rapidity. May I venture to offer my most sincere sympathy to her mother and sisters in their trouble?

> With Kind Regards,
> Very sincerely yours,
> Annie Berkley[25]

Sept 12, 1899

Dear Gilbert,

. . . though I have known the Bloggs most with Gertrude and I cannot conceive what it will be like without her. There was so much of her in everything that was said and done. You showed me once how sorrow and death add to the vividness of the world's joys and beauties. One's own do, but is it so with another's? It seems suddenly to work a disenchantment, as the sudden sense of the death that lurks in a beautiful but plague-stricken spot . . .

. . . You know what I want to hear. How are the Bloggs? I have written twice and heard from Mrs. Blogg, but that was long ago and I find it too hard to write again. I only once wrote a letter that pleased me . . . never heard whether it pleased anyone else. Now I find myself utterly unable to get anywhere near to my correspondence or even to say exactly what I mean . . .

What are you doing and how are you? These are things I always want to know and never hear. Let me know now.

> Yours ever,
> Lucian Oldershaw.
> PS Love to the Bloggs.[26]

---

[25] Wade Center folder 236.

[26] *Ibid.*

The Bloggs were absolutely shattered.[27] Blanche's tendency toward depression resurfaced. Knollys descended even further. So devastated were they that they could not even be supportive of one another; each of them was trapped and isolated under a dark cloud of grief.

Ethel and Frances found a means for consolation together: travel. Immediately after the funeral, Frances took an extended leave of absence from the P.N.E.U. to travel abroad, hoping to rest and recover from the shock. She believed in the power of natural beauty to heal. In August she and her sister Ethel traveled to France and Switzerland with a larger party of men and women (including Frances's cousin Cordelia as well as her Aunt Rhoda, who served as chaperone). A mixed group would work, they all determined, only if there were no attachments. Consequently, Gilbert was not allowed to come. Gilbert disapproved of the scheme, especially as Frances was still in deep mourning. He felt he should come so he could comfort her.

Frances's decision to travel without Gilbert, in spite of his objection, may have resulted from the keenness of the spiritual struggle in which she found herself. Frances was not only grieving her sister's loss, but also was striving to reconcile in her mind the tragedy with the idea of a loving God.[28] Restless and aching, Frances climbed mountains in the Swiss Alps, where their hotel had a view of beautiful Mount Rigi.[29] Poetry, always so dear to her heart, ever more poignantly spoke to her wounded soul. She might have quoted to herself the words of Henley's "When You Are Old" (one of her favorites):

---

[27] *Gilbert Keith Chesterton*, 108.

[28] Ker, 56.

[29] Courtesy of John M. Kelly Library Rare Books, Archival & Manuscript Collection's G.K. Chesterton Microfiche Collection.

When you are old, and I am passed away—
Passed, and your face, your golden face is gray—
I think, whate'er the end, this dream of mine,
Comforting you, a friendly star will shine
Down the dim slope where you still stumble and stray.
So may it be: that so dead Yesterday,
Not sad-eyed ghost but generous and gay,
May serve your memories like almighty wine,
When you are old!

Dear Heart, it shall be so. Under the sway
Of death the past's enormous disarray
Lies hushed and dark. Yet though there come no sign,
Live on well pleased: immortal and divine
Love shall still tend you, as God's angels may,
When you are old.

Gilbert later wrote that Gertrude's death was a wound from which she never fully recovered. Her faith would survive, however, as her faith always did in the face of every trial. Gilbert himself instinctively knew that reliance on God was the only true means for healing. Writing to her during her travels, Gilbert said that he did not know how to comfort her (although he did write a poem for her), and he suggested she read the Bible. The one whose strong faith had so attracted Gilbert was now faltering, and Gilbert urged her to rely on her faith as a consolation.

When she returned home and to work in mid-December 1899, her five months of convalescence and travel had restored her spiritual and emotional health, though her grief was still strong. As the couple made preparations to marry, Gilbert worked diligently to build up his writing career sufficient to the support of a family. He believed the best way to help Frances deal with her grief was to marry her as soon as possible.

Their circle of friends expanded, especially with the natural intermingling that occurred during their engagement. Gilbert became well-known in the offices of the P.N.E.U.[30] from his visits to Frances, just as Frances grew to know Gilbert's Junior Debating Club (J.D.C.) and literary friends. Gilbert had by this time left his work at Fisher Unwin to become a freelance writer. He started by writing for the *Bookman* in December of 1899, but had little income from writing till he was hired by *The Speaker* in April 1900. He continued his friendships with the former JDC, and his delight at their reunion banquet was shared by Frances. It was at around this time that he met Hilaire Belloc, the prolific Anglo-French writer who would become one of his closest friends and most successful collaborators. Hilaire's wife Elodie and Frances developed a friendship as well.

1900, the dawn of a new century, marked the beginning of a new stage in Gilbert's career with the publication of his first two books: *Greybeards at Play* and *The Wild Knight*. Both works owe a great deal to Frances's encouragement. Rex Brimley Johnson, who was to have been Gilbert's brother-in-law, published *Greybeards*, with money provided from Edward Chesterton. When Johnson would not publish the second and more serious book of poetry, *The Wild Knight*, Frances discussed the matter with Gilbert's father, and Edward again provided the capital for its publication with Grant Richards. Edward also negotiated pay raises for his son,[31] a task Frances would take over once they married. After Edward negotiated the contract for *The Wild Knight*, he hired an agent, A.P. Watt, to act on Gilbert's behalf. Frances would do business with Watt from then on regarding her soon-to-be husband's books.

---

[30] Gilbert called it "The Parents' National Highly Rational Educational Union".

[31] Ker, 59.

The Wild Knight contains several of Gilbert's most famous poems, including "The Donkey" and "By the Babe Unborn". His success with this venture was indicative of the new circle of possibilities that had opened to this up-and-coming poet. Gilbert demonstrated his knowledge of Frances's contribution to his life and his work when he inscribed Frances's copy of the volume:

> They love (the bonfire and sparks and stars)
> They fight (the war)
> She wards off the press
> He loves her like a princess
> She's all the world to him
> She takes sorrow in, and doesn't let it out
> She is wise
> (They are engaged but not yet married)

The couple never planned on a three-year engagement. Some of their letters indicate impatience; a year before they actually married, Gilbert wrote that he saw no reason why they could not be married in April 1900 (and, as they were not married at that time, his eager suggestion obviously did not bear fruit). April 1900 was not, however, an utter disappointment; while Frances was away from her home that month, Gilbert was in the neighborhood for a political meeting at the Macgregors'. Gilbert had a cold, and the meeting ran late, so Ethel Blogg invited him to stay the night. To his own entertainment, he was thus enabled to write to Frances from her own home address. In his letter, he enthusiastically described the meeting and the speakers, including Belloc.

It was around this time that Frances expressed her concerns about Gilbert's appearance, and in particular, his hair. Gilbert told her that he considered that his hair grew out and at some point reached perfection, at which it only remained for three minutes, immediately returning to wild, long, unmanageability. Frances eventually solved the problem with a hat.

By autumn 1900, they were finally planning the wedding. In October, Frances gave notice at the P.N.E.U. that she was resigning. She quit at the end of December. Her ending salary was £80 a year. The P.N.E.U. advertised her departure with a brief commendation:

> We have another loss to deplore this New Year, and though there is an element of happiness in this loss—for we all congratulate Miss Frances Blogg on her approaching marriage with Mr. Gilbert Chesterton, yet we must regret the loss of a Secretary so indefatigable in her labours for the Parents' National Educational Union, and so steadfast in upholding its principles. We have much reason to be grateful to Miss Frances Blogg for five years of always sympathetic, kindly and enthusiastic work amongst us. It is a pleasure to know that her interest in the Union will not cease with her resignation of office.[32]

After her resignation, Frances and Miss Evans, a P.N.E.U. co-worker, took a long trip Florence, Italy, remaining until the early spring. It was a delightful trip, if cold. Frances's letter to her friend Isabel Sieveking captures her enthusiasm—describing the ice blocks floating on the river, the fashions she admired, her enjoyment of this time of leisure, her love of being surrounded by beautiful things:

> And yet it is not the treasures of art and architecture that attract me most, but the life of the town—the lightness of the Atmosphere, the colours and movement in the streets, the voices of the people, the grouping of the gossips at the

---

[32] *Parents' Review* Vol. 12.

street-corners. The whole revelation of an attitude towards life with which we are quite unfamiliar. They are a happy-go-lucky people, these Italians, but I am perfectly horrified at the misery and poverty that meets one at every turn . . .

. . . You must let me know when I return if I can help your Branch in any way. I am feeling a little as if the threads of the P.N.E.U. had suddenly snapped in my hands and that I have no clue, and you know I care enough about the work to still wish to help when I get the chance. I did not find it an easy task to give up . . .

. . . my love to the "tame lion [Lance]." How I should like to show him the sights of Florence. I can imagine Lance's delight at Cellini's "Perseus" or the Boar in the market place.[33]

Frances and Gilbert may have had some sort of lovers' quarrel during this period; Gilbert sent Frances a poem while she was in Florence entitled "An Apology."[34]

Nameless and gay my days have been,
Nameless and gay my life could pass
Finding no trumpet like the birds
No laurel greener than the grass.

But if I look but once again
Into that princely face and pale
I lose my oldest liberty
The peerless liberty to fail.[35]

This is not the only example of an apologetic poem from Gilbert to Frances. Though they were singularly well matched in every

---

[33] Courtesy of The Lilly Library, Indiana University, Bloomington, Indiana.

[34] Barker, 109.

[35] *Return To Chesterton*, 41.

respect, they were deeply human and their union was very much a *labor* of love. Another poem, written at about this time, seems to indicate that Gilbert was paying attention to an "old love," oblivious to the hurt or perhaps jealousy it caused Frances. He describes her as calm, reasonable, wise, and thoughtful; while he himself is a wild, swaggering fool:

THE HOUSE OF CHARITY

I know that Wisdom is throned among you—
Our Lady of laurels, Our Lady of scrolls.
You that take heed of your ways and ponder—
The choosing of roads, the weighing of souls.

In the new calm air of the age of reason
I swagger foolishly unafraid
With one poor tune amid all your music,
The tinkling tune of a man and a maid.

Ye that are wise—ye are also pitiful
Though I have smitten you—you can smile,
Thus have I walked from the womb of my mother
Never reeking of ditch or stile.

Waste it is in the well-laid garden
When into its boundaries breaks the sea
But the old wild ocean hath one law only—
—Ponder a little: and pardon me.

Ah love, I love in the old plain fashion,
With the old god's curse on this coward's head.
Heeds any eyes less bright than the dearest
Hears any words out of lips less red.

I sinned: I fell: and all about me
Is darkness: Can you forgive me, dear?
I loved old Love to ride with banners
And blow the trumpet and shake the spear.

I lie in the wreck of my own strange folly
With a faint, fierce hope—that far within
In the shade of your face may be God's own secret
A hidden smile and a pardoned sin.[36]

Whatever the "sin", it was clearly pardoned. Frances returned from Florence ready for her new and greatest challenge. As a former coworker put it: "Frances Blogg had been General Secretary to the P.N.E.U., but after a time, abandoned that arduous task to take up the still more arduous one of being the wife of G.K. Chesterton."[37] This was a task she was now prepared to face.

---

[36] Courtesy of John M. Kelly Library Rare Books, Archival & Manuscript Collection's G.K. Chesterton Microfiche Collection.

[37] Monk Gibbon, *Netta* (London: Routledge and Kegan Paul Limited, 1960), 175.

Chapter Three

WEDDED TO A RISING STAR (1901–1908)

A knight comes riding by, he enters
Ah no! Tis gone, and now I see a lion
With looks as gentle as fair Luna's guide
Again, the great lion-head is but an angel's wing
With calm face turned toward the changeless blue.

The wedding of Gilbert Keith Chesterton and Frances Alice Blogg took place on Friday, June 28, 1901, Frances's thirty-second birthday. After a three-year engagement, the couple finally united in matrimony at St. Mary Abbot, the Kensington Parish Church, with Fr. Conrad Noel presiding, assisted by Reverend C.H. Nicholson.[1] Rhoda Bastable, Frances's fifteen-year-old cousin[2], was her bridesmaid, along with the eight-year-old "infant" bridesmaid, Doris Child.[3] (Doris was the daughter of a woman working in the home of Blanche Blogg at the time; Frances had been teaching the girl arithmetic.[4]) The stories of their wedding day have been told from Gilbert's point of view, and there are no accounts

---

[1] *The Morning Leader* notice, recorded in the notes of the St. Stephen's College alumni magazine.

[2] Daughter of Aunt Julia Marsden Blogg Bastable, now a widow.

[3] *The Collected Works of G.K. Chesterton* Vol. 10-C (San Francisco: Ignatius Press, 2008), 463.

[4] *Return To Chesterton*, 100.

of Frances's point of view. There are no photographs of their wedding day extant in Chesterton archives.

Wedding guests included John Butler Yeats, Miss Elizabeth "Lollie" and Miss Susan "Lily" Yeats, the father and sisters of the poet William Butler Yeats. Lollie recalled:

> My sister and I were at the Chestertons' wedding at St. Mary Abbot in Kensington. Gilbert wanted the ceremony as ceremonial as possible—but Frances, who then belonged to some new thought people in religious matters, wanted everything possible cut from the Church of England Service—except just the legal parts. Gilbert had been, of course, brought up a nonconformist.

It was a day of laughter and love—and joyful mishaps—a foretaste of their future life together. Frances's nephew, Charles Bastable, age twelve, was sent out at the last minute before the service to buy Gilbert a tie, which he had forgotten. Annie Fermin, Gilbert's childhood friend, sat with Marie Louise, his mother, and laughed together at a forgotten price tag on the bottom of Gilbert's shoe, fully visible once he kneeled in front of the congregation.

Their honeymoon fared no better. Lucian Oldershaw, soon to be Frances's brother-in-law, reliably deposited the couple's luggage on the train—the train they failed to catch. On their way to the station, they stopped so Gilbert could drink a glass of milk at a restaurant where he and his mother often stopped. After the milk, they visited another shop where Gilbert bought a new revolver so he could protect his wife. Arriving belatedly at the train station, they caught a slow train for Ipswich and stayed the first night on their way to Norfolk at the White Horse Inn. By this time Frances was tired, so Gilbert suggested she lie down while he went for a walk, and he promptly lost his way.

It was quite a honeymoon: robbed of her luggage because of her husband's loving gesture toward his mother, waylaid at an Inn, and deserted by her bridegroom. After so unpromising a beginning, the couple enjoyed their six-day honeymoon. They spent their time happily on Norfolk Broads, the place that was to give the future Father Brown his dumpling description.[5]

It may seem an unconventional move in a biography of one person to shift at this critical nuptial moment to focus on someone else entirely, but two circumstances have combined to make this briefly necessary in any biography of Frances Chesterton: the couple's infertility and the odd personality that was Ada Chesterton, Frances's future sister-in-law.

Ada Eliza Jones was a street reporter who wrote under the penname of J.K. Prothero. Gilbert and Cecil Chesterton met Ada sometime in 1899, when Cecil was about twenty-one. Ada was thirty-one.

Cecil and Ada were an unlikely couple. Ada was extroverted and a sensationalist, writing romance novels under another *nom de plume*, and always pressing her editors to print material that bordered on libelous.[6] A "scoop" was her goal and delight. Cecil, meanwhile, was introverted, loved intellectual argument, and wrote political and economic articles.

For seventeen years, Ada and Cecil remained friendly co-workers, with the slight complication that Cecil fell in love with

---

[5] ". . . he had a face as round and dull as a Norfolk dumpling . . ." G.K. Chesterton, *The Annotated Innocence of Father Brown*, ed. Martin Gardner (Mineola: Dover Publications, 1998), 18.

[6] Mrs. Cecil Chesteron, *The Chestertons* (London: Chapman and Hall, 1941), 95.

her. He asked her over and over again to marry him, and she always refused.[7]

Seventeen years passed. Cecil was then thirty-seven and Ada was forty-seven; he was a Roman Catholic convert, and she was a Communist.[8] War was then devastating Europe. Cecil extracted a promise from Ada that, if he were ever sent to the front, she would marry him. He enlisted and received his orders. They married during his three-day leave. (Ada lied on the marriage certificate, making herself ten years younger and writing the wrong name for her father.) Their honeymoon was less than one week long and logistically challenged: Cecil was on duty and Ada stayed in a hotel nearby with her mother. Then he went off to France. Cecil fell ill during the war and died at the end of it. Their marriage lasted nineteen months on the calendar, but with only part of one week of that time together.

In 1941, Ada Chesterton published a "tell-all" book entitled *The Chestertons*. In it, among other things, she concocted a lurid tale of the couple's wedding night, where a repressed Frances shrieked, repulsed, from Gilbert's embrace, condemning him to a life of wedded virginity. Ada claimed Cecil as her source, and that it was "old news" by the time she heard it.

Biographers have universally condemned this as an invasive invention on the part of Ada, and this for many reasons. Ada herself is roundly described as an unreliable witness.[9] Whatever the degree of intimacy in friendship, the actual marriage of Ada

---

[7] According to Aidan Mackey, we must be just as skeptical about this remark of Ada's as we are with anything else she said. Mr. Mackey states, "I am very cautious about accepting Keith's assertions. She was given to high inflation in recounting her life and memories."

[8] Ada Jones wrote for the Communist paper *The Daily Worker*.

[9] See Appendix in Ward's *Gilbert Keith Chesterton*. Frances was a good friend of Maisie Ward's mother, Josephine. And as she adored her friend's children, so Frances lavished attention on Maisie as she grew. Maisie met and married Frank Sheed and together

and Cecil was brief. The union bound Ada to the Chesterton family without deeply incorporating her into their ranks. It is difficult to believe they would have discussed the intimate details of Gilbert and Frances's private lives before they were married, and even more difficult to believe they had time or inclination to discuss it after their marriage.

Further, Frances herself was a deeply private person, unlikely to discuss details regarding her wedding night difficulties—if, indeed, there were any. England in 1901, though hardly prurient, was not a time in which such a conversation would be common. It is, of course, quite possible that the most intimate aspects of marriage proved anxious or even challenging, as they might to any virginal young couple. For detailed suppositions, we should only follow the advice of Victor Hugo, when he wrote that: "At the door of every bridal bedchamber an angel stands, smiling, with a finger to his lips." As to the seemingly spiteful suggestion by Ada that Frances doggedly refused Gilbert access to her bed and her person, this is well answered in the long and tragic struggle by the couple against infertility (a struggle that would have been spurious if they had not actively striven to conceive a child).

Little knowing the energy that would be expended in lurid hypothesis about their wedding night, Gilbert and Frances settled into married life. They adopted a host of nicknames. Frances called herself "the wife of the Innocent" when Gilbert called himself "an Innocent at Home."[10] She called him "The Mighty

---

they published books under the name Sheed & Ward. Maisie would be the only author Frances allowed access to materials to write Gilbert's biography.

[10] *Chesterton as Seen by His Contemporaries*, 114.

Atom."[11] He called himself "The White Elephant." He called her "the Queen,"[12] and "Carp."[13] She was also called "Francesca" by Gilbert, as well as by Margaret Heaton.

When they returned from the honeymoon, they lived temporarily in the Georgian house of the Bloggs' family friend, Mr. William Boore, in Edwardes Square, Kensington. They only lived there a few months—and certainly could not have afforded to live there—before moving to Overstrand Mansions, in Battersea, where they took a flat.[14]

Frances set up housekeeping as best she could, cleaning and straightening the house as well as her husband. She had tried to keep Gilbert as neat in appearance as possible during their engagement—something Gilbert called Frances's "crusade of tidiness"[15]—but early in their married life, she decided to work *with* Gilbert rather than fight nature. She outfitted him with a large hat and cape coat; he finished it off with a swordstick. His theatrical appearance brought him notice and recognition wherever he went.

Frances set new rules for the Chesterton household. She put up a board on the wall, over which hung the words "Lest We Forget". Here she kept track of Gilbert's comings and goings, trying to help him stay on schedule and on time. Another rule

---

[11] G.K. Chesterton, "Chesterton on Dickens," *Collected Works* Vol. 15. Alzina Stone Dale, *The Outline of Sanity: A Biography of G.K. Chesterton* (Grand Rapids: Eerdmans, 1982), 96. See also *Chesterton as Seen by His Contemporaries*, 164-65.

[12] Ker, pg. 60.

[13] *Collected Works* Vol. 10-A, 317. There is one reference to "Carp" in the Ward biography—"There will be a select store of chocolate-creams (to make you do the Carp with) . . ." in *Gilbert Keith Chesterton*, 98.

[14] No. 60 first, then No. 48.

[15] Ker, 58.

was particularly challenging for Gilbert: there was to be no reading at the table. Since Gilbert mentions this rule several times in letters, he must have been in the habit of enjoying a book over a meal—but he would give it up for the sake of his new wife. He was also trying to brush his hair more often, all in an effort to be good and please Frances.

In these early years of their marriage, Frances organized all of her husband's lectures, even negotiating payment, in addition to supervising his correspondence, as shown by this 1903 letter:

> My dear Isabel,[16]
> I ought to refuse your P.N.E.U. invitation to Gilbert but he is anxious to accept. He is so full up with lectures, meetings and work of all sorts, it seems impossible to fit in any more. However, he might arrange for the 10th or 11th November. Either afternoon or evening. Let me know. Excuse such a hurried line—I have arrears and arrears of work and correspondence. Love to you all including my brother.[17] Tell him I should like to see him.
>
> > Yours ever affectionately,
> > Frances Chesterton
> > Can the Branch afford any fee?[18]

In the beginning, when money was tight, they lived thriftily from week to week as Gilbert's various articles and books were published. They had decided even before the wedding that Frances should handle the money and the shopping. Gilbert needed his mind free to think about other things. Frances was frugal because she had to be. Gilbert would leave the house

---

[16] Isabel Sieveking.

[17] Knollys was working as a tutor for the Sieveking household at this time.

[18] Courtesy of The Lilly Library, Indiana University, Bloomington, Indiana.

with money in his pocket, and come home with nothing, and not know where it went. Frances had to watch things closely and work hard at the maintenance of the household. She would often sit by the fire patching clothes and darning socks. (The kitchen fireplace was her favorite cozy place to be.)

Throughout their life together, Frances took Gilbert in stride. Her calm demeanor surprised other women, including her sister Ethel, who found Gilbert eccentric. A neighbor, Mrs. Saxon-Mills, lived close enough to hear Gilbert through the walls, and she wondered at his bloodcurdling cries in the morning when he needed Frances to help him dress—and Frances's serenity in the midst of such monumental oddness.[19]

Gilbert's joy in marriage is expressed in backwards fashion in a letter to his old friend and neighbor, Annie Fermin, upon the announcement of Annie's engagement:

> . . . my wife recalls herself to me continuously by virtues, splendors, agreeable memories, screams, pokers, brickbats and other things . . . I know you will be happy (married) . . . I know it because my wife is happy with me . . ."

This comical transformation of gentle Frances into an abusive, blunt-instrument-wielding harridan clearly delights its inventor. The triumphant flourish comes at the end: *my wife is happy with me.*

Literary endeavors and Frances's interest in publication grew apace—and her attention was not confined to Gilbert. Edward Chesterton had written and illustrated a book called *The Wonderful Story of Dunder van Haeden and His Seven Little Daughters* when Gilbert was young. In his autobiography, Gilbert mentioned that the book was for home consumption

---

[19] Ker, 83.

and never published. However, Rex Brimley Johnson actually published the book in 1901. Edward Chesterton's drawings are intricately detailed, demonstrating his considerable artistic talent. A copy inscribed to Frances shows that she must have had some influence in the publication:

> Frances Chesterton,
> with the author's love,
> November 1901.
> (All your fault!)[20]

At around this time, Rex also published Frances's Uncle and Godfather Cosmo Monkhouse's book, *Nonsense Rhymes,* in the same style as *Greybeards*, illustrated by G.K. Chesterton.

Frances's married life was busy and ordered. Weekdays she took dictation from Gilbert as he wrote his articles and essays. Weekends they both regularly attended the Anglican Church and visited their parents and families. Frances continued to teach Sunday school, and was active in the local parish. She could often be found at the rectory on a Sunday afternoon, having tea with the rector's wife and other ladies from the parish.

Under Frances's influence, Gilbert had made many strides in his journey toward Christianity. He had also gained an appreciation for sacramental Christianity. Early in their married life, Frances was attracted to the high Anglican Church as well as to Christian Socialism, which has been described as Catholic Action plus popular reform. This latter attraction seems obvious; she had a love for the poor, for education for those who could not afford it, for visiting the sick and the elderly; she believed her faith ought to be put into action. She was grateful for her opportunities at St. Stephen's College, and wanted to share her

---

[20] Courtesy of Aidan Mackey.

faith. The sisters had taught her the importance of caring for the poor. Later, while working as a tutor and governess till she obtained employment at the P.N.E.U., she began teaching as a volunteer in the evenings at local schools, which held "Happy Evenings" for poor children to get caught up on their education.[21]

There were many socialists among their friends, preeminent among them the playwright George Bernard Shaw. Besides Shaw, C.F.G. Masterman, a liberal member of Parliament, and a cabinet minister, was an active member of the Anglo-Catholic Christian Social Union, along with Conrad Noel, the Anglican priest who had married Gilbert and Frances. Gilbert says in his autobiography that he was considerably influenced by Noel, and his brother Cecil even more so. Gilbert's sympathies with Christian Socialism were shown in a primarily literary light, as in his admiration for the novelist Charles Dickens (identified by Gilbert as such a Christian Socialist). Early in their marriage, Frances started a Christian Social Union group out of their home, which Noel directed. Gilbert gave talks at their events.

These men each represented a different aspect of Socialism, reflected through their distinct personalities. This popular school, self-identified as progressive and open-minded, was attractive in its most secular iteration to a mind like George Bernard Shaw. With his like-minded friends, Shaw became a charter member of the Fabian Society to bring about social justice in a secular organization.

Noel was considered a controversialist and an eccentric. He was the son of a famous poet, and a leading member of the Christian Social Union, which combined religion with politics: the religion was Anglo-Catholic; the politics were a

---

[21] "Ladies' Gossip," *Otago Witness* (June 2, 1909). See also "Happy Evenings," *Gilbert* Vol.15, no. 8 (2012).

radical socialism. In addition, Noel was involved in the Christo-Theosophic Society. Gilbert related that when he and Cecil first met Noel, they were both more or less anti-religion. Under his influence, they both became open to the idea of the church, even as they became interested with socialist ideals.

The Chestertons' support for the Christian Social Union came at a time before their thoughts had converged on the idea of Distributism. At this time, Gilbert's passion for politics led him to hope that change could be brought about politically. (His friendship with Hilaire Belloc would eventually give him a close view of the workings of the government, as Belloc served as a member of Parliament from 1906 until 1910.)

Beyond politics and personalities, Frances Chesterton's interest in socialism was imbued with a special flavor by her quiet passion for Christian service to others. This was shown in her innumerable charitable efforts, as well as within their growing circle of friends. Belloc had cause to be grateful for her selfless goodness: in 1902, he became very ill while visiting, and Gilbert and Frances set up a sick bed for him in their home. He developed pneumonia, and Frances nursed him through it.

The family grew. On July 16, 1902, the couple attended the marriage of Frances's sister Ethel to Gilbert's longtime friend Lucian Oldershaw at St. Peter's parish church in Bayswater. Lucian was working full-time as a tutor. Ethel and Lucian had their first baby a year later in September 1903, a girl they named Gertrude in honor of the lost Blogg sister. When Ethel brought the baby over for Frances to see, Frances admitted she could hardly bear it. Her unfulfilled dream, expressed to one of the Chesterton secretaries, to have "seven beautiful children", was a devastating cross.

1903 brought yet another critical shift in the development of both Chestertons, with the acquaintance of a Catholic priest named Fr. John O'Connor. O'Connor wrote to Gilbert, introducing himself and stating exactly why he loved Chesterton's work.[22] O'Connor asked if he could send Gilbert a sonnet he had written. The correspondence began, and they quickly discovered they had a mutual acquaintance in Belloc. Within a short time, they also discovered another mutual friend: Walter Crawley, who had participated in the I.D.K. society in Bedford Park, and was (according to Frances) "a very old friend, my brother's greatest friend."[23]

Despite the fact that Frances would not meet O'Connor in person until the following year, O'Connor became one of the dearest and closest in their circle of friends. After responding to O'Connor's letter the first time, Gilbert left the task of keeping up with him mainly to his wife. In fact, Frances seems to have maintained the correspondence not only with O'Connor, but with most of their friends, for once Gilbert started writing full time for a living, he no longer had much time for personal correspondence. Frances was a great correspondent and wrote many, many letters.

Frances and O'Connor shared a love of art, music, literature, sunshine—neither liked cloudy days. They were also both devout fans of Gilbert Chesterton. Frances made sure that O'Connor read Gilbert's latest essays, books, and poems. On Frances's recommendation, O'Connor searched out *The Wild Knight*, and wrote to her of his enjoyment of it. The priest let her know how much he enjoyed Chesterton in person as well as in print. They also discussed new books Chesterton should be encouraged to write: a book on George Meredith and a book of verse.

---

[22] British Library folder 73196.

[23] British Library folder 73196-65.

O'Connor and Gilbert were well-suited to be friends as well. They were both writers, both poets, both well read. A striking mixture of the conventional and unconventional, O'Connor was a robustly swearing, motorcycle-riding,[24] art-collecting lover of the poor. He even came upon a set of vintage swords, and knowing Gilbert's love of weaponry, wrote Frances asking if they wanted to purchase the antiques. Frances sent the money and they hired someone to make a mount for them for display in their home.

The history of the correspondence between O'Connor and Frances is extremely long and those letters could fill a book. O'Connor listened and advised, sought advice and relayed stories, was sympathetic, religiously supportive, sought out gifts for their home and more. In all ways, he was a family friend.

By 1904, O'Connor wrote Frances with a correction of a grammatical error, which he found while reading "the Watts book":

> There is one slip, not exactly of grammar, but of the kind which impairs the perfection of diction. He joins an active verb with a passive and does not repeat the auxiliary.[25]

O'Connor continues on with a critique of *Napoleon of Notting Hill*, telling Frances it was too much of a compromise between grave and gay, irony and earnestness. Then he complimented the book by saying it was a rare achievement to make a wildly remote allegory so intimately credible by sheer lightness of touch. "What I admire most in your husband," wrote O'Connor,

---

[24] Julia Smith, *The Elusive Father Brown: The Life of Mgr. John O'Connor* (Herefordshire: Gracewing Publishing, 2010), 70.

[25] British Library folder 73196.

is his passion for the things of the mind. He was made for things both high and deep, and seems never so at home in conversation as when a metaphysical hare starts for a good run. There is then an exhilaration in his view-halloo which conciliates one's best attention.

Their relationship was not confined to literary subjects; O'Connor served Frances and her family pastorally many times. The following 1904 letter, often quoted in other biographies, though not in full, indicates the priest's closeness to their most intimate struggles:[26]

April 12th

My dear Father O'Connor,

Thank you for your letter. It is good of you to write to my brother, please don't be put off by any rebuffs & encourage him when you can—

You will see us, I hope, before very long.

On Saturday week I am going into a Nursing Home for a month to get satisfactorily through an operation. After that I am to go to Ilkley and go in for a course of bed and massage. And I trust nevertheless you will come over and see me & leave me your priestly blessing.

It's all very horrid and I hate leaving my husband but I've been obliged at last to give in and I hope to end as an Amazon.

All good wishes for a Blessed Easter.

Yours gratefully,

Frances Chesterton

---

[26] British Library folder 73196.

Her mixture of sadness and hope of triumph is all there in that "Amazonian" sentence. So many of her deepest concerns are here: Knollys, her health, her marriage. The relationship had already developed to the point that Frances felt comfortable speaking to O'Connor when she was upset with Gilbert.[27] The closeness was reciprocal; he called upon Frances for advice on running a dancing class for children, and to ask for donations when needed.[28]

Because of this, the correspondence grants special access and illumination regarding Frances herself. When O'Connor wrote in 1905 that he was praying for Gilbert and Frances that "all things may work together unto good", it gives a small indication of the suffering to be found even in a happy marriage.[29] This is explored even more fully in O'Connor's letter of May 17, 1905:

> . . . I should think that the very intensity of his cerebration would be a positive physical bar to his staying long enough still to give the passive sympathy or power of listening which I believe the only real help we can give one another in trouble. I speak from experience. Advice is good, but it is the silence of the other party while we blow off steam that is the really soothing influence. Hence God, being the most passive of listeners, is the only perfect sympathizer. I have to warn young brides before their marriage that even the most ideal husband will have them lonesome at times, and often as they grow older, and that it is important never to put trust in any human relation for the final intimacy which we all do seek.

---

[27] O'Connor, letter dated 17 May 1905, 57-56, British Library folder 73196.

[28] *The Elusive Father Brown*, 48-49.

[29] British Library folder 73196-61.

This seems hard in prose, but read Francis Thompson's "Yew Tree" in his first book, and you will see.[30] But perhaps I am misreading your letter . . .

One thing I do know I do not misread. You are carrying the Cross, and whether you want another to help you or not, you are distressed that you are not carrying it well, nobly, gracefully. That is the Cross within the Cross, to find that there is no knack nor deftness of handling which will make it less cumbersome, that one must stagger, and even fall, and find that rising is harder than walking as the Cross is still on top. Yet these details of the way which assail one's hope of the end, have to be disregarded, in a sense. I would tell you of times when I have gone at work in a cursing—rather than a praying spirit, wildly determined to go through, even as a panic-stricken soldier rushes mad with fear against the enemy. Yet looking back on those times I feel really proud and useful and "worthied" as Shakespeare's subtle word has it, at an hour when lack of routine or slackness of nerves would make me despair of being fit for the Kingdom of God. From the penances of the skies gladness of the streams.[31]

Here is the famous phrase of St. Augustine, presented pastorally: *Our hearts are restless, O Lord, until we rest in Thee.* Loneliness is essential to the human condition, and marriage—even the happiest of marriages—cannot bring satisfaction. Thus: O'Connor advised her to rely more on God than on Gilbert.

During this same time, Frances must have written to O'Connor about a deep depression she was feeling. He writes:

---

[30] Francis Thompson, "A Fallen Yew," in *Selected Poems of Francis Thompson* (New York: John Lane and Company, 1908).

[31] Wade Center folder 234.

... I wonder if the "black despair" you mention is a mental or nervous malady—the latter I should think, and if so, surely a passing cloud. I do not know the priest you mention. I wish I did know the right person to commend to you.[32]

Frances knew well her family history of mental illness, an affliction from which her mother and brother both suffered. She perhaps worried that she might be similarly afflicted, and O'Connor tried to reassure her that he believed it was temporary—which indeed it must have been, for there is no evidence of severe mental illness in Frances.

Her depression may also have been occasioned by the circumstances of her life. Frances loved the privacy of the home and disliked publicity. Her husband's popularity brought joy, but also disruption to what might have been a quiet domestic life. On the other hand, it brought many special people into their lives she might not have met otherwise, like O'Connor. There were many people in Frances's inner circle: Isabel Sieveking, Elodie Belloc, Frances's sister Ethel Oldershaw, her cousins Margaret Arndt and Rhoda Bastable, and Alice Meynell,[33] the poet and author, Freda Rivière, a friend from Bedford Park;[34] as well as their many private secretaries. For those interested in Frances, these relationships all grant invaluable insight into

---

[32] *Ibid.*, letter dated September 18, 1905.

[33] Meynell, an Anglo-Catholic who converted to Roman Catholicism, was famous for her poetry and was a prolific writer. Although she was twenty-two years older, she and Frances became friends and had much in common. When they first met, Frances found the Meynells dull, and wrote in her private diary that Alice's husband Wilfrid was a snob; and that Alice was nice and intelligent, but affected. Frances must have changed her mind about them afterwards.

[34] Ker, 162.

her character, since Frances wrote hundreds if not thousands of letters to intimate friends as well as distant acquaintances.

These letters only partially fill the documentary void. Frances kept notebooks and diaries throughout her life. Gilbert's biographer Maisie Ward saw Frances's diaries and quotes from them, but only to the extent that secretary Dorothy Collins allowed her to. Many papers and journals were destroyed by Dorothy at Frances's request. In the 1990s, Aidan Mackey made the remarkable discovery of a partial diary of Frances's.[35] That discovery allows access into the social life of the couple for one year, 1904 to 1905.[36] In the Mackey diary, Frances confesses that Gilbert had asked her to write her memoirs, which she stated she would not do, not even for money. She would only attempt to write down the people they met and got to know. On April 5, 1904, the entry states that Frances met O'Connor in person for the first time. She immediately liked him, saying he was delightful, so wise, and so dazzling in appearance.

Invitations to go out to dinner were frequent for the couple, and they had dinner parties at their home, too. It was largely a delight for Frances. She noted when people complimented Gilbert's work, which she loved. Her diary, she wrote, was never to be published, so she felt free to comment on the beauty of one hostess and the snobbery of another.

Throughout the diary, Frances drops name after notable name. Some are authors, some politicians, some playwrights, and some artists. All were well-known people of the day, but now most are forgotten. They sometimes mingled with high society,

---

[35] Aidan Mackey, "Diary of Frances Chesterton, 1904-1905," *The Chesterton Review* Vol. 25, no. 3 (1999).

[36] There were also two diaries that Frances kept in 1919-1920 for trips to Egypt, Jerusalem, and Rome, and another for the trip to America they took in 1921.

in which Frances did not feel at home. She complained that she encountered "too many clever people" or that they were "very aristocratic and interesting and detached." She would have the time of her life one night, laughing with Belloc and Conrad Noel, and then record an event the following day as a "dull affair" with a hostess who was a "good-hearted snob," in whose company Frances felt "too uncultivated to talk much."

Throughout the diaries and letters, especially in the letters to O'Connor, themes repeat: admiration and support of Gilbert (who was endlessly busy and relied on her organization in all things), concern for her family members, especially Knollys, and her own physical suffering.

In 1907, Frances caught pneumonia, and wrote to O'Connor of it:

April 12

Dear Fr. O'Connor,
I fear you may not get this letter & that you may have made a fruitless journey to the Battersea flat.

I have been very ill, pneumonia following influenza and now after 5 weeks am only able to walk across a room & have sunk to the awful degradation of a bath chair,[37] though it is not allowed to be seen on the public highway.

I should have been so delighted to see you & should gladly have housed you if it could have been arranged—but the luck is all against me just now.

We are staying here for a week with my sister & so our time is mostly taken up in persuading Gilbert not to go to London, a hopeless mission . . .

---

[37] A wheelchair, so named because it originated in Bath, England.

Have you seen his poem in "The Albany Review"?[38]

After the pneumonia, Frances remained weakened throughout the summer. She herself traced the beginning of her illness to her April 1906 operation:

August 1907

My dear Isabel,
I ought to have written to you ever so long ago . . .

. . . I have been ill off and on, since an operation in April 1906, and this spring I had pneumonia rather badly and everything got out of hand.

I am so glad my brother is with you, after his terrible illness I am so happy and thankful to have him almost well again. . . . Mother and I are very conscious to keep him away as long as possible if it suits you at all to have him with you let me know—I would gladly pay for his holiday with you as I am sure he cannot have much money—having been idle so long—Please don't say anything to him about this, but tell me what you would charge per week, and if you could keep him a little longer. . . . We are here with Gilbert's people for another ten days and very jolly it is—though the weather leaves a good deal to be desired.

My love to the boys and the girlie.[39]

The suffering of Knollys throughout these years were considerable. He suffered a complete nervous breakdown in 1905, and had spent a year at Holloway Sanatorium, which Gilbert and Frances subsidized. During that time, he injured himself with

---

[38] Frances is referring to "Fragment from a Ballad Epic of 'Alfred'" published in 1907, Wade Center folder 308. This would become *The Ballad of the White Horse*, and would be dedicated to Frances.

[39] Courtesy of The Lilly Library, Indiana University, Bloomington, Indiana.

self-inflicted wounds, breaking his own elbow and leg. After he left there, "almost well" as Frances cautiously states in her letter, he returned to the Sieveking house. In this letter, she offers to pay her friend to house Knollys, not as a tutor but merely to reside in the Sieveking home. Gilbert and Frances, despite their frugality, still had money to spare to send for the care of her brother.

Additionally, the letter above is evidence of yet another operation which Frances underwent. It seems she had three—1904, 1906 and 1908. Each attempt to cure her infertility failed.

In addition, Frances suffered more each year from the constant strain of having to compensate for the shorter leg. There were pressure and wear on her hips, her knees, neck, and spine from being out of alignment. Frances also suffered from rheumatism,[40] and Gilbert told Belloc that Frances had trouble sleeping. Later when Frances did consult a doctor, the cause of the insomnia was revealed. Frances has been suffering in silence for years, in pain from her back, neck, and hips.

In the midst of her illnesses and suffering, Frances rekindled her publishing career. On March 25, 1908, Frances's poem "Lady Day" was published in the *Westminster Gazette*. Before her marriage, her articles had appeared in *Parents' Review* and *L'Umile Pianta*, the publications of the P.N.E.U. This was her first foray into print since her marriage. After "Lady Day", Frances's poems appeared regularly in the papers. "Midsummer Day" was published in June of 1908 in the same paper.

In August 1908, Isabel Sieveking must have written Frances asking her to give a talk on behalf of the P.N.E.U. Frances's response is friendly but tentative, and Knollys remains a clear concern:

---

[40] A. Chesterton, *The Chestertons*, 285.

My dear Isabel,

I have been hoping to hear from you. Re: P.N.E.U., I would so gladly help if I could. I only wanted to explain that I am no longer authorized from head quarters, so they might not think [I] am qualified to speak on their behalf. Do write and tell me what you think about the matter. Of course I could work up the affairs of the Union and be up to date, but I feel sure they would not think me representative. Do you see what I mean?

I must try and see you. I suppose you never come to town. We are such busy people—I never have a moment and all the people I love best are neglected (you included.) I feel so happy at thinking of Knollys with you, after all our anxiety about him.

Excuse a short scribble, it is just on 12 o'clock, and I must go to bed—I feel dazed after writing 15 letters this evening.

Ever yours affectionately,

Frances Chesterton[41]

The intimacy with Isabel was founded on many points: suffragettes, co-workers at the P.N.E.U., concern over Knollys, and, finally, fellow writers. Isabel had several books published. (Isabel was also an amateur photographer. She took a portrait of Knollys in her home.)

The summer of 1908 brought an appalling tragedy into all of their lives, and particularly affected Frances: the death of Knollys. His emotional and mental turmoil was well-known to all who were close to him. By the end of summer 1908 though, Knollys seemed better—although he was still prone to occasional despondency. With his conversion to Roman Catholicism, Knollys' black cloud seemed to have partially lifted. He had recited his own poetry at a public hall and had planned out tutoring work for the following school year. His article on Gilbert's Japanese

---

[41] Courtesy of The Lilly Library, Indiana University, Bloomington, Indiana.

dolls was going to be published soon in *Girl's Realm* magazine. He was a quiet man, and the intensity of his suffering was not revealed until his death.

In late August, Frances was shocked to receive the worst of news: her brother had been found dead, floating in the middle of a river in Sussex. He had committed suicide on August 16 at age thirty-six.

Knollys' writings, especially in his book *Ledgers & Literature,* are full of strange, poignant touches. One chapter extolled the existence of an imaginary friend. Another described the advantages of living in a lunatic asylum. Knollys informed sane men how to get committed to an asylum.[42] "It is an infinitely pathetic collection of essays and poems, some of which only too clearly foreshadowed his end," wrote Lance Sieveking.[43] It appears Sieveking was right.

So much of Knollys can be seen in the writings of his friends and family as well. Knollys' suicide coincides with the publication of Gilbert's *Orthodoxy.* The chapter "The Maniac," and the line, "The men who really believe in themselves are all in lunatic asylums", may be drawn from Gilbert's personal familiarity with lunatic asylums from visiting Knollys. At that time, if your relative was confined, the family was responsible for bringing the patient food. Frances would have taken a turn bringing food regularly to Knollys during his year at Holloway.

Knollys, who loved to do quadratic equations in his head, and had earned a living as a bookkeeper and accountant as well as through tutoring, was possibly also the inspiration behind

---

[42] For more about Knollys Blogg, see Nancy Carpentier Brown, "Brother-in-Law of G.K. Chesterton, George Alfred Knollys Blogg (1871-1908)," *Gilbert* Vol. 17, no. 2-3 (2013): 8-10.

[43] Lance Sieveking, *The Eye of the Beholder* (London: Hulton Press, 1957), 19.

Chesterton's line, "Mathematicians go mad, and cashiers; but creative artists very seldom." Perhaps this was why Gilbert and Frances encouraged Knollys to write poetry, to try to improve his mental health by fostering creativity.

Frances went to Newhaven to assist in identifying her brother's body, along with her brother-in-law Lucian Oldershaw. The body had been in the water for days and the face was unrecognizable. Lucian identified Knollys[44] based on previous injuries and a ring on one of his fingers. The coroner determined that drowning had not caused death, but rather the self-inflicted wounds to the neck, one of which had severed the artery. Based on his history, the death was determined to be suicide.

Frances met with a Catholic priest to arrange a funeral Mass. Her mother was away visiting family in Germany and changed plans abruptly to return home.

Frances had allowed herself not to worry so much about her brother, as he had seemed to be better since his conversion. She found out that the Sunday prior to his suicide, he had gone to Mass. This appeared ironic to her, and these circumstances were to become a part of the delay in her future conversion.

Frances had lost another sibling, and she was miserable. She turned to her husband first, and they shared their sorrow in tears. Frances wrote to her friend and confidant O'Connor, who had been praying for Knollys.

> Dear Father O'Connor,
> I have to write in great trouble—my dear brother was found drowned[45] at Seaford a few days ago. It is a terrible shock

---

[44] *East Sussex News*, 28 August 1908 and reported in Ker, 203.

[45] "Found drowned" was the polite term used in those days for suicide. G.F. Watts, the painter Gilbert wrote a biography of in 1904, painted "Found Drowned," picturing a young lady, lying half out of the sea, clutching a locket in her hand.

to us all—we were so happy about him. He seemed to have quite recovered from his terrible illness—But he sought death himself . . ."

Once again, intense suffering flooded into Frances's life, and she struggled to understand. She felt suddenly lost, floundering, not knowing how to handle yet another family crisis. Inconsistent with her usual response, Frances consulted with a medium in an attempt to contact the spirits of her dead brother and sister. Why did she do this? She wanted to know where they were. She needed assurance: were they at peace or not? In heaven or not? Whatever she saw in the glass ball made her scream. Gilbert wrote a poem, "The Crystal,"[46] which tells of his anger at her for choosing this way of dealing with the death of her brother.

Although out of character, the lapse to spiritualism is not completely without foundation. Raised in bohemian Bedford Park, she must have been familiar with crystal gazing and planchette boards. Her cousin Margaret, who was interested in the occult, may also have influenced Frances. Frances's temporary foray into the world of spiritualism she later described as, "an old and ugly practice . . . powered by evil."[47] (Gilbert's anger may also have come from his past life; he had a similar experience with the planchette board, and an encounter with the devil, which took him to his lowest point, when he was at Slade School.)

Meanwhile, woven through all the turmoil of getting married, moving house, keeping track of the growing career of a popular author, living through the grief and stigma of her brother's suicide, was the fading dream of a family with "seven beautiful

---

[46] *The Collected Works* Vol. 10-A, 345-46.

[47] *The New Witness* (Feb. 16, 1923).

children."[48] She had married at age thirty-two, at a time when most women who married did so in their early twenties. With each passing year, Frances must have felt this emptiness more acutely.

Further, and possibly related to this infertility, Frances's health was fragile. She and Gilbert consulted with doctors about her health. Therapies, massages, rest cures and the best medical suggestions of the early twentieth century all followed. And despite the fact that it appears from her personal correspondence that Frances spent a lot of time in rest cures, special baths, and massage therapies, she always cut her time there shorter than doctor recommendations because of her desire either to do work or to travel with Gilbert.[49]

The couple visited yet another doctor in 1908. Once again, an operation was advised. The desperate but hopeful couple agreed, and Frances made plans to recuperate in a nursing facility. Some scholars have suggested that the operation in question was an operation called a hymenectomy, a procedure for a rare but not dangerous condition which renders marital intercourse painful, if not practicably impossible. Since Frances's medical records do not exist from that time, there is simply no way to know (though the nature of that operation is such that it seems unlikely with two previous infertility-related surgeries). Whether it was this condition or not, the operation did not produce the intended results. After this third operation, Frances was moved to Maidenhead where her sister and brother-in-law lived, and Ethel looked after her until she regained her strength.

---

[48] Told to Dorothy Collins and recorded in *Return to Chesterton*, 324.

[49] Bakewell letter file, Courtesy of John M. Kelly Library Rare Books, Archival & Manuscript Collection's G.K. Chesterton Microfiche Collection.

Gilbert and Frances had tried for eight years to conceive. During this time, Frances had aged from thirty-two to forty; now at that age—considered elderly by obstetricians—she had a much smaller chance of getting pregnant.

Because of the unsubstantiated rumors begun by Ada Chesterton, some have speculated that perhaps their marriage was never consummated. However, many a wedding night may not attain the heights of hyper-romantic imagination, though no one in polite company would ever speak of this. Even Belloc, that man of enormous bravado, described as powerfully built, with great stamina, wrote in a letter to Elodie a short while after the wedding that he was quite frustrated with their "physical problem." However, six months later, Elodie was expecting their first child. Couples figure out how things work. It would be an *extremely* rare case if they did not.

Gilbert and Frances likely worked out the details of their private life like any other normal couple. They suffered from infertility, like many other couples. They visited more than one specialist regarding their infertility. Unless the visits to infertility specialists were a charade, there is simply no reason to believe they failed to consummate their marriage. Unfortunately, Gilbert and Frances's infertility gave fodder to Ada's imagination.

Frances was not physically fertile; still, she loved to tend and care for the young. She was a very caring person, who always surrounded herself with her nieces and nephews, her godchildren, the neighbor's children and the children of her cousins. In addition, she tended their garden, houseplants, and pets. She was able to create a home where her need to nurture was fulfilled in other ways, and that seems to be the sign of healthy acceptance of the burden of infertility.

Frances's life after these eventful eight first years of marriage was a mixture of sorrows and promise. The former seemed to be in greater evidence for a long time—death, infertility, the struggles of domesticity while Gilbert established himself in his chosen profession, the challenges of achieving and maintaining a respectable place in an exacting society. Soon the promise would reach concrete fulfillment, bringing in its own wake both delights and new challenges. One delight was certain: the fulfillment of a dream to live in the country. Gilbert had even posited it as a possibility during their engagement, when he suggested they might be married in April 1900: "I have been making some money calculations with the kind assistance of Rex,[50] and as far as I can see we could live in the country on quite a small amount of regular literary work. . ."[51] After their marriage, during one of the weekend excursions on which Gilbert took Frances, on a Saturday in 1901, they arrived at a train station. Enquiring as to the next train, they were told it went to Beaconsfield, Buckinghamshire. On a whim, they took the train. They stayed the night at the White Hart and decided that someday this quaint village should become their home.[52] In 1909, the country life they had talked about since their engagement was to become a reality.

---

[50] Reginald Brimley Johnson, fiancé of Gertrude Blogg and publisher of Gilbert's first book of poems, *Greybeards at Play*.

[51] Letter dated "Good Friday, 1900," quoted in *Gilbert Keith Chesterton*, 140.

[52] *G.K. Chesterton: A Centenary Appraisal*, 156.

Chapter Four

FAME AND FORTUNE (1909–1915)

*Mr. Gatty turned up with the Duke of Westminster. My
goodness, how he sings—he sang us your translations—
& Wagner & Bach & I was awfully happy—*

In the summer of 1909, Gilbert and Frances bought
Overroads, a house on Grove Road in Beaconsfield.[1]
During the time they lived there, Frances heard that
across the street, someone planned to build a laundry. The idea
of the noise, the steam and the traffic caused her to consider
purchasing the land for themselves. They did purchase the
lot across the street and begin building a new home, which
they called Top Meadow, the historical name of the land.[2] At
first, they just built a studio there, but eventually, they built a
home around the studio building. They would move into Top
Meadow in 1922.

Many Fleet Streeters, including the irascible Ada Jones,
complained that Frances had taken Gilbert away from them.
Frances did take Gilbert away—away from what she saw was too
much drink, too much smoking, and too much food. Gilbert's
health was not as robust as some of his habits, so a move to the

---

[1] G.K. Chesterton, "On Being Moved," in *Lunacy and Letters* (New York: Sheed &
Ward, 1958).

[2] Information provided by Aidan Mackey.

country could certainly have been his wife's effort to improve his well-being.

However, the argument can be made that Gilbert wanted to move Frances away from London. Depression and its various temptations had followed after Knollys' death. Gilbert felt he had to do something. Perhaps Gilbert moved Frances, willingly giving up the London life he was so fond of for the sake of his wife, who loved the country.

Whatever the primary reason for their relocation, Frances settled in happily and began meeting the neighbors. Mrs. Walpole and her daughter Felicity lived close by. Frances immediately befriended them, and invited them over frequently. She wrote this poem to Felicity:

> When I was but a tiny child, they chose for me a saint,
> Fulfilled of Christian charity and heavenly restraint;
> But you have called me Mary, and oh! I joy to hear
> The name of God's own Mother come so gaily on the air.
>
> What though my arms be empty, and hers for ever press
> The Eternal Child who touches you with such divine caress.
> Here's another love, Felicity, and oh, sweetheart, drink deep.
> That you may laugh more easily, and I forget to weep.
> For you have called me Mary, making bitter waters sweet.[3]

This was, perhaps, the most important poem Frances had yet written, revealing deeply her pain and sorrow. *You have called me Mary, making bitter waters sweet.* This play on the Hebrew name, which combines the meanings of "desired child" and "bitter", captures the suffering of the childless Frances. She could

---

[3] Frances A. Chesterton, *How Far Is It To Bethlehem: The Plays and Poetry of Frances Chesterton*, ed. Nancy Carpentier Brown (Antioch: Chesterton & Brown Publishing, 2012), 228.

look to the Blessed Virgin Mary for solace, she who caresses the "Eternal Child" in her arms.

Such themes of longing for a family are to be found throughout Frances's poetry. In "The Small Dreams", Frances said she dreamed of tiny feet that falter, and tiny songs unsung.[4] Frances's plays, too, reveal a longing for a wee babe. In *The Christmas Gift*, a soldier finds an infant on the battlefield and brings the baby home to the family, who welcome the child. In another play, *The Three Kings*, the dispute over who will take the throne as the next king of Spain is answered by the arrival of a baby.

To Frances's mind, the country was the perfect setting for a home. It was fruitfully full of the things she loved. How could this recognition of fruitfulness and home be resolved with her infertility, especially since she and Gilbert seemed by this time to have accepted the fact that they could not have children of their own? They seemed to have come to a resolve, after the last failed operation; they made perhaps some sort of secret pact. Many people have noted that it was not their decision to adopt. This is true, although they did discuss the idea of adopting one of their nieces.[5] However, never again did Frances say that it was hard for her to see babies: now she welcomed them.

The couple now gave preferential treatment to children. When traveling, they would choose the train compartment with children in it; they planned activities for children's amusements, and they gave presents to the children of all their relatives and friends.[6] There were many children familiar to them: nieces,

---

[4] *Ibid.*, 211.

[5] Geoffrey Guinness writes, "My mother, Catherine Oldershaw, was a favourite of Frances & GKC. Since they could not have children, there was, at some point discussion as to whether my mother might not be adopted by them but it came to nothing."

[6] *Gilbert Keith Chesterton*, 258.

nephews, and numerous friends' and cousins' children. They would welcome children to Beaconsfield; entertain them, spoil them, play with them, read to them, write plays and songs for them, do puppet shows and toy theater productions, provide a listening ear and a welcoming hearth.

Extended stays at the Chesterton home were not uncommon. Frances's two small nieces came for a week visit to Beaconsfield. While they visited, they both came down with chicken pox and Frances nursed them. They stayed for six weeks.[7] The children whom they welcomed felt the warmth of love from Gilbert and Frances. If there were quarantines and the children could not go to school, they came to stay with Gilbert and Frances. School vacations were spent with Gilbert and Frances. They teased back and forth, often creating their own nicknames for Aunt Frances and Uncle Gilbert: Auntlet and Unclet, Auntie Dibbs and Uncle Blobs, Auntie Frances and Uncle Chestnut, Mr. and Mrs. Tame Lion, Aunt Harriet and Uncle Humphrey.

> Of Uncle Humphrey who can sing? (wrote Gilbert)
> His name can't rhyme with anything.
> How much superior is Aunt Harriet
> Who rhymes correctly to Iscariot.

Many, many children were born during the Chesterton marriage, and Gilbert and Frances either together or separately were asked regularly to be godparents. The final count is at about twenty-five, illustrative of friendships and bonds with all these children and their families.

Frances's sister Ethel had three girls—Gertrude Monica (nicknamed "Woozle"), Pamela Frances, and Catherine Cordelia Alice—and two boys—Peter Hubert Walter and Basil

---

[7] British Library folder 73196-0180.

Lawrence—who all attended Oakdene School in Beaconsfield during the first war. The Chesterton place was their second home, and Catherine, known as "Kate," was a favorite. Frances developed a close connection to Oakdene School. She wrote their school song, and many of her plays and skits were performed at the school, with her nieces and nephews as actors.

Additionally, Gilbert and Frances took financial responsibility for the education of a number of their relatives' children.[8] Michael Knollys, Patrick[9] and Arthur (known as "Rossi") Braybrooke were the sons of Frances's cousin. When their father deserted the family, Gilbert and Frances paid for the boys' education. Michael spent all school holidays and leaves with the Chestertons during the ten years from 1907-1917. He became a doctor; Gilbert and Frances also covered his medical school expenses.

The couple seemed to prefer the company of the children to that of their parents; however, perhaps it was just an honest desire to give the children a good time. The annual Christmas party was a children-only event, and Gilbert and Frances could indulge the children to their hearts' content. Aunt Frances and Uncle Gilbert devised endless games for young people. Frances wrote plays for them, at least four of which were published.[10] The children memorized lines, created sets, found props, built swords, painted shields, and sewed costumes. The plays almost all had a Christmas theme, and were performed for the entertainment

---

[8] *G.K. Chesterton: A Centenary Appraisal*, 158.

[9] Patrick Braybrooke became a prolific writer and fellow of the Royal Society of Literature, and wrote many books about Chesterton, as well as Conrad Noel, Belloc, Barrie, Kipling, Wilde, Stevenson, Dickens, Shaw, etc.

[10] See *How Far Is It To Bethlehem: The Plays and Poetry of Frances Chesterton*.

of the children at the annual Christmas Eve party.[11] In addition to the plays, Gilbert continually created figures and made up stories for the toy theaters he loved so well.

The children loved Frances in a different way than the way they loved Gilbert. Gilbert was sometimes loud and boisterous; Frances was quiet and loved tea and conversations. Many a young child found in Frances a tender-hearted listener.

Frances cared about people. Her personality was such that she was deeply interested in making sure the people around her were happy and knew someone cared about them. She was humble and selfless, and she rarely spoke about herself, preferring to stay in the background and let the other have center stage. She had a good memory. Frances would patiently listen, and was carefully observant and noticed if someone was feeling out of sorts.

She had already found ways to cope with tremendously difficult situations. As we have seen, her father, with whom Frances had a deep and close relationship, died at a critical time in her development, when she was just fourteen. After recovering from the tragedy of their father's sudden death, the family had to face death with Gertrude's bicycle accident. Then, Frances's brother committed suicide. No sooner did that happen, but the last hope for children of her own faded as the operations she underwent failed to help her conceive. And, on top of all of this, she was nearly always sick with something or other. Gilbert wrote a letter to Fr. Ronald Knox stating that Frances was "one of the good who mysteriously suffer."[12]

---

[11] In addition, Frances also wrote plays for a mixed set of adults and children, which were put on in Beaconsfield and Bath for the entertainment of the community.

[12] *Gilbert Keith Chesterton*, 460.

However, she did not falter—much. Yes, she had periods when she strayed or her struggle caused her to break out of quiet serenity: the trip to Europe to rest and recover from Gertrude's death prior to her marriage, the letters to Fr. John O'Connor expressing her disappointments, her conversations with close friends when she allowed the sadness to bring her to tears; the foray into the occult. And yet, these were few and far between, and she always rose above the trials. She found strength in talking to people, in sharing the grief with Gilbert, O'Connor, and friends. And she found strength in her faith, which shone through her poetry and plays, letters and articles. She developed her sympathetic listening skills.

Someone who had experienced the number of tragedies that Frances experienced could either become bitter or make an excellent listener and sympathizer. Those who confided in her found strength, and also reported that she never talked about herself. That is where the "heroic" part of Gilbert's statement (that Frances's life was a very "heroic tragedy") really means something. It would have been so easy for a person who had experienced that number of bereavements and disappointments to find opportunities to talk about herself, but Frances never gave in to that.

This found special expression after the move to Beaconsfield, particularly the decision to welcome all children. Frances seemed to become a new woman, richly realizing the promise of her earlier years. She faced life with faith, hope, and love, focusing her energy outward, rather than inward. This is what made her truly heroic.

These days, Gilbert was a busy writer. He wrote all his usual newspaper columns—those for the *Illustrated London News* and *Daily News* were both weekly columns. Books that appeared during these first years after the move to Beaconsfield included

George Bernard Shaw, Tremendous Trifles, The Ball and the Cross, William Blake, Alarms and Discursions, What's Wrong With the World, and *The Ballad of the White Horse.* His introductions to the works of Charles Dickens, and the publication of his own book on Dickens in 1906, inspired so much enthusiasm among readers, that the introductions were compiled into a work in 1911 called *Appreciations and Criticisms of the Works of Charles Dickens. The Innocence of Father Brown* was first collected, *A Miscellany of Men, Manalive, Lepanto, The Victorian Age in Literature, Magic, The Flying Inn,* and a second collection of Father Brown, *The Wisdom of Father Brown,* all appeared within a short span of years. In 1911, Frances selected quotes of her husband's already popular phrases—one quote for each day of the year—and the resulting book was published as *The Wit and Wisdom of G.K. Chesterton.* It was advertised as "selected and arranged by his wife."

Meanwhile, Frances continued to be busy. In the June 2, 1909, issue of the *Otago Witness*[13] this most interesting item appeared under the title: "Ladies' Gossip."

> Mrs. G.K. Chesterton, like so many other clever wives of distinguished husbands, runs the risk, perhaps, of lacking that justice from the public which is her due. Yet, Mrs. Chesterton has several titles to distinction; she is not only a spirited and practiced debater, but she writes "occasional verse" of a most rare and delicate beauty. She is likewise keenly interested in social reform; she constantly presides at "happy evenings" for the children of the slums, and is a prominent supporter of the "Christian Socialist" ideals.

---

[13] A New Zealand paper that probably picked up London news items.

High praise indeed for Frances—ever active, ever engaged, and ever putting her faith into action.

Frances found a parish home at the local Anglican church of Saint Mary and All Saints in downtown Beaconsfield. Gilbert attended with her, but his heart was slowly turning towards the idea of conversion to the Catholic faith—an idea which Frances found difficult to swallow. She was at that time still content with the faith she adopted at St. Stephen's from the Clewer Sisters. Additionally, the "failure" of conversion to save her brother still rankled in her heart.

Her family remained close, emotionally and geographically. Frances's sister Ethel and her husband Lucian were by this time living at Fernley, a huge twenty-five room house in Maidenhead, only about nine miles from Beaconsfield. Lucian was still tutoring students for a living. Frances's mother lived with them, as well as another tutor, four students and five house servants, and their own five children as well: eighteen people living under one roof. The families visited back and forth frequently.[14] Frances and Ethel had always gotten along well; now they had similar husbands who were good friends. Both had struggled to make ends meet in the early years of marriage, and later supported their husbands in success and fame (Ethel's husband Lucian went into politics and became mayor of Maidenhead). The two sisters might be taken as a living imitation of the conclusion of Jane Austen's first novel, *Sense and Sensibility*: "there was that constant communication which strong family affection would naturally dictate;—and among the merits and the happiness of [the sisters], let it not be ranked as the least considerable, that though sisters, and living almost within sight of each other,

---

[14] For more information about Ethel, please see "Ethel Laura Blogg Oldershaw," in *Gilbert* Vol 17, no. 4 (2014): 10-11.

they could live without disagreement between themselves, or producing coolness between their husbands."

Success brought many changes. In July 1912, because Gilbert had broken his right arm, Nellie Allport was working part-time as Gilbert's secretary. Allport was an old friend from the I.D.K. Society in Bedford Park. She could not type, so she wrote letters longhand for both Gilbert and Frances. During this time, O'Connor sent holy water from Lourdes to help heal Gilbert's arm, and a beautiful statue of the Madonna, which Frances set prominently on a shelf in their home.

This same year, the couple bought two additional acres of land across Grove Road from Overroads and began building on it. They first built a studio. They used this to put on plays, and also as a quiet place for Gilbert to write when Overroads became too noisy. They gradually built their home around the studio, and this second house became known as Top Meadow, which was built in the shape of a cross. Gilbert enjoyed knowing that the land once had belonged to Edmund Burke.

Frances continued to take Gilbert's dictation whenever there was a need; she organized his publishing work, and scheduled increasing requests for appearances, speeches, lectures, and dinner engagements. For household help, she kept a cook, a housemaid and a gardener. The place was large, and Frances had her own work of writing and secretarial duties to Gilbert, not to mention the letter writing, and the constant stream of household guests who seemed to stay not just days, but often weeks or months. Her active life is clearly shown in her letters:

Dear Padre,[15]
I have only time for a line. . . . Mr. Gatty turned up with the
Duke of Westminster. My goodness, how he sings—he sang

---

[15] Father John O'Connor.

us your translations— & Wagner & Bach & I was awfully happy—Lady Grosvenor sent you all kinds of messages . . . I am churning butter, with grateful thanks—[16]

In 1913, trouble came in the form of the Marconi scandal, which involved allegations that members of the government abused their high positions and knowledge of the government's plans regarding the Marconi Wireless Telegraph Company. The government was about to award a huge contract to the English Marconi Company. Marconi's general manager was Godfrey Isaacs. Knowing that the government was about to award the contract, Isaacs and two of his brothers bought stock in the American Marconi company, before that contract was made publically known—thousands of shares. One brother, Rufus— attorney general at the time—sold stock to Lloyd George—the future prime minister.

The English people were primed to the scandal, as 1913 was already a time of political unrest. On April 3, 1913, Emmeline Pankhurst was put on trial for bombing the house of David Lloyd George—then chancellor of the Exchequer, and the same man to whom Isaacs would sell stock. Every suffragette in the city attended the trial, many of whom were Frances's friends.

Then came Marconi. Cecil—or Ada Jones—had discovered the insider trading. Cecil published a story rightly accusing the men, but Isaacs hired an attorney to prove that Cecil had damaged his reputation. Cecil, confident in himself, had refused to hire his own attorney to answer this accusation. Gilbert and Frances were present all ten days in court during the trial. On the ninth day Gilbert was called to the witness stand and questioned.

---

[16] Wade Center folder 309.

Cecil was found guilty. He avoided jail and was fined instead. But in the midst of the trial, a surprising event took place. On June 7, 1913, Cecil was received into the Catholic Church.

Gilbert was bitterly disappointed in the trial and its outcome. The scandal led to his total disillusionment of the Liberal Party, of which George Cadbury was a leading supporter. Gilbert made constant attacks on Cadbury—the chocolate manufacturer and *Daily News* owner—in the pages of Cecil's *New Witness*. Another consequence of the scandal and trial, was Gilbert's removal of himself from the *Daily News,* where he had started writing in 1901. Gilbert began writing for the *Daily Herald* instead.

At around this time, recorded history affords a detailed glance into the Chesterton home. A young cousin of Gilbert's, Lilian, from a branch of the Chesterton family that had immigrated to Canada, came to visit. She stayed with the Chestertons from June until November 1913. She recalled her visit:

> Gilbert and Frances were now living at 'Overroads' Beaconsfield. The former had just built what he called 'the studio;' a large hall, on the other side of the road, to which he retired when too many visitors arrived.
>
> I suggested that he build an underground passage connecting the two houses so that he could easily escape all intruders.
>
> "Yes, I have thought of that," he said and smiled.
>
> "Only," I added, "it would have to be a large one."
>
> "That is exactly why it has not been done," he replied laughing.
>
> I spent very pleasant days there, Frances always bright and genial, and Gilbert charming. They took me for some lovely drives . . . more enjoyable even than the scenery was Gilbert's conversation or to be exact, his commentary on all things as we passed.

[One thing] that amused me greatly, (though I am sure it did not amuse Frances) was seeing her, trying to make Gilbert finish his article for the *Illustrated London News*, in time for the train. It happened at lunch, while he was launched on some knotty discussion, and did not remember, or anyway was not bothering. She gently reminded him that his article was not quite finished. As gently, he vaguely answered that there would be time after lunch. He continued to talk . . . . A maid came in to say the messenger boy had arrived. Gilbert turned his head saying, "Have him wait," then went on with his discourse. Frances, looking worried said, "I shall have to ask them to hold the train, if you do not go at once."

"Yes, do that," he answered brightly, as if it were a happy thought, and turning . . . continued, "As I was saying. . . ." By this time I had almost reached the stage where it was impossible not to laugh, but fortunately I managed it, as no one else seemed at all amused. Finally, Frances brought the article and a pencil, placed them in front of him, standing with the addressed envelope in her hand, while he finished it. This he did after many apologies to us for interrupting the conversation.

She folded it quickly in silence, and sealed the envelope; the waiting maid hurried to the hall, the boy sprang onto his bicycle and raced to the station. In a very few minutes the whistle blew and we all sighed with relief, peace for another week! Then—it would happen all over again![17]

Frances invited Lilian to the opening of *Magic*, but sadly, the young lady had to depart a few days before that date. She was glad when Frances mailed her a copy of the poster for the play.

---

[17] Lilian Chesterton, "Further Chesterton Recollections," *Mark Twain Quarterly* Vol. 5, no. 4 (1943).

Frances enjoyed Gilbert's popularity, including opening nights of his play *Magic*. Shaw had done his utmost to persuade Frances to persuade Gilbert to produce dramas. He believed the Chestertons' financial situation would improve if Gilbert could use his talent and write plays. Frances and Shaw carried on a playful and conspiratorial correspondence. (Although it is often repeated that Gilbert remained friends with many of his intellectual enemies like Shaw and Wells, this is a reminder that Frances remained friends with them, too. She once nursed Wells' estranged wife during an illness, and entertained both Shaw and Wells in her home.)

Shaw was not the only person urging Gilbert to produce plays; Frances mentions in her diary that George Alexander, the actor and theater manager,[18] and Granville Barker, another actor, producer, and theater director, both asked Gilbert[19] to write a play. Finally, Gilbert wrote *Magic*.

Ada Chesterton's description of the opening night captures the scene:

> It was a memorable evening. Gilbert and Frances were almost mobbed in the foyer, and at every interval were eagerly surrounded. She wore a quite charming gown of a pre-Raphaelite cut in blue and gold, and I think was genuinely overcome by their reception.[20]
>
> There was an immense ovation when the curtain rang down, and Gilbert made one of his wittiest and most delightful speeches. There were demands from the management that he

---

[18] "The Diary of Frances Chesterton, 1904-1905," *The Chesterton Review* Vol. 25, no. 3 (1999): 283-293. See entry date December 8, 1904. Incidentally, George Alexander is the great-great-uncle of actor Hugh Laurie.

[19] *Ibid.*

[20] A. Chesterton, *The Chestertons*, 135.

and his wife should go to supper at the Savoy with the members of the company. . . . But it was not to be, and the Chestertons returned with us to Warwick Gardens, where a huge sheaf of wires attracted G.K.'s attention. . . . Frances eagerly opened and read the messages. Later, Marie Louise gathered the telegrams together, and put them carefully away. She kept them for a long time, right up to her last illness, when she decided to destroy the less intimate of her mementoes. All sorts of things relating to her sons were stored at Warwick Gardens, letters from Edward and both her boys, and some from Frances to G.K. during their engagement and his to her.[21]

Patrick Braybrooke was also in attendance at the play that evening. He recalled George Bernard Shaw seated in one of the boxes, and heard him yell out "Bravo!" and "Speech!" at the fall of the final curtain. The Little Theatre was packed with all the leading critics of the day, as well as many notable members of London society. The audience howled with merriment at the Duke, and sympathized with Patricia. Kenelm Foss, who produced the play, considered that night the highlight of his life.[22]

Frances continued to enjoy her own mild success. She had a very small item published in 1913, the first under the heading, "Thoughts for the Day: Wisdom and Experience":

The stronger and wiser men grow, the less they are superior to anything. —Mrs. G.K. Chesterton

In addition to this short quotation, a lengthy poem was published in the *Westminster Gazette* on January 7, and in the *Ashburton Guardian* on March 27, 1913, entitled "The Small Dreams." The

---

[21] *Ibid.*, 136.

[22] Braybrooke, 24.

poem was also reprinted in *The Living Age* magazine on March 29, 1913.[23,24]

After its publication, Frances received fan mail:

My Dear Mrs. Chesterton,
I feel that I must write and tell you how beautiful I think <u>The Small Dreams</u> in the Westminster and how much I thank you . . . . I hope there are many others there where that came from, for it would be to the general sweetening of the world.

I am very glad and proud to be associated with GKC and with his brother. I'll always read GKC, with the greatest appreciation: and if he finds his left ear burning it may be because . . . we are talking about his work. I could not tell you how often we say—"Chuck it, Smith!" It has become a sort of [code] word.

Please forgive this intrusion, and believe me, Mrs. Chesterton,

Yours very sincerely,
Katharine Tynan Hinkson[25]

On the same day "The Small Dreams" first appeared, another poem, "Our Lady's Day",[26] appeared in *The New Witness*.[27]

Gilbert's impressive, prolific literary output did not flag. Everything Gilbert wrote delighted his wife; poetry brought special joy. Frances and O'Connor spent numerous hours discussing

---

[23] *The Living Age* (March 29, 1913): 276, 3586, American Periodicals, 770.

[24] *How Far Is It To Bethlehem*, 211.

[25] Hinkson was a poet and author of note. She was friends with Gerard Manley Hopkins, cousin of Frances Chesterton's good friend Isabel de Giberne Sieveking; and a close associate of W.B. Yeats, who proposed to her in 1885. She wrote over 100 novels.

[26] *Ibid.*, 274.

[27] *The New Witness* (March 27, 1913): 657.

The Ballad of the White Horse in the months leading up to its publication. Frances described the *Ballad* to O'Connor, who could see that she greatly loved the poem. He made suggestions of a historical nature; and eventually, when the great poem was near completion, Frances gave him the manuscript for a final proofreading. O'Connor describes his input on this poem as much greater than his input ever was for *Father Brown*.[28]

Gilbert's research for the poem prompted many trips out to the land of King Alfred. He and Frances hired a car and drove to Glastonbury and the Isle of Athelney to see the river and the marshes. Frances enjoyed this "lovely though all too short holiday of a fortnight in Devon and Cornwall, searching about for memories of King Arthur".[29] They both had a deep love of England and its history, and the poem was a labor of love for them. Gilbert dedicated this poem to Frances.

Much of 1913 was full of joy for the couple. At Christmas 1913, Frances wrote a letter to O'Connor telling him to excuse her penmanship as Gilbert was talking to her while she was writing, mostly, she says, about O'Connor's excellent translations of Latin hymns. She invited him to come and see *Magic*.

As the year moved toward its conclusion, there was one cause of sadness. Frances's friend and Hilaire Belloc's wife Elodie became ill. She deteriorated as the new year began, progressively worsening as the days went by. On February 2, 1914, she died at the age of forty-five.

Gilbert's book *The Flying Inn* first appeared in print at the start of 1914. Gilbert said this was the book he most enjoyed writing. But in 1914, it seemed the tide of happy success seemed to have turned, for the Chestertons and for all of Europe. On

---

[28] *The Elusive Father Brown.*

[29] Wade Center folder 301, unidentified correspondent.

June 28, a Serbian nationalist assassinated Archduke Franz Ferdinand, nephew of Emperor Franz Josef and heir to the Austro-Hungarian Empire, an act which catapulted the world into war.

Gilbert became ill with a cough, and Frances wrote O'Connor in October that Gilbert had just got over bronchitis, still had a lingering cough and was overworked. Cecil was in the trenches— at the *New Witness*, not in Europe (he had not yet enlisted)—and Gilbert was writing for the government (his personal war effort), which was wearing, difficult, and tired him. (Frances also asked O'Connor to review a book for the *New Witness*, saying that Gilbert said he could have as much space as he needed to do it justice.)

By November Gilbert was quite ill. Overweight, overworked, stressed by Cecil's trial, and the start of war, Gilbert could not seem to shake the cough he had picked up. Frances wrote to O'Connor on November 25 saying Gilbert was very sick, and that it was heart trouble with complications. She had two nurses to assist.

On Christmas Eve, 1914, Gilbert suffered a complete collapse. He was only forty years old. The established retrospective diagnosis is that his condition was prompted by some sort of heart trouble. Gilbert passed in and out of a coma—induced by the doctor, a common treatment at the time—until the following Easter. Newspapers prepared Chesterton's fans for the worst. The *New York Times*, January 4, 1915, had this report:

> The announcement in the cable dispatches of *The Sunday Times* of the grave, perhaps fatal, illness of Gilbert K. Chesterton was surprising, not only because of the comparative youth and supposed robust constitution of the man, but on account of the extraordinary vitality of his latest writings. His discussions

of international relations, and particularly of the British Spirit in contrast with the German since the war began, which have been published in *The New York Times*, have been regarded by some of his warmest admirers as the best expression of his character and convictions. They assuredly have possessed an unmistakable tone of sincerity and feeling which not all his readers have found in his most highly extolled books, from the exceedingly clever studies of Browning and Dickens to "What's Wrong with the World." In the prodigious volume of literary discussion inspired by the war, assuredly nothing more readable than Chesterton's articles has appeared.

On January 9, Frances wrote that she had three nurses for him, and everything possible was being done. It was a time of singular fear and suffering for Frances. They had been married for fourteen years and Gilbert was clearly the center of her life. Further, she was burdened with his unfulfilled desire for conversion. She was conscious of it from the beginning of his illness, telling O'Connor that Gilbert was in and out of consciousness, very weak, and she had a feeling when he woke up he might ask for the Catholic priest. Now, he appeared to be dying. He was rarely conscious, and when he was, he was very weak. She was in a bind. Not knowing what to do, she had written to O'Connor for advice.

January 7, 1915

. . . His heart is stronger and he is able to take plenty of nourishment. Under the circumstances therefore I am hoping and praying he may soon be sufficiently himself to tell us what he wants done. I am dreadfully unhappy at not knowing how he would wish me to act. His parents would never forgive me if

I acted only on my own authority. I do pray to God He will restore him to himself that we may know . . .

O'Connor advised her to wait till Gilbert was recovered enough to express his wishes clearly. She and Gilbert received many supportive letters during this time. Writer Max Beerbohm wrote at length:

Jan 10, 1915

My dear GKC,
I am most sorry to hear that you are—or have been—very ill. I hope you will get well very quickly. In such times as these, people need all the cheer and inspiration they can get; and a break in your writing must be even more of a loss than it would be at other times.

I think "The Flying Inn" is quite one of the very best of all your things. I constantly—though unmelodiously—sing snatches from the songs that are there. Especially—

"Old Squire is gone to the Meet today
All in his — — —"

And I find it hard to forgive you for not having carried that song further. I should like to have ALL the "forty-seven verses."

My best remembrances to Mrs. Chesterton, and all my sympathy with her in this anxious time she must have been having. And again all best wishes for a quick and happy convalescence.

Yours ever,
Max Beerbohm[30]

There were glimpses of hope and relief. One day, Gilbert called for Frances. Frances wrote to her friend Josephine Ward—Gilbert

---

[30] Wade Center folder 24.

biographer Maisie Ward's mother—and told her she was so happy Gilbert called for her; that he had given her a hug, and Frances felt she could carry on for forty more days on the strength of that hug alone. Frances's tender bedside care and constant vigilance would help Gilbert to make a full recovery.

While Gilbert lay sick, Frances worked on a collection of his poetry for publication, correcting proofs—and much more. The book, called *Poems,* had a section called "Love Poems"—which Frances selected and added herself—all but one of which had never been published before. Frances worked beside her ill husband, searching through the love poems he'd written to her years before, selecting the less personal of them. Re-reading the poems must have brought back many keen feelings and affections for the man she had known and loved for so long, bringing special intensity to her hope and prayer that he would get well again.

Many things may have prompted her to work toward publication of these most private poems. Frances may have decided that it was time to share with the public how much Gilbert loved her. In addition, she may have been working on the poetry book to provide income while Gilbert was ill. She also added some poetry of Gilbert's that he had published during his Junior Debating Club days. Interestingly, later on, when Gilbert was well and the book was reprinted, he removed some of these early poems from the book.

Frances also worked on a collection of her own poetry, gathering some particularly beautiful poems together to give to friends as a gift book.[31] Inside the pages of Frances's book,

---

[31] A copy of this book, which I had long heard of, was finally located in the special collection of rare books in the library of the University of British Columbia. The book was printed in Beaconsfield at the Excelsior Printing Works at 24 Aylesbury Street. "For Private Circulation only," was the printed warning on top of the first page. The

she wrote, "These poems, with one or two exceptions, have already appeared in *The Daily Chronicle, Westminster Gazette* and *New Witness.*"[32]

---

particular copy at the University of British Columbia was labeled "Kidd" and signed by Frances, "With her love to you, Christmas 1915." Mrs. Robert Kidd was Gilbert Chesterton's childhood friend, Annie Fermin—the young lady Gilbert's mother wished he had married. Annie and her husband moved to Vancouver, British Columbia, and left photograph albums and books to the university after her death.

[32] The first poem in this collection is "The Small Dreams." This was published on January 7, 1913 in the *Westminster Gazette* and on March 27, 1913 in the *Ashburton Guardian.* See *How Far Is It To Bethlehem*, 211.

Next is, "An Unknown April." This poem was published in the Westminster Gazette on April 12, 1910. Here Frances is longing for April and spring, saying some go south to find spring, but we will find spring right here in England; after all, spring is just hiding.

> Oh, some have been to seek you where the winter never comes,
> And some have thought to find you where the scent of palm is sweet;
> But you were hiding, hiding in the woods and fields of home,
> And in the lands of England are the traces of your feet.

Often while reading Frances Chesterton's poetry, we are reminded that they sound sing-songy, and would make good lyrics.

"Of Your Charity" is the same as Frances called "All Souls' Day." This, as we saw above, was published in *The New Witness* on November 7, 1912. See *How Far Is It To Bethlehem*, 237.

"Mater Invicta" is a poem about Mary and Baby Jesus, and appeared in the Westminster Gazette on December 19, 1909. Mary asks the sun, the river, the cornfields, and the sheep to take care of her Son by providing warmth, water, food and clothing for him.

> Our Lady stood at the open door,
> Her Babe lay folded warm asleep,
> Deep nestled in the sheltering straw
> He shared with ox, and ass, and sheep.

"Bluebells," is a new poem. The sky bowed down and touched a lake—

> And lingered for a moment
> To kiss the green earth's face,
> Earth and sky were wedded
> In rapturous embrace.

In this time of sickness, Frances's character was once again tested, and shone forth in all of its beauty. Like Gilbert, Frances saw earthly life as a battle, the Church Militant as a reality, and All Saints' and All Souls' days as celebrating the battle won. Her life certainly was a battle, and her victory was her cheerfulness, unselfishness, and sacrificial love, shown through her ability to constantly give herself to others in the forms of service to the sick, listening ears to children and friends, and, of course, the physical, emotional, intellectual, psychological and spiritual caring and sharing with her husband, Gilbert.

And the kiss of the sky turned into bluebells—a sweet floral poem, of which Frances has quite a few. "Ode to a Hydrangea," "Spring," "Red Anemones," and "Poppies" come to mind, See *How Far Is It To Bethlehem*, 265-66, and 280.

"Winter's Prisoners" was printed on March 2, 1909, in the *Westminster Gazette*. And, like "An Unknown April," it asks longingly why spring is tarrying. How Frances hated long winters.

> Our very souls are sick with vain desire,
> With imprecation of the loitering spring;
> Why halt her footsteps on her seaward way,
> Have English woods for her no welcoming?

"Midsummer Day" is a much happier poem about the bright days, the golden corn, the blue skies, and the whole earth is laughing, she says. It appeared in the June 24, 1908, *Westminster Gazette*.

> The blue sky opening outwards
> For infinite miles and miles,
> Have you seen the whole earth laughing?
> Midsummer smiles. Oh! Midsummer smiles.

"Lady Day" is the same as in *How Far Is It To Bethlehem*, 273. "To Gertrude Monica" is the same as in *How Far Is It To Bethlehem*, 207. "Is There Freedom Left in England? The Question and The Answer" are in *How Far Is It To Bethlehem*, 213-17.

"Une Nuit Blanche: To M.H.W." This poem is most likely dedicated to Mildred Wain, a close friend of Gilbert and Frances's who married one of the Junior Debating Club members, Waldo D'Avigdor. Frances had had a nightmare, and Mildred came in the night and calmed her.

Some women have a sort of inborn charism to care for others, and it could be said that Frances had this personality trait, or cultivated it. However, it still takes someone with extraordinary strength to refrain from becoming frustrated, angry, or simply tired of giving after so many years. Many women, who start out easily giving when they fall in love, discover later in life that they want "their turn," and become selfish, angry, frustrated, and bitter. Frances easily could have—her life was not what she had hoped—but she never did. This is just one example out of

---

You came swift-footed in the night,
A night of black, unlovely things,
Your very candle seemed the light
Of solid day's quiet happenings.

"The Unforgotten Feet," is the same as *How Far Is It To Bethlehem*, 299. "The Vale of Avalon" was printed in *The New Witness* on May 21, 1914.

My soul has found a palfrey
To climb St. Michael's Tor
To see the shrine of Glastonbury,
The Holy Well of Glastonbury,
And touch the live and blossoming tree
That stands beside the door.

"To Felicity, Who Calls Me Mary," is the same as *How Far Is It To Bethlehem*, 228-29.
"The Longest Day," is about Midsummer's Day again (see above, "Midsummer Day") and was in the *Westminster Gazette* on June 26, 1910.

Oh June, lavish June enthroned in glory,
O bountiful lady of healing and balms;
We souls that are starving, whom winter had beggared,
Stand in thy sunlight and ask of thee alms.

More evidence with this poem of Frances's need for sun and how much the winter and cloudy days affected her.
"To a Rich Man," was published in *The New Witness* on September 10, 1914.

You call across the roll of drums, across the drums of death,
To us who served you blindly in your days of pomp and ease,
While the sweat poured off our bodies with every laboring breath,

many that shows the different paths Frances *could* have taken in life. She chose the self-sacrificing way—she gave herself away to Gilbert, friends, family, nieces and nephews, even the cook and the maid, whom she tended during their illnesses. She was consistently generous, kind, caring and loving, even when she herself felt ill. These traits may have come naturally, but to continue to carry on that way is to overcome one's natural inclinations.

And we drank our cup of agony from the first drop to the lees.

"Les Jour Des Morts," is another new poem. Not only is this poem here, but also it was published in 1915 in an anthology called *Lest We Forget: A War Anthology,* [*Foreword by Baroness Orczy*] (London: Jarrold & Sons).

The day of the dead, the day of the dead;
Down on your knees and pray
For the souls of the living, the souls of the dying,
The souls that have passed away.

> And the great bell tolls
> For the treasure of souls
> Delivered into His hand;
> Gabriel, Michael, Uriel reap
> Souls as a measure of sand,
> Souls from the restless deep,
> Souls from the blood-red land.

"All Saints' and All Souls'" was published on November 2, 1915, in the *Daily Chronicle*.

The armies of earth and the armies of Heaven,
On this day of days, uncounted but one,
Earth's little number, God's hierarchies seven,
> With plumes all a-toss
> They bear up the Cross
In the light of the moon, in the light of the sun,
> The battle is done.

Then last of all are "Three Christmas Carols," all three we have seen: "In Her Warm Arms our Lady holds her Son" is simply titled "1912" and just to confuse us is listed for 1911

Gilbert regained his health in 1915. He and Frances happily resumed their work together, but his health would never be the same. His wife had willed him to live, nursed him back to health, and kept busy with his writing work and her own. She kept the home fires burning, added to his collection of books, managed their finances, and kept up her strength so she could care for him. Now they could move forward, once again, to face the drama of the unfolding war and the growing success of the resurrected giant. The flood of published writings would increase from a trickle to a roar—a roar that would startle the world with its ferocity and vigor.

---

in *How Far Is It To Bethlehem*, 318, because it actually was the Christmas poem on the 1911 Christmas card; "Upon a Little Bank of Grass," is simply titled "1913" and is listed for 1912 in *How Far Is It To Bethlehem*, 319 because it was the Christmas poem on the 1912 Christmas card; "The Kings of Old Came to Thy Bed," is simply titled "1914" and is listed in *How Far Is It To Bethlehem*, 363, as a probable Christmas card poem, and from the Notebook we know that this was actually the Christmas poem from 1914. There were a total of twenty-one poems published in Frances's gift book.

Chapter Five

POETRY AND PLAYS (1915–1922)

*Interviewers, photographers, film men all seized on
us and we spent our last hours on the boat in a mob
of what I can only term lunatics. Gilbert bore it all
with imperturbably good humour but I was feeling
so sick and tired.*

Gilbert, a thinner man after his long illness, recovered
his health and resumed his writing, debating and
lecturing. He spoke of his experience being so close
to death, and realizing how marvelous it was to have remained
alive. Frances, always conscious of his food intake, tried to limit
his portions, and restrict his smoking and drinking—all part
of her devoted effort to make sure he would never suffer such
a collapse again. Her care of his health—which he, due to his
father's influence and personal philosophy, (which was that in
order to maintain one's health, one should pay no attention to
one's health) tried to ignore—certainly gave the future a gift of
more years, and many more words of wisdom.

Plans multiplied even before he was truly convalesced.
Gilbert was invited to the United States to lecture and began
planning the trip for sometime in the next few years. When
Gilbert finally was up and ready to write again, he composed
his first post-illness column for the *Illustrated London News*.

It was published on May 22, 1915.[1] He immediately received so much fan mail in response to his return to journalism that he and Frances needed to hire a secretary just to handle the correspondence. They hired Freda Spencer, who was Winston Churchill's cousin. This young lady came to love Gilbert and Frances and they her—and was the object of many teasing stories and poems. The typewriter was a Corona, and the cigars Gilbert smoked were Coronas. In order to differentiate, Gilbert named the typewriter "Ursula" to avoid confusion. The picture on the box of cigars was of a swarthy dark-skinned gentleman—Julian Alvarez—and Gilbert kept up a running joke about the famous lovers, Freda and Julian.[2]

Every day as Gilbert worked, Frances kept house, read, and worked on her poetry. And every afternoon, Frances served tea, as was the British custom; this ritual was sacred. Friends, secretaries, family, and reporters were served tea. In a *New York Times* article of May 21, 1916, "India for Indians, says Gilbert K. Chesterton," the reporter stated near the end of the piece that during the interview "Mrs. Chesterton interrupted and came into the room to ask us to have tea."

As Gilbert recovered from his illness, and adjusted to working with a new secretary, war fervor increased. Gilbert's brother Cecil felt the patriotic urge to enlist. After a few refusals due to his health—he had Bright's disease—he was accepted into the Highland Light Infantry as a private soldier in 1916.

For many years Cecil had been in love with Ada Jones, and now he had an opportunity to act on his intention to propose marriage to her.

---

[1] "Taking a Proper View of the Prussians," *Collected Works* Vol. 30. As originally appeared in *Illustrated London News*, May 22, 1915.

[2] *The Collected Works* Vol. 10-C, 257.

This impasse in the life of Cecil makes it incumbent upon us to revisit Ada. She was born on June 30, 1869, exactly two days after Frances. She was, therefore, ten years older than Cecil. Jones was born into an interesting family. Her father, Frederick John Jones, a Manchester warehouseman, married his first wife, Eliza, and had seven children.[3] At the birth of the last child, Eliza died.

Meanwhile, the woman who was to become Ada's mother, Ada Charlotte Sheridan, married her first husband, Charles Francis McDonald, a doctor, had one daughter, and shortly afterwards, her husband died. According to family legend, Ada Charlotte was a descendant of Richard Brinsley Sheridan, the famous owner of Drury Lane and playwright best known for writing *The School for Scandal.*

Frederick Jones married Ada Sheridan McDonald in 1865.[4] Their combined families included eight children, and they added three more: a boy, Sheridan, born in 1866; Ada Eliza, born 1869; and a boy, Charles Sheridan, born 1874.[5]

---

[3] Sefton William, Alice Emma, Gertrude Elizabeth, Ethel Emily, Laura Maria, Rosa Evelyn, and Frederick John Junior.

[4] Frederick John Jones was listed as a "Manchester Warehouseman," and despite the way it sounds, he was a middle-class business owner. A Manchester warehouseman, as he was listed in the 1861 census and on the birth certificate of Charles Sheridan in 1874, was not a stock-keeper in a warehouse-type occupation. It was the term used for an importer of cloth—usually varieties of linen. He was also listed as Merchant when he married Ada Charlotte in 1865 and in the 1871 census: that applies as well to a cloth importer and tends to indicate a reasonably high social status, and as a "Fancy Leather Goods Maker" in the 1881 census. He was a businessman, not an artisan—like James Keymer, Frances's grandfather.

[5] Now we can see the curious thing Ada's parents accomplished: They named the first boy Sheridan, most likely, as stated above, because of the mother's connection to Richard Brinsley. Then they named their daughter after Frederick's two wives, Ada and Eliza. They named the next son after Ada Charlotte's first husband, and then the Sheridan

Even these early details were muddled by Ada throughout her life. She often claimed her middle name was Elizabeth, even though she was born and baptized Ada Eliza. An early mini-biography of her even called her Elizabeth Jones. She made out her own will in 1950 using the name Ada Elizabeth. The Central and Cecil Housing Care Support, which claims her as its founder, refers to her as Elizabeth Chesterton.[6]

Not only did Ada falsify her name and age, but she also misled people about her past. On her marriage certificate she listed her father as Frederick Charles, rather than his true name Frederick John. Were these inconsistencies simply symptoms of Ada's passion for self-invention? Perhaps so. In any case, these have led to questions about the truthfulness of her writing.

What was Ada Eliza Jones like? She had a forceful, outgoing personality and a loud, penetrating voice; she loved to escape by reading books. She was out on the street at sixteen, insisting that she wanted to become a journalist, and she began earning her own living as a reporter. In those days, few women worked in the newspaper world, but Ada was a hard worker and tough. She could drink and swear with the men and often did after work. She maintained a feminine appearance, however, wearing high heels, plucking her eyebrows, and wearing thick make-up.

She wrote for *The Eye-Witness* with Belloc as her boss. Her younger brother, who used "C. Sheridan Jones" as his byline, was also a reporter, connected with the Chesterton circle in multiple ways: he was a special correspondent to the *Daily News*, an editor at the *Daily Herald*, the London editor of

---

name *again*. Perhaps they were attempting with names, to connect the "yours, mine, and ours" family together.

[6] "History," *Central and Cecil Housing Trust*, accessed March 2012, http://www.ccht.org.uk/history.

the *Everyman*, and was part of the group, along with Cecil Chesterton, that started *The New Witness*, for which he was a regular contributor; he was an actor in the *Trial of John Jasper for the Murder of Edwin Drood* along with Gilbert, Ada, Cecil, and George Bernard Shaw in 1914.

Ada's strong personality created challenges for those who worked with her. When *The Eye-Witness*, the newspaper that preceded *The New Witness*, was experiencing difficulties, Ada only made things worse. Ada and Cecil had crossed paths as reporters before at *The New Age*, but in 1911 when Belloc and Cecil started up *The Eye-Witness*, the younger Chesterton brother invited her to come work there. Not everyone was happy working with Ada:

> The troubles were aggravated by Ada Jones, who became imperious and, after a difficulty about unpaid salaries, plotted for the dismissal of the company's secretary, one Bowerman, the only efficient man of business in the ramshackle organization. Bowerman went to the literary solicitor, E.S.P. Haynes (who had an interest in the company), intending to sue. Haynes wrote despairingly to Gilbert Chesterton, since it was useless, he claimed, to deal with his brother, who was completely under Ada's thumb. "And she is a perfectly impossible person to have in control of a paper . . . I am absolutely convinced that if Bowerman goes and she remains, the paper cannot last three weeks." Belloc and [Gilbert] Chesterton hastened to London to talk sense to Cecil Chesterton, and that particular crisis was passed."[7]

A few other clues about Ada can be gleaned from her book, *In Darkest London*, written many years after Cecil died—1926—in

[7] Dudley Barker, *G.K. Chesterton*, 212.

which she admitted that she went out on the streets with "nothing but my personality." She was an agnostic, although later, during World War II, Father Vincent McNabb received her into the Catholic Church. McNabb had been a close friend to both Cecil and Gilbert. Ada wrote a biography of St. Teresa of Avila, another woman with a strong personality, whom she admired.

The observant Ada had known and enjoyed the camaraderie of the tavern, which nothing, she said, can excel. She stated she was not a feminist, in that she refused to believe that man was the cause of injustice to woman. But, she stated,

> I could not have dreamed that in this day of feminine emancipation from political disabilities, that trade union leaders, women preachers, doctors, barristers, lawyers and under secretaries, would all have passed by on the other side, leaving their sisters to find refuge in squalor, or to spend the night walking the inhospitable streets.[8]

To earn money, Ada wrote many books in addition to *In Darkest London* and *St. Teresa: I Lived in a Slum, Women of the London Underworld, Sickle or Swastika? Young China and New Japan, Salute the Soviet, What Price Youth? My Russian Venture, This is Thy Body: An Experience in Osteopathy,* and *The Chestertons.* She wrote the stage play of Gilbert's *The Man Who Was Thursday*; she wrote romances under another *nom de plume,* Margaret Hamilton. Her books often subsidized her newspaper work, and she primarily thought of herself, like Gilbert, as a journalist. She was a first-class reporter, and for years was the foreign correspondent for the *Daily Mail.*[9] The public's positive reaction

---

[8] Ada Eliza Chesterton, *In Darkest London* (London: Stanley Paul, 1926), 45.

[9] According to Aidan Mackey, personal recollections.

to *In Darkest London* is understandable, when one reads such a paragraph as this:

> And if we get down to bed-rock fundamentals, a homeless woman, whatsoever her moral character, is still a terrible indictment of society. But if Society refuses to act with moral courage, our streets will be full of derelict women, quite as many of them physically as chaste as the most bigoted puritan.[10]

And indeed, after publication, it seems many in London did discover that the women of the underworld were under-served. Her book caused a sensation. And so Cecil Houses began, places for destitute women to sleep and rest, wash and get back on their feet again.[11]

Social concern seemingly was a cause to unite Ada and Frances. Their different personalities, however, made it unlikely that the two would become close. Ada herself wrote this of Frances in her book about the Chestertons:

> She had a queer elusive attraction in those days, with her pale face, quite devoid of powder or the least tinge of make-up, and curiously vague eyes. She looked charming in blue or green, but she rarely wore those shades, and usually affected dim browns or greys. We did not find much mutual ground of understanding. She and I looked at life from a radically different standpoint. She had never had to earn her living in the ordinary strenuous sense, and her experience of employment had been confined to the secretaryship of a society called, I think, "The Parents' Reform League," or something of that kind. I was out in the world at sixteen years of age learning

---

[10] *In Darkest London*, 182.

[11] These homes are still open and run by the Central and Cecil Housing Trust today.

my job as a news reporter, moreover, I loved adventure, and wanted to go everywhere and see as much as possible. Even our domestic reactions differed. I revelled in cooking and housewifery, while Frances was not interested in food and really did not mind what she ate. A garden was her delight and she had the green hands of the flower grower. But the essential difference between us lay in our respective attitudes to Fleet Street—a difference which coloured the greater part of our association.[12]

In some ways, this passage demonstrates how little Ada really knew Frances. Frances's father had died when she was fourteen and her life changed. During her youth, Frances worked to educate herself while engaged in tutoring and governess-type work.

The crux of the difference lay in their attitudes, not necessarily their experience: Frances valued formal education and Ada did not. Ada's dismissal of Frances's life as less physically strenuous than working on the street as a reporter is accurate, but Ada preferred "the school of hard knocks". Ada loved wearing makeup, and noticed that Frances wore none. Again, this is a personal preference, not a matter of fundamental difference.

Much of the description is clearly inaccurate. Frances did like cooking and her favorite place in the whole house was the kitchen fireplace. Frances loved to serve tea; she made fudge and other treats to go with the tea, and at the start of their married life, she did all the shopping, cooking, and baking. Later on, when they could afford it, they hired a cook and housekeeper,

---

[12] *The Chestertons*, 26-27.

as well as a gardener to help tend Frances's gardens. Ada calls Frances the "average housewife,"[13] which for her was censure.

Ada's "Fleet Street" comment is correct. Ada loved the pub scene as much as many men, drinking, smoking, and laughing until late in the night. Frances knew Gilbert had greatness in him and needed time to write. Further, that environment was not conducive to her husband's health. She not surprisingly wanted to limit his time there, granting him opportunities to create the literature Frances knew he was meant to write. Ada seems to have loved Gilbert's fun-loving company too much to think of this.

Ada appears to have been addicted to the most thrilling aspects of her profession. Ada and Cecil often put *The New Witness* to bed—finished up writing and submitted it for publication—after long debates about what legally constituted libel.[14] She loved controversy; she had no fear of the consequences to herself—she was hiding safely behind a *nom de plume*.

In June of 1917, Cecil came home from training, eagerly seeking out Ada, whom he called, "Kiddy." He had been sent to the front. He needed to be back in service in less than a week. The wedding was quickly arranged. They married on June 9 in two ceremonies: the civil service at the local Church of England and the Catholic ceremony at Corpus Christi for Cecil. Cecil visited his lawyer and made out a will to his new wife, and after the briefest of honeymoons, he was gone.

When Cecil left for the war, his newspaper *The New Witness*, which he and Hilaire Belloc had begun, was left in Gilbert's hands. Gilbert had never been an editor, and did not necessarily

---

[13] *Ibid.,* 69.

[14] *Ibid.,* 72.

want to be one,[15] but became an editor for the sake of his brother. He came to the office once a week, and was in constant contact either by phone or telegraph. Ada, along with Elizabeth "Bunny" Dunham, the office assistant, W.R. Titterton, and his other reporters, kept up the day-to-day activity on the paper.

As the war went on, Gilbert and Frances visited wounded servicemen in the hospital.[16] On one occasion, they met a young injured pilot Hugh Paynter, and Frances invited him to Beaconsfield when he recovered. It was the beginning of a lasting friendship.

During the war, Frances worked to maintain her other interests. In late 1917, she was invited to give a speech at Highfield in Maidenhead, where Ethel and Lucian lived. Highfield had just re-formed a branch of the Parents' National Educational Union. The influential crowd included Lady Ethel "Ettie" Desborough, who was a friend to Gilbert and Frances as well as to Ethel.[17] Frances chose as her topic "Children and Poetry."

Frances had started a poetry circle in Beaconsfield, which encouraged adults and children to read and write poetry. Frances also taught a poetry class to children in Beaconsfield: some of the children had come to her hating poetry, but later were able to read and enjoy poetry and write their own poems. Frances talked about all of this in her speech and encouraged the parents in the audience to help their children enjoy and write poetry, too.

Like everyone else in England, the Chestertons were never far from the war. By the end of 1918, Cecil had been wounded

---

[15] W.R. Titterton, *G.K. Chesterton: A Portrait* (London: Alexander Ouseley, 1936), 123.

[16] Pearce, 232; see also: *Catholic Truth*, Autumn, 1916.

[17] Richard Davenport-Hines, *Ettie: The Intimate Life and Dauntless Spirit of Lady Desborough* (London: Weidenfeld & Nicolson, 2008).

three times fighting in France, and had developed a kidney infection; less than a month after the Armistice, on December 6, 1918, he died in a hospital in France. Ada was the only family member there at the end, and she alone was present for his funeral and burial. Gilbert and his friend Maurice Baring had worked through diplomatic contacts to help her travel to France at this time.

Gilbert naturally took the news hard. Cecil's death was a wound from which Gilbert never really recovered. Gilbert coped by dedicating himself to the memory of Cecil in carrying on his newspaper.

Small consolation came that month when Frances's poem "Here is the Little Door" was published as a Christmas carol by Stainer & Bell. The composer of the melody was Herbert Howells.[18]

The following year was mostly taken up with the everyday labors of writing, editing, and struggling through grief, limited rations, and political tenseness. At the year's conclusion, with the war winding down to the uncertain peace of the 1920 Armistice, the Chestertons decided to act on a desire they had to travel to Palestine. Gilbert was writing a book about Jerusalem; in addition to this, he had a personal reason for traveling, as he explained in a letter to Baring:

> I have another motive for wanting to go there, which is much stronger than the desire to write the book. . . . Frances is to come with me, and all the doctors in creation tell her she can only get rid of her neuritis if she goes to some such place and misses part of an English winter. I would do anything to bring it off. . . . If you could help in this matter, I really

---

[18] A quick check on iTunes shows thirty-seven different recordings of the song today, most which give no credit to the author of the lyrics.

think you would be helping things you yourself care about; and one person, not myself, who deserves it.[19]

The Chestertons began their journey on December 29, 1919. Frances kept a detailed diary of the trip. They saw Rome for one day on the journey; they traveled through Paris, to Alexandria and Cairo in Egypt; saw the Nile, visited two mosques. Gilbert gave a lecture, "Sightseeing for the Blind." During the sea leg of the journey, Frances was seasick for the first two days on the boat. When they arrived in Alexandria, they visited a Catholic church, still beautifully festive for the Christmas season. Frances, always attracted to a Nativity scene, wrote in her diary that this was the most beautiful crib she had ever seen.[20]

Gilbert gave an address at the Bishop's chapel in Cairo clad in cassock and surplice (Frances said he did very well). In Damascus, Gilbert was so busy writing that Frances hired a typist for him. They visited the tombs of Godfrey de Bouillon and his brother, Baldwin.

While they stayed in Damascus, Frances was invited to a "Mohammadan" wedding. She wrote up her strange experiences in a letter on which was written, "For Ladies Only!"

As they traveled, Frances kept up a correspondence with family and friends at home. Addressing letters to her mother-in-law, Marie Louise, whom she addressed as "Mater," she wrote about their travels and of Gilbert's successes. Then she asked Marie Louise to pass the letters along to her own mother, who should then send them on to her sister Ethel.

This trip clearly contributed to the spiritual growth of both Gilbert and Frances. The former, by this time, was reaching

---

[19] *Gilbert Keith Chesterton*, 442-43.

[20] Pearce, 249.

PHOTOGRAPHS

Frances Chesterton's father, George
William Blogg, circa 1880

The Blogg Family Crest

George Blogg in an unknown
military uniform, circa 1878

Frances Chesterton's mother,
Blanche Blogg, circa 1925

*Frances Chesterton's sister
Gertrude Blogg, circa 1899*

*Frances Blogg about the time of
her engagement, 1898*

Frances Chesterton's sister, Ethel

*Frances Chesterton's brother George
"Knollys" Blogg, circa 1906*

(left) Gilbert and Frances, possible wedding day photo, 1901

(far left) Frances Chesterton's sister Ethel and brother-in-law, Lucian Oldershaw

Sketch made of Frances about 1906

*Portrait of Frances
by photographer
Richard Speaight,
circa 1908*

*Gilbert and Frances attend
the christening of their
niece, Pamela Oldershaw.*

Portrait of Frances Chesterton by Alfred Priest, 1909

Frances Chesterton, circa 1910

Gilbert and Frances at Overroads circa 1911

Frances Chesterton, circa 1914

Frances Chesterton sitting in her favorite place by the kitchen fireplace.

Gilbert and Frances, trip to Palestine, 1919

*Gilbert giving a talk at Fernley, the home of Ethel and Lucian Oldershaw.
To Gilbert's left: Lucian Oldershaw, Frances, an unknown minister, and
Blanche Blogg. To Gilbert's right is his father, Edward Chesterton.*

*Frances Chesterton's mother, Blanche
Blogg, along with her sister Ethel, niece
Gertrude (Woozle), grand-niece Sheila,
and Lucian Oldershaw's mother.*

*Frances Chesterton,
circa 1921*

Frances Chesterton, after
Gilbert died, about 1937

The Blogg Family grave at Highgate
Cemetery, London. Frances's parents,
George, Blanche, and sisters Gertrude,
Helen and Rachel are buried here.

a new crisis of faith. This was shown when, in the summer of 1920, Gilbert was asked to speak to a large gathering of Anglo-Catholics. He felt a bit uncomfortable; he had agreed to do the speech before realizing his own discomfort in going through with the promised speech. He tried to get out of it, but was held to his promise. He felt it was something of a farewell speech, as in his heart, he was feeling as though his Anglo-Catholic days were behind him. He wrote to Baring:

> I am concerned most, however, about somebody I value more than the Archbishop of Canterbury; Frances, to whom I owe much of my own faith, and to whom therefore (as far as I can see my way) I also owe every decent chance for the controversial defence of her faith. If her side can convince me, they have a right to do so; if not, I shall go hot and strong to convince her. . . . I must await answers from Waggett and Gore as well as Knox and McNabb; and talk the whole thing over with her, and then act as I believe.[21]

Besides the serious contemplation of his conversion, Gilbert and Frances were preparing for their upcoming trip to America, which would take place in early 1921. Between Jerusalem, which they had returned from in April 1920, and America, in early 1921, Gilbert completed several projects: *The Uses of Diversity*, *The New Jerusalem*, and *The Superstition of Divorce*. All the while he kept up with his regular work at *The New Witness* and the *Illustrated London News*.

These were critical months for Gilbert. Frances had not yet felt the call to convert with her husband, but she did not knowingly hinder him. She told Fr. O'Connor that she asked God to show her the way, but that as of that moment, she

---

[21] Pearce, 251-52.

could not see how He would do so. Frances noticed Gilbert's increasing restlessness of spirit, but was at a loss as to what to do. Her feelings, though, remained strong: she was not ready to convert.

In addition, Frances was visibly unwell. She visited her doctor, who sent her on for several consultations. The doctors all agreed that there was something wrong; they could see she was in pain. She needed to regain her health for the trip to America, and they worked together to see what they could do. But first, they needed to diagnose what was wrong.

On October 19, 1920, Dr. Mennell saw Frances for the first time. Her regular doctor, Dr. Bakewell, had sent her to a Dr. Pococh, who sent her to Mennell. From that consultation, Dr. Mennell diagnosed the cause (and outlined it in detail in a letter to Bakewell). Mennell said Frances's problem originated in childhood. As she grew, one leg had grown longer than the other. This situation tipped the pelvis to one side, which resulted in all kinds of trouble, from her knees to her spine to her neck. She had been in pain for years, but thought it was something to bear in silence until the pain became so intense that she agreed to seek help.

Frances was advised to see a shoemaker and have a shoe manufactured with a heel raised to support her shorter leg. She was also given a belt of some sort to help correct her posture. In addition, massage, heat, and rest were recommended. These were the days before pain-killers were simply and readily available. In addition to everything else, the pain had caused Frances to have difficulty sleeping. The doctors considered a number of options as treatments, but it was not something easily remedied. Resting helped, and Frances began to feel better.[22] She stayed at the hospital under Dr. Mennell's supervision until December 17, 1920—resting, working through therapy, and thereby restoring her sleep habits. She remained just under two months. Dr. Mennell wrote to Dr. Bakewell that he would have liked to keep her longer, but he thought she was healed sufficiently to weather the trip to America.

With such a medical blessing, the Chestertons departed for the United States. (Before they even departed, Gilbert gave two newspaper interviews on the boat.) Once again, Frances kept a diary of the trip, full of many little details and notes, as well as saving newspaper clippings of all their interviews while in America.[23]

Frances enjoyed the trans-oceanic trip. She took hot sea baths on the journey, and was happy they had a lending library. One evening, the ship's band gave a concert, after which Gilbert delivered a speech on behalf of the Merchant Service Orphanage. To Frances's delight and pride, they brought in a record-breaking collection. The steward, the son of a famous conjuror, thrilled Frances by performing some sleight-of-hand tricks at the table. Frances attended a shipboard religious service conducted by the captain on a Sunday. On another day she saw a group of dolphins leaping out of the water.

They played cards—Poker Patience—after dinner one night. There was also dancing to the ship's band. When the trip got a little long, as they had to make a detour due to icebergs, the captain took a few of the passengers on an extended behind-the-scenes tour. Frances saw store rooms, cold storage, the crew

---

[22] Courtesy of John M. Kelly Library Rare Books, Archival & Manuscript Collection's G.K. Chesterton Microfiche Collection.

[23] *Gilbert Keith Chesterton*, 477.

compartments, third-class accommodations; she even saw the captain's cabin, his instruments—everything, she said, except the bridge. The chief engineer later took them to see the actual workings of the ship, with its immense machinery.

The first thing Frances saw in New York Harbor was the Statue of Liberty, and then some skyscrapers. When they landed, the fun ("or the horrors", as Frances called it) began. They were greeted everywhere as celebrities.

> Interviewers, photographers, film men all seized on us and we spent our last hours on the boat in a mob of what I can only term lunatics. Gilbert bore it all with imperturbably good humour but I was feeling so sick and tired. After getting off and through customs Mr. Lee Keedick[24] met us and took us to the Biltmore Hotel, where another frenzied mob of newspapermen attacked us and even penetrated to our room and took photographs there! When they at last departed, I went to bed, though I had to unpack and re-pack as we are to go to Boston by the 10 o'clock train tomorrow.

Despite her intense tiredness, she visited with her cousin, Harriet Monkhouse, and, always a faithful chronicler, took time to write in her diary.

They arrived in Boston. ("More interviews—more photographers," said Frances.) They had a Mr. Widdicombe with them, who had arranged some of the details of the trip. They reached their hotel, and "Gilbert was again assaulted by a waiting crowd of journalists."

The next day, Gilbert escaped the journalists, and Frances stayed in the hotel room, trying to catch up on necessary correspondence.

---

[24] Keedick was their US agent.

"So far my feelings towards this country are entirely hostile," she wrote in her diary. "But it would be unfair to judge too soon. We have refused all invitations, it's the only thing to do. The first lecture took place at 8:30 in the Jordan's Hall." The Jordan Hall[25] lecture was covered in the newspapers and periodicals.[26]

On January 13, 1921, Frances experienced a surprising first: "I was interviewed to my amusement. But insisted on seeing a proof so that nothing too outrageous should be printed." She later explained that this was the first time anyone had ever asked to interview her, an interesting and somewhat amazing fact, considering her husband's fame in Britain.

In one interview, she was asked her views on America, Americans, American literature versus British literature, American journalists versus British journalists, and jazz music. In another interview, she was reportedly enticed to read from a book she was keeping, a journal she called *The Book of Likes and Dislikes*. She liked the way American women dressed so smartly, but found they kept to the style of the day and failed to express their individuality; she said all the women's silhouettes looked the same, although she did see some distinctive hats; she did not like that her husband's answer to a reporter's question was misquoted; she did not like ice cream or ice water; and so on. Another article stated that Frances spoke at a luncheon where Gilbert was also invited to speak.

After Gilbert had given a lecture at Smith College, Frances wrote, "I had a delightful conversation in the train with a

---

[25] "Chesterton Expresses Ideas on Modern Education," *The Harvard Crimson*, January 14, 1921, http://www.thecrimson.com/article/1921/1/14/chesterton-expresses-ideas-on-modern-education/.

[26] "The Perils of Health," *The Nation's Health: Continuing Modern Medicine* Vol. 3, no. 2 (Chicago: The Modern Hospital Publishing Co., 1921): 126.

lady, Miss Salton of Smith College. I should imagine a typical American cultured woman of ideas."

Her reflections and commentary ran the spectrum from thoughts regarding the culture at large to observations about smaller archetypal American details. For example, we find this entry:

> Gilbert spoke [at the] Brooklyn Institute in the evening. Very, very successful. We went by subway—a new experience, like our tube but not so good. Returned in a car. New York is a wonderful sight at night, especially the view from Brooklyn Bridge.

Frances took a walk in Central Park, and visited nearly every day with friends or relatives of friends from England. The Rann Kennedys, old neighbors from the Chesterton's first flat in Battersea, were living in America and came by, as did the brother of a former pupil of Frances's brother-in-law Lucian Oldershaw. They met Gerald Stanley Lee, a famous literary figure at the time, as well as his wife. Another evening, Frances met Aline Kilmer, wife of poet Joyce Kilmer. The two wives had lunch one day at India House near Wall Street.

Frances's health seemed to stand the test of travel. She did complain occasionally of a headache, or that it was too warm indoors. She loved fireplaces and thought furnace heat uncomfortable. She lay in bed one day until noon, but otherwise, she was up and writing all morning every morning. On Dr. Mennell's advice, Frances visited a Dr. Osgood in Boston. She mentioned in her diary that Dr. Osgood felt her leg support was too heavy, and that she needed something lighter. He sent a most "lugubrious" report.

In spite of imperfect health, she was present and attentive for and with her husband. Gilbert was delighted to have her as his companion. He particularly looked forward to some time alone with her, without the mountains of writing work between them. He needed to discuss conversion, faith; and these important topics were difficult to bring up in the course of a normal day at home.

Their schedule was tightly packed with engagements. On January 26, Professor Arthur Hadley, the president of Yale, met the Chestertons at the train station and welcomed them into his home. At the university, Gilbert gave a talk in a lecture hall to an enthusiastic audience. The Yale boys, Frances says, stormed the platform for handshakes and autographs. Another day, Mr. Phelps, a professor of literature at Yale, drove Frances to a ladies' tea where the women gathered there had been anxious to meet the wife of Mr. Chesterton.

On January 28, they arrived in Philadelphia. Gilbert was whisked off to a lunch with some press people, and Frances went to the hotel. "There," she states, "I was besieged and made to give an interview and taken to a photographer's."

At first, the reporters and requests for interviews amused the British couple, but soon they began to annoy them both. They could not go anywhere without a gang of journalists asking questions, or cameramen thrusting lenses in front of them.

Even as Gilbert left a sea of admiration in his wake, Frances made a quiet but favorable impression as well. She told a reporter in Philadelphia[27] that she was acting as her husband's private secretary, answering social and professional invitations at a rate of fifty to sixty a week, and had arranged many of the details for their three-month itinerary in America. Cosmo Hamilton, one of Chesterton's debate partners during the American tour, said this describing Frances:

---

[27] *Evening Public Ledger* (Philadelphia, Monday, Feb. 7, 1921).

> ... and dear Mrs. Chesterton, more than wife and something of
> [a] mother, with a wonderful touch of governess, valet, Cook's
> guide and protecting angel, who whispered encouragement to
> G.K. before he mounted the creaking platform and brushed
> the crumbs from his clothes.

Everywhere they went, Frances made sure Gilbert was dressed, pressed, his hat dusted, and the crumbs brushed off. The press interviews were a necessary evil; they ensured that his lectures were well attended. They continued on from Boston to Oklahoma, and then traveled into Canada.

After they visited with Murray Hill, an American writer, Hill jotted down these thoughts about his visit with the Chestertons:

> The two of them were framed in their doorway as we got into
> the "foreigner's" car[28]... Mrs. Chesterton called to us that she
> hoped to see us all in England. ... As the car dropped from
> their floor both were beaming a merry, friendly farewell.
> Suddenly it struck me that they were very like a pair of chil-
> dren—they were so happy, so natural, so innocent of guile,
> and obviously so fond of one another."[29]

As their visit wound down to its close, the Chestertons were invited to a luncheon given by the Dickens Fellowship in the National Arts Club and were the guests of honor. Gilbert spoke on Anglo-American friendship. A few others spoke at the luncheon, including Frances.

The exhausted couple returned to England on April 12, 1921. They had departed on their trip on New Year's Day. Frances was homesick, yearning for her home, her garden, her dog and

---

[28] Elevator operated by an American.

[29] Murray Hill, "Murray Hill Bids Mr. Chesterton Goodby," *The Bookman: A Review of Books and Life* Vol. 53 (1921): 311.

cats and even her donkey—but relieved to have been spared a brutal English winter.

Almost as soon as she got home, she went back to Dr. Mennell, and again complained of insomnia. He told Frances that before he had only treated symptoms; now he needed to do more work to discover the cause that underlay them. Blood work and x-rays followed. Mennell determined that her major problem was an abscess in a couple of teeth. He cultured the infection, and prepared a "vaccine". Additionally, he wrote Dr. Bakewell that Frances was obviously trying to do too much, more than her condition warranted, and suggested ordering her to a rest cure. Dr. Mennell believed Frances could not get better at home, because she saw all the work to be done there. In order for her to get well, she needed to get away. Her heart rate was very high, so he recommended digitalis.

Frances was unlikely to comply with any recommendation that would remove her from her husband and their unflaggingly active life. Instead of a rest cure, upon their return they hired a new secretary, Kathleen Chesshire. Frances once told her that there were three things she would never do: cut her hair, engage an efficient secretary, or become a Roman Catholic.

Additionally, they prepared to move. 1921 marked their last Christmas at Overroads.

At this time, Gilbert remained perched on the brink of conversion. He endeavored to explain his dilemma to his close Catholic friend, the author Maurice Baring.[30] Gilbert wrote Baring on Christmas Day, 1921:

> For deeper reasons that I could ever explain, my mind
> has to turn especially on the thought of my wife, whose
> life has been in many ways a very heroic tragedy; and to

---

[30] These letters are included in both the Ward and the Pearce biographies.

whom I am so much in debt of honour that I cannot bear to leave her, even psychologically, if it be possible by tact and sympathy to take her with me. We have had a very difficult time lately; but the other day she rather abruptly faced the thing herself in a new way, and spoke as if she knew where we would both end. But she asked for a little time; as a great friend of hers is also (with the approval of the priest whom she consulted) delaying for the moment till she is more certain. She and Frances want to meet and have it out, I think, and I cannot imagine any way in which Frances is more likely to be moved in that direction than by an Anglican or ex-Anglican friend of exactly that type. . . . I only write this to tell you the thing may look rather stationary, 'and yet it moves'.[31]

It was not an easy time for discussing conversion (if such a thing truly exists). Frances's father-in-law was dying. Gilbert and Frances visited Marie Louise and tried to assist and console as they were able. In the spring of 1922 they were present when Edward Chesterton died.

Grief, softened by the comparatively peaceful passing of Gilbert's father, would heal quietly. Meanwhile, the Chestertons moved across the street into Top Meadow, their second Beaconsfield home. One great benefit of the American lecture tour was the extra money the trip had made for them. These funds sufficed for them to finish the addition onto Top Meadow, enabling their move.

Top Meadow was a sprawling home, with a lovely garden, a donkey shed, a greenhouse, a garage, a small orchard, and a small vineyard. Over the garage was a storeroom for apples

---

[31] Pearce, 260.

and potatoes. Adjoining it was a log shed and boiler house, and at the other end, the greenhouse.[32]

The gardens were perhaps the most wonderful aspect of the new home. Ada Chesterton described them enthusiastically:

> The gardens stretching luxuriantly at the back were always a joy. Frances I think found undiluted happiness in their superintendence. They were lavishly kept and a local man worked unremittingly. I remember one gorgeous summer day when flaming pokers, delphiniums, lupine, peonies, sunflowers—all the piled-up wealth of scent and colour—streamed across the lawn.[33]

The main garden was laid out to the south of the house with four York paths radiating from a pond; the flower beds were sheltered by low stone walls on the top of which was space for small plants. On the north side of the house were some old field hedges, some lime and cherry trees, ornamental hollies, and a few small cypresses. There was a large kitchen garden. A shoot of honeysuckle from Frances's wedding bouquet had been rooted following the wedding in 1901 and was transplanted to the new home; the bush grew in the meadow nearby. Frances delighted in picking and choosing plants and found joy in the beauty of a flower border.[34]

The house was built of brick and oak, with several fireplaces. (Frances loved a wood-burning fire far more than central heating, which she criticized. This was paradoxical, because she also hated winter and the cold, and central heating could have done

---

[32] Unpublished notes from Henry Reed, warden for the Converts Aid Society, which owned Top Meadow in 1945.

[33] *The Chestertons*, 257.

[34] *The New Witness* (January 5, 1923): 13.

much to increase her comfort during the cold months.) The bedrooms were fitted with oak wardrobes floor to ceiling. There was plenty of ironwork —door hinges, latches, and the window fittings were different in each room. Beaten iron vinework on the chandelier added character to the home. And off the kitchen was a room called the maid's and cook's sitting room with its own brick fireplace, the coziest room in the house.

Top Meadow featured a south-facing bow window on the first floor overlooking the garden and meadow, which Frances called an afternoon room. Frances loved the room, and placed in it a cupboard for her miniature dolls. Frances had her own set of puppets with which she made up stories for the children who visited. In addition, the toy cupboard was filled with boxes of dress-up clothes for amateur theater productions, and plenty of sheets for swathing Gilbert during games of charades. The couple would invite all the children they knew out to Top Meadow for visits; they commissioned an indoor stage for home theatricals.

Frances's domestic duties increased exponentially with the new home, and she embraced her multifarious tasks with fervor. She supervised the making of marmalade, and churned butter. She kept chickens and collected the eggs. She kept milk goats,[35] and she darned socks by the fire. She tended her gardens and her pets—they kept cats, dogs, chickens, ducks, rabbits, goats, the donkey, and bees for honey. In her play *The Children's Crusade*, one of her characters describes simply what women do at home: they cook, clean, mend, and pray.[36] With the additional task of being all things to Gilbert, such was the life of Frances.

Their various dogs, cats, and donkey figured into Chesterton's poetry. Dogs included the purebred Winkle ("Wink"), a Scottish

---

[35] *The Chestertons*, 160.

[36] *How Far Is It To Bethlehem*, 24.

Aberdeen terrier; Quoodle ("Quo") the first and second; Bingie, and Dolfuss. Names of cats included Perky, Stanley Baldwin, Not-a-Man, Mrs. Whitehouse, Bonrick, Post, and Maud; the name of the donkey was Trotsky—according to Gilbert, because he would not "walk-skee."

In addition to the chaos of moving and the busy work of helping his mother deal with the estate of his father, and in spite of the fact that Frances had a nurse staying in their home to give her heat treatments for her back, Gilbert had to go on another lecture tour—this time to the Netherlands. It was much shorter than his American tour, lasting only ten days, but he went without Frances.

Gilbert was moving toward a critical moment. Frances's health continued precarious. In the summer of 1922, pain again in her knees, hips, and back, prompted Dr. Mennell to arrange nurses to enter the Chesterton home and work with her. He described Frances to Dr. Bakewell as being in a "dilapidated condition".

Largely, perhaps, because of her physical suffering, Gilbert became increasingly restless. The problem of Frances perplexed him. He consulted with Fr. Ronald Knox, himself a convert from Anglicanism, writing that the issue for Frances was that it was difficult to wrench herself away from a religion which she had always practiced in good faith. Gilbert states he had never been able to feel that way about the Anglican faith, and so for him the problem was different.

Further, though it had been sixteen years since Knollys' suicide, Frances was still haunted by the knowledge that he had converted to Roman Catholicism before his death. In fact, the two events seemed linked in Frances's mind. She still could not see her way to conversion.

Nevertheless, the moment for taking action had come for Gilbert.

Frances and Gilbert had come to regard Fr. John O'Connor highly. Gilbert, writing to him in 1922, said, "You are the person that both Frances and I think of with most affection, of all who could help in such a matter."[37] Gilbert was finally ready to be received into the Catholic Church.

Knox had helped Gilbert with some theological questions, as had Fr. Ignatius Rice, a monk at the Douai Abbey in Berkshire. Rice had become interested in Gilbert's writings, and in particular, in his work on Distributism. When Rice was a young monk, he attended one of Chesterton's lectures at Oxford. The hall was packed, and the enormous speaker made a considerable impact on him. From that moment on, Rice read as much Chesterton as he could, and strove in all he did to put the ideas into practice, attempting, by his teaching of young men, to rear "a succession of Chestertonians."[38]

But now the person Gilbert called upon was his longest standing priestly friend, Father O'Connor. The very difficulty of that decision—without Frances—makes the conversion all the more important. Frances told Gilbert she wanted him to do what he felt was right. It was the permission he needed. Gilbert indicated to O'Connor he felt he would soon decide to enter the Church. O'Connor in turn wrote to the bishop of Northampton. On July 13, 1922, he received a note from Bishop Dudley Charles Cary-Elwes:

> Please God what you anticipate may be true about Mr. Chesterton. I enclose a form of delegation for receiving a

---

[37] British Library file 73196-0192.

[38] *The Chesterton Review* Vol. 15, no. 3 (1989): 355.

Convert in case it is needed, and another, which I leave blank
in your hands, in case his wife is also on the way.

O'Connor came for a visit on a Wednesday, July 26, 1922, and
stayed overnight. On Thursday, he and Frances went for a long
walk, and O'Connor tried to ascertain her feelings on Gilbert's
conversion—and her own. She said she would be relieved if he
converted, as Gilbert had been so fidgety lately, especially the
last three months. She said she could not come along yet, as
she felt the way was not clear.

O'Connor wrote Rice to come to Beaconsfield. On Sunday,
July 30, the two priests met with Gilbert and Frances in a make-
shift church, located in a tin shed at the back of the Railway Hotel,
directly across the tracks from the train station. Afterwards
Gilbert loved to tell the story of how he was received in a pub.

While Gilbert was making his confession to Fr. O'Connor
for the first time, Frances was emotionally overcome, weeping
continually. A.N. Wilson, in his biography of Hilaire Belloc
(who was invited to attend), relates that everyone

> . . . sat awaiting the appearance of Mr. Belloc. The moments
> ticked by, turning first into a half an hour and then an hour.
> Frances Chesterton, still loyal to her Anglicanism and bro-
> ken-hearted by her husband's defection, was in floods of tears,
> and Father Rice had to take her into the bar of the hotel for
> a drink to calm her nerves, while Father O'Connor heard
> Chesterton's confession in the tin tabernacle. At length, they
> abandoned any hope of Belloc's appearing, and they proceed-
> ed with the ceremony in an agony of awkwardness. . . . The
> perfunctory rite was performed to the accompaniment of
> Frances Chesterton's lachrymose sniffing, and Ronald Knox

felt afterwards that the occasion had been 'spoilt' by Belloc's negligent failure to appear.[39]

Colorful though the description is, there are several inconsistencies. There is no recorded reason for Belloc's absence. Frances was not quite as broken-hearted as this story relates, as was shown in her conversation with O'Connor beforehand. In addition to that, Knox was not actually present at the conversion rite. He had been in close contact with Gilbert during his long, slow march toward conversion, but he was not there the day of the actual ceremony.

Gilbert, however, was mostly happy—except for the part of him that wished for Frances to have converted with him. He no longer had to live two lives, and was at peace with the change. He immediately wrote to his mother, saying he had joined because he came to the same conclusions Cecil had.

Frances's resistance to converting alongside her husband came from many sources. She may even have been resistant because of his very enthusiasm. From Gilbert's previous comments, he felt a responsibility towards Frances for bringing her to the truth, once he converted. Frances nearly always believed Gilbert was right about things, and almost always shared his opinions. She seemed to know she would convert eventually, but wanted to do it in her own time, at her own pace. In a way, this provided Gilbert with the ultimate test of his own decision, as a mutual friend, Fr. Vincent McNabb, noted in a letter to O'Connor:

2 August 1922

My Dearest Father,

---

[39] A.N. Wilson, *Hilaire Belloc: A Biography* (New York: Atheneum Books, 1984), 249-50.

How good of you to make me so soon a partner in the good news of Gilbert's homecoming. . . . As Mrs. Chesterton has not, for the moment found herself able to go where he has gone, his will must have been fast set on the Will of God! There was a time when his wife seemed so undeniably sent of God that he had no will to go elsewhere then where she went. If now he has loved God more than "father & mother and wife" I feel sure that this love of God must be a sword piercing him to the very division of the soul and spirit.

We must pray that the pain he is suffering on her account will be to her profit. Ever since I spoke with her and heard from others some of the sad story of a convert kinsman of hers I have felt that her difficulties were psychological rather than logical; and that nothing would be so strong to help her as prayer to God. . . .[40]

The diagnosis of the priest seems likely. The convert kinsman, of course, was her brother Knollys. Frances had linked her brother's conversion with his mental instability and suicide. Furthermore, she was content with Anglo-Catholicism. It had benefited her spiritually and was familiar and comforting. While she could accept the logical reasons for converting with her mind, she could not easily realize the thought with an active decision of her heart. Her mind would not need as much convincing. Intellectually, she knew, even when Gilbert converted, where she would end one day.

---

[40] Fr. Vincent McNabb, O.P., Wade Center folder 216.

Chapter Six

FOLLOWING FAITH (1922–1926)

*You will I know be glad to hear that I received my first
Communion at Wycombe last Sunday and was confirmed
in the Cathedral in the afternoon—I am very happy*

The first book Gilbert wrote after his conversion
was a biography of his and Frances's favorite saint:
Francis of Assisi. Gilbert had loved St. Francis since
childhood. He and Frances both based their admiration for
the saint in a belief in the superiority of childlike innocence.[1]
Gilbert's book was a success. Catholics and non-Catholics alike
admired the saint, and Gilbert's book transformed Francis' story
into a romance.

The holy man of Assisi was a happy point of unity between the
two. They had, by now, settled comfortably into their closely-knit
relationship. They were so comfortable they could even tease
each other—even regarding Gilbert's old girlfriends. They wrote
poems together and for each other, and they helped each other
during illnesses. Gilbert said the time he felt most helpless was
when Frances needed him when she was ill. Frances was the one
great light of his life. It was she who lavished upon him all the
affection of a woman and the homage of an ardent admirer.[2] But
now, there was a form of separation between them, as they did

---

[1] Pearce, 293.

[2] Braybrooke, 22.

not share the thing that was most important to both of them. St. Francis was, therefore, a happy consolation, and a reminder that they shared a great deal in faith, though divided by affiliation.

With her father-in-law's death and her husband's conversion, and her own physical condition, Frances suffered a great deal in 1922. To her great relief, she returned to the doctor in October, and he found that she was much improved. His only suggestion now was that she would be much better off if she could get to a warmer climate sometime after Christmas. He suggested Morocco, Madeira, or the West Indies. They never went.

Her work continued as ever. Frances wrote a play for the children to perform at the annual children's Christmas party, and enthusiastically announced it to Fr. O'Connor:

> December 4, 1922
>
> ... I've written a Children's play called the Children's Crusade which is being acted here—If you want anything for children to perform you might like it. Doggerel verse but it acts all right and Geoffrey Shaw HMI has written music for the carol. Gilbert is well. Writing an opposition [to] Wells' *History of the World*! Save us!
>
> Yours ever, Frances Chesterton[3]

The song was published as "Crusader's Carol" (also known as "The Shepherds Found Thee by Night") by Novello & Co. In addition, the poem Frances had written as a Christmas card in 1917—"How Far Is It To Bethlehem"—also known as "The Children's Song of the Nativity" and "A Nativity Song"—was also set to music and published in 1922 by Novello & Co. as a musical score.

---

[3] British Library folder 73196-0203.

At the end of the year, Gilbert attempted a daring adventure: traveling alone to attend a theater production of *The Man Who Was Thursday*. It was an unmitigated disaster. He forgot his dress clothes, and someone had to run for them, arriving only ten minutes before the train started that was to take him to the theater for the opening night of the play. Frances decided he should never again go anywhere without her.

Six months after Gilbert's conversion, in January of 1923, Frances wrote to O'Connor concerning the possibility of her own conversion: "I am better, but still unable to get about much, and longing so desperately for a little time in which to find my own soul and lose my own body . . . we are neither of us ever left alone for a moment."

Life continued at its relentless rate, and that "little time" still did not come. In May of 1923, the *New Witness* halted production due to lack of funds—although it was not initially apparent to Gilbert that it was finished completely. He still hoped it could be revived. In November, Bernard Gilbert offered to buy the *New Witness* from Gilbert, who refused, kindly, saying he could not really sell it, believing he owed it to his brother either to save it or sink it himself. Gilbert went on to praise Bernard Gilbert for his book, *Tyler of Barnet*, which had been published in early 1923, which he was reading while getting over a cold:

> I think "Tyler of Barnet" quite admirable; a very original and imaginative scheme of work achieved with a success which I should have thought impossible for it. My wife began to read it when I was *hors de combat*, and came to me with such a fire of appreciation that I started on it in preference to the murder stories in the magazines. If you knew how fond I am of murder stories, you would appreciate that compliment more than you probably do.

The months passed. In a letter from July 1923, Frances wrote again to O'Connor: "I am feeling my way into the Catholic fold, but it is a difficult load for me, and I ask your prayers—I will write when I want definite help. Yours affectionately, Frances Chesterton."[4]

As 1924 dawned, conversion continued to come slowly. This year Gilbert attained the honorable age of fifty (Frances would turn fifty-five). Their writing output continued on a prolific scale, as always. Frances enjoyed particular success. Samuel French, Ltd. published three of her verse children's plays—*The Children's Crusade*, *Sir Cleges*, and *The Christmas Gift*—as a set.

The plays, Frances stated in her preface, "make no pretense to any historical or literary value. They merely serve as a text or background for the exercise of that ingenuity and love of pageantry and even rhetoric which is the common heritage of all children." Frances then goes on to explain that the only reason she sought publication was that others had encouraged her to do so after noting the sheer number of requests she had for copies of the plays for others to put on in their own homes or schools. She also noted that, although the children enjoyed putting on the plays, it was quite possible that the making of the scenery, creating costumes, and painting heraldic shields was an even greater part of the enjoyment.

The Children's Crusade is a sweet story of a medieval Christmas where three children grieve because their father is missing. He has gone to fight in the crusade. The play begins with a triolet, a popular poetical form Gilbert, his wife, and their friends all enjoyed:[5]

---

[4] British Library folder 73196-0206.

[5] Ada Chesterton had mentioned earlier that a well-planned meal took as much creativity, in her mind, as a novel or a triolet.

Sorrow fills my heart,
Oh Richard, oh my King,
That you and I did part
Sorrow fills my heart.
But Blondel with his art
Will strive awhile to sing,
Though sorrow fills his heart,
Oh Richard, oh my King!

Sir Cleges is an Arthurian story, which includes the song "How Far Is It to Bethlehem." It was performed locally for the benefit of the Bromley Cottage Hospital and the National Society for the Prevention of Cruelty to Children. *Sir Cleges* was also performed at the Dickens Fair at Sutton Surrey on December 1 and 2, 1926, by the children of the congregation of Our Lady of the Rosary. The third play, *The Christmas Gift*, takes place during World War I in Flanders.

In December 1924, Frances again went to the doctor, who sent her on to see an endocrinologist, Dr. Gardiner-Hill at St. Thomas' Hospital, London. Based on blood work, Gardiner-Hill suspected a problem with her pituitary gland, and started her on a course of pituitary and thyroid drops for six months.

At around this time, yet another of Frances's plays appeared. The children of Oakdene School performed *Piers Plowman's Pilgrimage: A Morality Play in Five Scenes* for Christmas. There were two performances, December 16 and 17. Two of the Chesterton's nieces, Kate and Pamela Oldershaw, were part of the cast. The play was written up in the newspaper on December 17, 1924.

On January 23, 1925, Gilbert and Frances were guests of honor at a dinner held at the Grand Pump Room Hotel in Bath, where Frances would have *Piers Plowman* performed later in the year. They were seated with the mayor of Bath, and afforded all courtesy and attention.

Unfortunately, the trip was not simply one of delight; Frances once again fell ill. This doctor she visited in Bath wrote to Dr. Bakewell, reporting the incident and offering his diagnosis. Her complaint was general muscular rheumatism. Her pulse, as before, was too fast: 140. Her blood pressure was too high: 180 over 100. She had a fine tremor, palpitations upon exertion, and swelling in her feet. He prescribed medicine and suggested to Bakewell that she might have an overactive thyroid.

Four months later, on May 7, 1925, the Citizen House Players performed *Piers Plowman's Pilgrimage* at the Pump Room in Bath. Saturday, May 9, the *Bath Chronicle* wrote a glowing review. The play reminded the reviewer of earlier mystery plays: "Surely here there is symbology enshrined within symbology, and a parallel is presented with the adoration of the Blessed Virgin and the Holy Child."

Bridget Muller was praised for the beautiful songs she composed for the play (Samuel French published the score soon after, much to the benefit of would-be future performances). During intermissions, the string section of the Pump Room Orchestra played. "The performance was enthusiastically received," notes the reviewer, "and at its conclusion Mrs. Chesterton was called before the curtain and presented with a bouquet." The very youngest performer presented the delighted Frances with the flowers.

Mr. Fred E. Weatherly, one of the members of the audience, wrote a letter to the editor of the newspaper, and Frances cut it out and saved it:

To the Editor:

Sir—Will you allow me to add a few words of appreciation to the tribute which I am sure will be paid in your columns to Mrs. Gilbert Chesterton's "Piers Plowman's Pilgrimage," given so successfully at the Pump Room on Thursday night?

I am, as I think you know, a very old play-goer, and I find benefit and pleasure in every form of dramatic art, and, as such, may I say that Mrs. Chesterton's play impressed me with a delighted admiration which it has seldom been my good fortune to feel.

And why? I have no doubt why. It is because the subject of the play is a straight-forward, wholesome, and noble one, one which all can understand, and by which most of us can profit.

It is because the language of Mrs. Chesterton is simple, strong, pure English.

The following week, the Players put on *Piers Plowman* at the Little Theatre, from Saturday through Thursday, performing it six times. Yet again, it was afforded a favorable newspaper review (complete with several photographs of the performance):

This play, founded on the 14th century poem, reproduces with reasonable fidelity the language of the period, and contains many aspects of a distinctly mystic character. While the play is written for acting, it contains many passages, notably in the dignified prologue and epilogue, of literary power. This play, which was very favourably received on Thursday evening is still in manuscript. . . .

In 1925, *Piers Plowman* was formally published. Frances wrote two longer plays this year, *The Three Kings* and *Faith and Fable: A Masque*,[6] both of which were for a mixed group of adult and child actors. These plays were performed in community theater

---

[6] Also known as *Legends of the Gods and Saints*.

productions, schools, and as benefit performances to raise donations for causes that the Chestertons supported.

Even as her theatrical light glowed so brightly, another light was fading. In early 1925, the *New Witness* was finally allowed to rest in peace, and a new periodical was about to rise phoenix-like from its ashes. Gilbert, after many delays and debates over the naming of it, dubbed the resurrected paper *G.K.'s Weekly*. The first issue came out on March 21, 1925.[7] As usual, he had irons in many fires. *Tales of the Long Bow* appeared this year as well, and on September 30, Hodder & Stoughton published what is often considered Gilbert's most important work, his masterpiece: *The Everlasting Man*.

The theatrical endeavors were not solely Frances's; during the Christmas of 1925, Gilbert rewrote his own Christmas play about St. George and the dragon. He had begun working on this play as early as 1907.

During the following year, however, his primary concern was *G.K.'s Weekly*, an enterprise that was already foundering. It needed capital and there were no sources from which to tap, other than the Chestertons' own bank account, which they regularly raided. The Distributist League was initially founded to support the paper financially. However, it quickly took on a life of its own as a society for the discussion of economic ideas that would help make England a better country in which to live. The *Weekly* became the mouthpiece for articles in support of Distributism; branches of the league quickly sprang up all over the country.

Gilbert, to Frances's mild frustration, wanted to continue to run the newspaper despite its uncertain funding. Her complaints

---

[7] A pilot edition was released in late 1924, but regular editions did not begin until March 21, 1925.

and her concerns notwithstanding, Frances still fully supported her husband and the Distributist League. Nevertheless, she admitted freely that the paper had never made money and Gilbert continued to rescue it. Here, for example, is a letter Frances wrote to Fr. Charles O'Donnell, of Notre Dame, November 17, 1930:

> ... My husband wants me to add a line to thank the University very warmly for their generosity in the matter of payment for his lectures. He is very grateful indeed. The money is badly needed if he is to keep the flag flying in the [G.K.'s] *Weekly* & elsewhere.
>
> There is such a heavy debt on the paper, & Notre Dame has lightened a very heavy burden for him. It is very difficult to keep a paper going without any capital or subsidy—and one way or another he has tried to preach. . . .—ever since he could run a paper at all—over twenty years now, & there has never been even a penny gained & the debts have been heavy, though he has always paid them—& kept the paper going. Forgive this little personal paragraph, but we wanted you to understand how much your generosity is appreciated. . . .

In addition to financial concern over the paper, Frances also began 1926 with severe back pain—her rheumatism was acting up. The doctors suggested she go to Biskra, in Algeria, for the winter; to which they once again never traveled.

As was common with the Chestertons, the new year was productive across the board. *The Man Who Was Thursday* (Ada Chesterton's theatrical adaptation of Gilbert's novel) opened at the Everyman Theater on January 19, 1926. Gilbert's *The Incredulity of Father Brown*, another collection of Father Brown stories, appeared in bookstalls.

In April of 1926, Gilbert and Frances, accompanied by Frances's cousin Rhoda Bastable, traveled to Spain. They visited

Toledo and Madrid before venturing in Barcelona, where Gilbert had been invited to speak. They stayed until early June. It was, alas, yet another challenging trip, with Frances ill with heart trouble.

On June 28, Gilbert and Frances celebrated their twenty-fifth wedding anniversary with a party. Every friend and relative was invited, and the evening included a play performed in honor of the guests and the couple. This play, which was held in the garden, was a triumph. It was like a toy theater romance—but for adults. Nearly everyone of literary note was there that evening; it was so crowded it was difficult to move around the house or garden, all gathered to celebrate twenty-five years of married harmony. "The marriage had survived a long road of success without there being in either of the Chestertons any self-satisfied worldliness," noted Patrick Braybrooke.[8]

It was at around this time that Gilbert and Frances, along with some local friends including Patricia Burke and Margaret Halford, formed a group in Beaconsfield called "The Players Club." These were people interested in putting on plays for the community—their own plays as well as Shakespeare's.[9]

In the midst of so much productivity, Frances finally felt ready to make her way into the Catholic Church. At this time, she was advised to see her local priest, rather than one of her more famous priestly friends. O'Connor was a wonderful friend, but he lived at a distance and was too busy to instruct Frances in the faith. (In those days, priests met regularly and individually with potential converts, instructing them on all points of the Roman Catholic faith.) Frances looked instead to Fr.

---

[8] Braybrooke, 65.

[9] The Players Club won the trophy in the final of the British Drama League's national festival at the Garrick Theatre in May, 1932 with Miss Margaret Halford as the producer.

Thomas Walker, soon to be the first priest at the new church of St. Teresa's in Beaconsfield, which had begun construction in 1926. Fr. Walker currently said Mass at St. Augustine in nearby High Wycombe. Fr. Walker was an excellent choice; he had already prepared Gilbert for his First Holy Communion.[10] He was also a discreet choice—above all, Frances wanted to avoid publicity, as is clearly shown in her letter to Father O'Connor at about this time:

> I wish you had been at the Catholic Congress to see or hear the ovation [Gilbert] received and how the Bishop of Salford spoke of the *Weekly*. <u>It was encouraging</u>. I have been meaning to write and tell you of myself, but it is so difficult to find time. Now I send a line, but am just off to the funeral of my cousin Rev. W. Braybrooke (Michael's father) but I am wondering if you are likely to be coming South in the 3rd or 4th week of October. I have been receiving instruction all this time from Father Walker and I am to be received into the Church when he returns from Spain on the 18th. I had hoped it might be managed before the Congress, but I could not rush it and also I wanted you to know. You will understand how dreadfully I hate the idea of publicity in such a matter but I think most of my friends know. I told the Bishop of Leeds (for I lost my heart to him completely) and he has asked me to let him know the date of my Reception and promises to say Mass for me that day—I am fairly well though my heart is a bit groggy after the bad time I had in Spain.
>
> Yours affectionately,
> Frances Chesterton.[11]

---

[10] Some of his memories of Gilbert were collected in Maisie Ward's biography of G.K. Chesterton.

[11] British Library folder 73196.

Meanwhile, Gilbert corresponded for a long time with Father Knox regarding the possibility of Frances's conversion. He did not specifically request Father Knox's assistance; on the contrary, Gilbert wrote that, especially since Frances has not yet met Father Knox, the most suitable priestly advocate for conversion must be O'Connor. He later wrote touchingly of her support for his conversion:

> I have had a serious and very moving talk with my wife. . . .
> In our conversation, my wife was all that I hope you will
> someday know her to be; she is incapable of wanting me
> to do anything but what I think right; and admits the same
> possibility for herself: but it is much more of a wrench for her,
> for she has been able to practice her religion in complete good
> faith; which my own doubts have prevented me from doing.[12]

After what must have seemed an exceptionally long wait to a man so eager to be always in accord with his beloved wife, Frances was able to announce her decision. On October 25, 1926, she wrote again to Father O'Connor:

> Dear Padre, I hope I am to be received into the Church at High
> Wycombe on All Saints' Day, but I am waiting to hear quite
> definitely from Father Walker. I suppose there is no chance
> that you could come South then? But I know you will think
> of me and pray for me and I would hate you to tire yourself
> out for me.

She was received on November 1, 1926, at High Wycombe. Her reception was a two-step process: the first, like Gilbert's reception in the Railway Hotel four years earlier, included her

---

[12] Wade Center folder 314.

first confession, and some prayers; the second would take place the following month, involving her reception of the sacraments.

To Frances's horror, the papers immediately reported the news, and it spread even across the Atlantic Ocean within a matter of days. Thus, on November 7, 1926 the *New York Times* published the following:

MRS. CHESTERTON'S FAITH

Novelist's Wife Reported to Have Joined Him as Catholic

London, Nov. 6—Mrs. G.K. Chesterton, wife of the famous English writer who became a Roman Catholic, has adopted her husband's faith, according to a report here.

Mr. Chesterton is one of England's leading Catholics and has crossed pens many times on questions of faith with other intellectuals such as G.B. Shaw and H.G. Wells.

It seems a disproportionate amount of interest to be paid to a personal decision regarding religious affiliation. Further, it may appear bizarre that so monumental a figure as her husband be reduced to "the famous English writer who became a Roman Catholic". The nature of the environment in which they lived, however, truly made this a remarkable characteristic and doomed to be noticed. Though the spiritual fervor that had so electrified the English public seventy-five years earlier at the conversion of John Henry Cardinal Newman was now dulled by the growth of liberal secularism, the entrenched bigotry retained its keenness. Chesterton, following several generations on the heels of the mid-Victorian century rush of conversion, now could engage publicly and proudly as "one of England's leading Catholics". Nevertheless, the stigma still remained: to be Catholic was somehow to be a threat to all that was truly English.

Frances was embarrassed by the publicity. She went to a church one day and discovered a large poster with her picture on it, announcing her conversion. She requested that the poster be removed. Fr. Basil Maturin, another Anglo-Catholic who converted to the Roman Catholic faith, described the feelings of a new convert:

> I have never been able to understand the mental attitude of people who speak of their reception in a state of exaltation. The more real the English Church has been to you, and all your past experiences in it, the more terrible the wrench. And there is added a kind of uncertainty as to what you will find after you are received, the fear of the unknown—and with me, and probably with you, moments of mental agony, lest through some unknown act of your own you are, after all, making a mistake and doing wrong. I had such feelings up to the last moment, and went through the reception like a stone. . . . At such a moment one feels utterly alone, and how little help one can get from anyone else![13]

The poignancy of that one line: "The more real the English Church has been to you. . . ." must have resonated with Frances. Indeed, the English Church had been very real to Frances. She followed that Church in good faith and with affection.

Her struggle remained, even weeks later when, on December 19, she received her First Holy Communion and Confirmation. A few days later, she wrote O'Connor:

> (December 23) Just a line of Christmas Greeting. I have been ill and all my Christmas letters, etc. are in arrears. You will I know be glad to hear that I received my first Communion at

---

[13] Maisie Ward, *Father Maturin: A Memoir* (London: Longmans, Green, and Co., 1920), 38-39.

Wycombe last Sunday and was confirmed in the Cathedral in the afternoon—I am very happy—though the wrench was rather terrible—It was hard to part with so many memories and traditions.

Pray for me please that I may make a good Catholic. Love from us both. . . .

Many people asked Frances over the years "who" converted her to the Catholic faith. The expected response was, of course, her husband. Frances, however, always replied: "The devil." This was not simply a witty rebuff; Frances shared with Gilbert a sense that sin was the one thing about religion that could be proved.[14]

Though the spiritual turmoil of day-to-day life was always ahead of them, at least this great battle was fought and won. Gilbert's happiness joined with that of his wife. Once again, the couple walked their spiritual path hand-in-hand.

---

[14] *The Collected Works* Vol. 1, 217.

Chapter Seven

SUCCESS AND SECRETARIES (1926–1929)

*A friend of mine, a convert of only a month's standing writes,
'The Church is so gracious and so roomy.' Just what I find.*

*C*hesterton was in demand as a speaker, and audiences did not particularly care what he said—or did—as long as they could see and hear him. His popularity was tremendous, though he remained his humble and absent-minded self.

At home, changes were taking place in the housing staff. Kathleen Chesshire was leaving her secretarial service, and a new secretary had to be hired. One candidate was Dorothy Collins, who frequently visited friends living next door to the Chestertons at Top Meadow. She was known to the Chestertons and was considered immediately when the vacancy loomed—although it took months of negotiations before she finally started working.

In August 1926, Frances wrote Collins a note, indicating that she was interested in Dorothy coming to work for them, but wanted Dorothy to meet Gilbert and "see the working conditions". She suggested that Dorothy begin working at the beginning of October, when she returned from a planned trip to Italy. Her plate would be full when she began: regular work for *G.K.'s Weekly* as well as assisting with organizing a trip to Poland.

Another letter follows. On October 12, Frances asked if Dorothy had yet returned. Frances had made inquiries about a room where Dorothy could stay, but there was a complicating factor—Dorothy had a dog. Frances was not sure the place she found would allow dogs. Further, she noted that they would travel to Cambridge and Bath in the beginning of November, and suggested a starting date of November 10. Frances suggested Dorothy come down to Beaconsfield and look for good accommodations for herself—some place that had room for the dog and a garage for her car. On October 19, Frances wrote that a starting date of November 15 would suit her excellently. The Chestertons would be in Bath the 11th and 12th. She invited Dorothy to stay at their home for a week or so while she was searching for lodgings. She let Dorothy know their cook had just left and wondered if Dorothy knew of another cook who was available.

On October 25, Frances wrote Dorothy yet again, imparting details as to the specific work outlined for her. She would start at 10:30 in the morning—they rose late in the Chesterton home and no work would be done before then. Gilbert worked until late in the night. She told Dorothy there was plenty of work to do, although it was irregular work. She then wrote that she was about to be received into the Catholic Church, that she was still looking for a cook, that she was finishing her children's play and must supervise rehearsals, and she looked forward to relying on Dorothy's support.[1]

The household secretaries employed by Gilbert and Frances bear explanation, as there has been confusion in the past about them. It is safe to say that biographies of Gilbert Chesterton have focused, for the main part, on Dorothy Collins exclusively. However, Dorothy was only the last in a long line of personal

---

[1] Courtesy of John M. Kelly Library Rare Books, Archival & Manuscript Collection's G.K. Chesterton Microfiche Collection.

secretaries Frances hired as delegates for her own self-appointed task of secretary and keeper of Gilbert's schedule.

The secretaries prior to Dorothy Collins were many. Miss Nellie Allport, the first regular secretary, worked on and off from 1901 to 1910.[2] Marjorie Biggs—Mrs. Peter Ramsden—was secretary in Battersea.[3] Rhoda Bastable, Frances's cousin, occasionally helped. Mrs. Meredith worked from 1910 to 1913. Mrs. Grace "Daisy" Saxon-Mills typed *Napoleon of Notting Hill*. Frederica "Freda" Elizabeth Spencer—who became Mrs. Thomas Bayley— worked from 1914 to 1919. Mrs. Walpole, mother of Felicity, "who calls me Mary," worked from 1917 to 1919—Gilbert, by the way, became Felicity's legal guardian. From 1922 to 1926 they had Kathleen Chesshire. In 1922 when the secretary was away on a holiday, Frances had her niece Gertrude[4] ("Woozle") come over and type for Gilbert. Winfred Pierpoint, along with Grace Saxon-Mills and Mrs. Walpole, were neighbors who served as occasional secretaries.

In essence, Frances was Gilbert's first, last, and best secretary. She was his sounding board, and so had input and made corrections where other secretaries would not. (She did playfully tell Gilbert that she would "charge" him for mistakes—, so many pennies for this kind of editing help, so many for that.) Besides writing up his words, however, Frances was doing everything else in the world for Gilbert, from tying his shoelaces to choosing his outfit for the day to keeping track of his numerous speaking engagements. In addition, Frances would have cared a great deal about whether or not Gilbert felt loved and cared

---

[2] British Library Folder 112; *Return to Chesterton*, 156.

[3] *The Collected Works* Vol. 10-B, 409.

[4] Gertrude, called "Woozle" all her life, was the eldest daughter of Ethel and Lucian Oldershaw.

for, whether or not he was feeling healthy or ill, whether he was feeling stressed or at ease, whether or not the newspapers were accurately quoting him, whether or not people like Robert Blatchford or George Coulton were criticizing him—in other words, all of the things a loving wife cares about in her husband's interior and exterior state.

All of the practical aspects of life were left to her; Gilbert was not a man who dealt in details, he was an ideas man. Frances not only prepared Gilbert for the public by dressing him, she coordinated his meals; shopped; negotiated with his agent and publishers; kept a kitchen and a flower garden; took care of the children and visitors constantly welcomed under their roof; hired the cooks, gardeners, secretaries, and housekeepers; cared for the pets; kept up the correspondence with everyone; paid bills and taxes. It is no wonder she was still up at midnight, finishing up the last of fifteen—or more—letters: "Since we came back from our holiday I have answered one hundred and seventeen letters for Gilbert," Frances once said.[5]

Frances kept track of everything, constantly looking through her purse for letters, and sending telegrams to confirm engagements. She was more organized than Gilbert, but not completely organized, either; Frances could be called practical only in comparison to him. She kept confused masses of papers, from which she had to find important documents. Thus, she welcomed Dorothy, who was organized and created a neat filing system.

One reads other biographies that state that once Dorothy Collins was hired, Frances gave her the appointment book and, from then on, if anyone wanted to schedule Gilbert, they had to talk to Dorothy. However, this "handing over" of the appointment book happened at least one secretary back: "I

[5] Braybrooke, 21.

think it would be safe to fix January 17," Frances wrote to Fr. John O'Connor, on July 19, 1923, "unless we are abroad, which may be possible—Miss Chesshire is away on her holiday, but I cannot find any engagements for next year—though she may have a separate note of them somewhere."

Chesshire and, following in her footsteps, Dorothy Collins, did represent a new degree of streamlined administration, as Ada Chesterton noted:

> The typists did not stay long. One inefficient quickly gave way to another. Occasionally a capable variety would intervene, but that did not help Gilbert very much. Their time was divided between him and the dog, Quoodle the First, who had to be combed, bathed and taken for walks. Household errands had to be fetched, and there was always a stock of woolen garments to be mended. All this held up the ordinary secretarial routine, so that carbon copies of important articles were unmade or mislaid and top copies were lost, and very frequently had to be re-dictated all over again. A new regime was instituted by Miss Collins' immediate predecessor [Chesshire], an experienced capable young woman who eased the strain.[6]

"Not only did [Dorothy] bring order out of chaos," wrote Maisie Ward, "but she became first the very dear friend of both Frances and Gilbert and finally all that their own daughter could have been." Biographers have followed Maisie in this, asserting a sort of unspoken adoption. Of course, the Chestertons adopted every secretary into the family;[7] but was there something special

---

[6] *The Chestertons*, 77-78.

[7] See the collected poems, and how many poems Gilbert wrote to Freda Spencer. Freda called Gilbert "Uncle Humphrey" and Frances was "Aunt Harriet."

about Dorothy? Or was she simply the last and the best known of a long line of secretaries?

In her published recollections[8] Dorothy herself refers to Frances as "a very great friend of mine . . ." The friendship was reciprocal, though with an added touch of maternal satisfaction for Frances. In a poem dedicated to Dorothy Collins, Frances wrote:

> There is an empty space that must be filled;
> there is an empty room that needs a guest;
> enter my daughter,
> here you shall find rest.[9]

They exchanged poetry in this vein, with the recurring motif of a mother and daughter relationship. The twenty-plus-year difference in their ages could easily lend to a maternal attitude on one side, and a filial affection on the other. Nevertheless, although Frances poured out love on her, Dorothy retained autonomy as a worker—a beloved worker, certainly—in their home. Collins was paid to work; she was an employee—and after Gilbert died, she went to work for another man as his secretary. She never lived with the Chestertons. Dorothy was a very independent lady, who worked for her living, and traveled for recreation. And although Frances came to depend on her a great deal, it was not true that Dorothy depended on Frances. Collins believed they had an amiable working relationship.

She was not, as was mentioned above, the first efficient secretary they employed. Dorothy stands out for several other reasons: she owned a car; she was last; she was older; she was

---

[8] *G.K. Chesterton: A Centenary Appraisal*, 160.

[9] *How Far Is It To Bethlehem*, 250.

single, and *stayed* single; and she became Gilbert's literary executrix.

Even Frances's pronounced fondness of Dorothy must be in context. She was "like a daughter", but blood relations were always first. (She considered her sister Ethel's children "hers"—as when she says "my Peter" or "my Catherine.") Her direct relatives would be considered family much more so than ever a secretary or housemaid would, no matter how fond she was of them.

When Dorothy came on board as secretary, as an independent, single, older woman with her own dog and her own car, the Chestertons did come to depend upon her. Frances handed over the appointment book. Dorothy took dictation from Gilbert, and typed it up efficiently. Dorothy had nine years' experience and could take shorthand and type quickly.

The car was a significant new asset to their lives because, up until then, the Chestertons had relied on trains, cabs, or hired drivers to get them where they needed to go; and often, especially if Gilbert traveled on his own, this meant he was late or missed appointments. With the car, Dorothy now became, effectively and in addition to being secretary—a chauffeur, and Gilbert became a much more reliable speaker.

A great deal of Dorothy Collins' perspective has come down to us through Judith Lea, Collins' assistant for almost forty years, starting in 1952. Judith had some knowledge of the Chesterton's circle as well; she had met Frances in 1937, and was acquainted with Hilaire Belloc. She came to live at Top Meadow Cottage— Dorothy's home on the Chesterton property, which was built after Frances died (the property was willed to her).[10]

> During all our time together, (Judith wrote) I never doubted
> Dorothy's total devotion to both Mr. and Mrs. Chesterton. . . .

---

[10] Lea was interviewed in *Gilbert* Vol. 3, no. 6 (2000).

Chesterton was very dependent on Dorothy and Frances for everything. They put on his tie, did up his shoelaces, that sort of thing. . . . Dorothy's one fear was that Mrs. Chesterton would die before Gilbert. She said she didn't know what she might do after that. She knew after Frances was gone, he would likely have depended totally on her. Dorothy never married, but not for lack of opportunities. Her work was everything.

Her work was everything. There was love, there was affection, there was devotion, but Dorothy claimed Frances was a "great friend," and considered what she did at the Chesterton home "work." Further, it was her choice not to marry, according to Judith, but to dedicate her life to her work. *She didn't know what she might do after that.* Dorothy was worried that Gilbert's daily care would be left to her, and she was not sure about taking on that responsibility.

Dorothy died in 1988 at the age of ninety-four. Judith Lea is, to the best of our knowledge, still alive and in her nineties.

Dorothy was, indeed, a new point of contact and a go-between. This is illustrated in two letters from Fr. Ronald Knox:

July 1

Dear Chesterton,

Is there really no chance of getting you down to the Newman next term? Here have I been in Oxford five years, and trying to get you all the time; and then Charles Wegg-Presser reported that he had a really firm promise at last. And now it seems your secretary refuses to let you lecture for the next few months, because you've gotten so bored with it in America. Well, there's no reason why it shouldn't be November, even the first Sunday in December if you like. But it's too maddening, after five years of being told you wouldn't come because you were lecturing so much, to be told now that you won't come because you're lecturing so little. I shall begin to believe you have a down on me, or Newman, or something.

Yours v. sincerely,

RA Knox.

To Dorothy, Knox wrote:

Dear Miss Collins,

Thank you for your letter. . . .We should very much like to get Mr. Chesterton even if it were late in the term. . . . I need hardly say that "reading a paper" is only a manner of speaking; most of our guests simply speak extempore, and we should be delighted to get Mr. Chesterton if he were prepared to come and catch buns in his mouth.

Yours sincerely,

RA Knox[11]

Father Knox's suffering notwithstanding, the efficiency and reliability of Dorothy Collins did free Frances for her innumerable other responsibilities.

Late in 1926, Ada published her most important work, *In Darkest London*, and Frances reviewed the work glowingly in *G.K.'s Weekly*. Ada was surprised at how sympathetic Frances was to the social cause of homeless women on the streets of London. Further, Frances supported Ada's "Cecil House" project, which Ada started after the book was published. Cecil Houses were homes where women could stay when they had nowhere else to go. Frances not only supported the work then, but she and Gilbert left money to the homes after they died.

On January 4, 1927, Frances told O'Connor that her mother, Blanche Blogg, had come to live with them and needed much

---

[11] Wade Center folder 185.

care—she was healthy, but very nearly blind and depended on Frances for everything. Dorothy Collins was an asset at such a time, indeed.

The Chestertons remained busy, with frequent travel. Early that year, Gilbert received an invitation to visit Poland, to give speeches and see the country. Dorothy was a great help to Gilbert and Frances on this trip—her first with the couple. When Frances tired from traveling, Dorothy accompanied Gilbert in the evenings so his wife could rest. The Polish people, Frances observed, knew Gilbert's work better than any Englishman.

That summer, Frances returned to Bath for another highlight: the production of her play, *Faith and Fable: A Masque*.[12] The public received it enthusiastically and publicity photos abounded. Frances was asked to give a speech at the Bath Festival of Drama on August 9, 1927.[13] Frances spoke on the subject of the children's play, and expressed the opinion that children should act in their own plays, not simply watch movies or listen to radio. Movies and radio, she believed, were for older people who could no longer entertain themselves.

Then came the "Last Family" (so dubbed by Maisie Ward). While visiting Lyme Regis in 1927, Gilbert and Frances found accommodations and were quietly walking down the street when they noticed some girls staring in at a toy shop window. The girls noticed the couple looking at them, and one of them immediately recognized Gilbert. She grabbed her sisters and dashed home to fetch their sister Clare—a devout G.K. Chesterton fan.

Clare immediately set out, telling her mother she was inviting the Chestertons to tea. She saw Gilbert and Frances at

---

[12] Listed as *Legends of the Gods and Saints* in *How Far Is It To Bethlehem*.

[13] "Kinema and Wireless Not For Children: Mrs. G.K. Chesterton's View," *The Manchester Guardian* (1927). Kinema is a British variant of cinema.

the Three Cups, and her courage momentarily failed her. She then wrote a note issuing her invitation. Gilbert and Frances delightedly accepted. This was the beginning of yet another wonderful friendship, one that lasted through the final nine years of Gilbert's life. After a few years, the Nicholl family actually moved to Beaconsfield, and lived in Christmas Cottage, on the same Grove Road as Top Meadow. Frequent visits, the exchange of poetry, plays, and toy theater productions all followed.

"Chesterton achieved so much," remarked one biographer, "that it is sometimes forgotten how much more he might have done.[14] In 1928, it was announced that Chesterton was to work on two biographies—of Savonarola and Napoleon. Neither was ever written.

Like her husband, Frances's work never ceased, but the nature of her labors rarely could be quantified simply in terms of completed books. On February 6, 1928, she commenced her tender care of her cousin Rhoda Bastable, afflicted with influenza. Frances initially had a hard time hiring a nurse and so stayed with the patient day and night.[15] Meanwhile, Gilbert sprained his ankle so Frances now had two patients—in addition to her mother.

Soon after she nursed Rhoda and Gilbert back to health, Frances began having pain in her lower back. The doctor

---

[14] Braybrooke, 22.

[15] Rhoda and Gilbert carried on a long-standing joke about Rhoda being the president of the "Society for the Encouragement of Rain," of which Gilbert was the secretary, and to which Frances Blogg was an eternal enemy. These clubs Chesterton was constantly making up with the help of young friends. With Patrick Braybrooke, he carried on the Mustard Club, in which all members had to put mustard on all food items. Very few members survived. He started a Toy Theater Club, which fizzled out, as the only toy theater in continual use was his own. These are just a few of the many other examples of these clubs which Chesterton encouraged.

diagnosed disease of the left sacro-iliac joint. She had gained weight, and the doctor suggested another course of pituitary and thyroid medicine.

This year as well, Frances collected together some of her Christmas card poetry, poems that had been or could be put to song, and Sheed & Ward published the collection as *How Far Is It To Bethlehem and Other Carols* by Frances Chesterton.[16] Frances gave copies of this book away as gifts.

She continued to be the primary support to Gilbert's personal (and much of his professional) correspondence. She even inherited a share in his lively exchanges with Fr. Knox, including an exchange regarding the possibility of a romance for one of her nieces:

July 29, 1928

Dear Mrs. Chesterton,
You have the habit of the Immortals—not dating your letters—so I don't know whether this is too late to be of any use. I did

---

[16] There are very few copies of this book to be found in the world. Most of the poems are directly from the Christmas card collection, but one was new and unknown, and is the Christmas card poem for a missing year in the Wade collection: 1924. The poem is entitled "Audiamus":

In the hush of the night
Did you hear a bird call?
His note rang clear
In the bitter air
From an ox's stall.

In the burst of the sun
An ecstasy wild
From a shelter of hay
At breaking of day
The cry of a Child.

rather scent a romance about Gerald and your niece—I don't know why; perhaps because she seemed a fallinginlovablewith [sic] person.

I don't really know Gerald awfully well, thought he's v[ery] kind to me. I think he ought to marry a Catholic, or someone who will keep him up to the mark. He comes to Mass on Sundays, mostly, but I've never seen him at Communion ... I gathered he had definitely decided to go down. I think it's a mistake, because obviously he must have enough brains to take a pass degree, and a pass degree is better than nothing. I don't see him farming in Canada—hasn't he any relations who can shove him into a business job? He strikes me as the kind of person who could sell water. I hope to goodness she won't marry him out of pity—a martyrdom, I always think. Anyhow, he ought to <u>earn</u> her, by doing some work. But I believe an extra year at Oxford wouldn't be wasted. Use my name if you like: it will have influence with him. People ought to leave Downside at 16, to avoid weltsdryerz.[17] (Is that the right word?) I do hope you'll be able to do something with him: I believe you can.

Yours sincerely,

RA Knox.[18]

These sorts of letters pepper the various collections of Chestertonian correspondence, combining to illustrate the breadth and depth and influence of Frances. She truly did serve Gilbert in every way—even, at times, issuing his apologies for him, as in the following letter:

---

[17] Perhaps Knox meant "weltschmertz."

[18] Wade Center folder 185.

August 26, 1928
Homestead

Dear Mr. Heseltine,

My husband asks me to send a note of apology with the enclosed letter which seems to have been in his pocket for some time!

He had a[n] appalling rush of work and was so knocked out when we got here that we had to send for the doctor who said he must take a complete rest immediately or he would be seriously ill. So we cut the communications cord and only today has he been able to attend to things a little.

He asks you to forgive him.

Yours sincerely,

Frances Chesterton

In September 1928, Gilbert had a swollen gland that needed to be opened, additionally requiring extensive dental work. Their planned trip to Rome was delayed. Frances wrote to O'Connor that Gilbert was slowly having his teeth removed and dentures were to be made. The process took months. Frances nursed Gilbert throughout the ordeal.[19]

The Church was a special source of consolation to Gilbert and now to his wife. She wrote to Maisie Ward in late October 1928, noting her anniversary:

> It is two years tomorrow 'All Saint's Day' I was received into the Church. A friend of mine, a convert of only a month's standing writes 'The Church is so gracious and so roomy.' Just what I find.[20]

---

[19] Gilbert had all his teeth pulled, and was "toothless until new ones are made." Frances Chesterton to Ward, "All Saint's Eve" letter in the Notre Dame Chesterton Collection.

[20] Frances Chesterton to Maisie Ward, Oct. 31, 1928, Notre Dame Chesterton Collection.

She added this enthusiastic report, regarding the completion of the first phase of construction of St. Teresa's in Beaconsfield:

> Great rejoicing here because at last we are able to have the little Church open—and the Blessed Sacrament reserved—but we have no resident priest.[21]

The union in faith was indeed a blessing. The removal of that burden from the couple liberated them to focus on all of the things that brought them joy—things that they did exceptionally well—such as bringing together a host of talented people for mutual edification and entertainment.

This is clearly shown in the Christmas of 1928. Frances long had labored at a clever scheme for the Oakdene students—a mixed revue of short skits, songs, dances and poetry readings. She called it *A Christmas Garland*. Gilbert contributed a poem; Hilaire Belloc contributed a skit ("Mrs. Markham on Christmas", in which the titular character explains to her children various Christmas traditions); Frances contributed a Christmas carol entitled "The Three Brothers," and a skit about twelve passengers (named for the months of the year) who arrive in a coach. The character named "December" remains to help create the Christmas Garland.

Each story is woven into the others—beautiful, delightful, and imaginative. Here we can see the Chestertons in a scene worthy of Dickens: a nestling community of enthusiastic life and love, reveling in the glorious Christmas season, with all of its festivity. The collaboration of minds begets this wondrous, happy place where family and friends come together to celebrate the birth of the Christ Child, so well beloved by Frances Chesterton. And it is this place where we see the quiet triumph of Frances,

---

[21] *Ibid.*

for it is her hospitable love and gracious guidance that makes such a gathering possible. *How Far is it to Bethlehem*? Verily, Bethlehem is right here.

Chapter Eight

THE INN AT THE END OF
THE WORLD (1929–1936)

*I am organizing a campaign for the
emancipation of the wives of famous men.*

In early 1929, Fr. O'Connor wrote to Dorothy Collins, advising her on the Chestertons' upcoming trip to Rome. His letter is full of useful instructions, including which cardinal they should approach to help them gain an audience with the pope (the answer was the cardinal most familiar with Gilbert's writing). Unfortunately, the trip, already repeatedly postponed, would be delayed once again. Just when they had their bags packed, Frances fell ill. The doctors diagnosed appendicitis and scheduled an operation for the day before they were scheduled to leave. She recovered well, staying at St. Joseph's Nursing Home in Beaconsfield.

Illness and physical discomfort for both Chestertons were the presiding influences on the first half of the year. In April of 1929, while Dorothy Collins was on vacation, Frances wrote to her, sadly noting another delay:

Dearest,
Your letter has just come.
    There is no doubt we must put off the start to Italy till next week anyhow.

G refuses to start for Paris, and that being the case, we will wait and go all together. Of course, I'm dreadfully disappointed about the Joan of Arc—I had rather set my heart on it. I hope Kathleen Chesshire can get rid of the tickets.

Let me hear how you go on—and don't attempt to do anything before you are quite fit. I am awfully, awfully sorry you've had such a bad time.

Dr. Bakewell has been in today and decided on a diet regime which will I hope do good and the dentist managed to get out two bits of teeth without any anesthetic and he seems better.

This year marked the five hundredth anniversary of Joan of Arc's famous march of 1429. There were celebrations and reenactments in France that year, and perhaps Frances had planned to attend something of the sort.

This long-awaited trip to the continent, and especially to Rome, was momentous to the couple. They had been to Rome once before, a decade earlier, but then it had just been to pass through. Even more significantly, neither Gilbert nor Frances was Roman Catholic at that time. When the trip finally came to pass, they remained in Rome for three months, October to December. They rented a hotel room overlooking the Spanish Steps. The trip brought many delights, with several personal and professional highlights. It was on this trip that Gilbert met Mussolini. He also had a private audience with Pope Pius XI at which the Pope stated his admiration for Gilbert's *St. Francis of Assisi*. Near the end of the visit, Gilbert was a guest at the North American College. The Chestertons returned home to England on December 20, just in time for Christmas.

The following year marked an important moment in one of Frances's closest relationships: for the first time, she signed a letter to O'Connor simply "Frances". They had now known each other for twenty-six years. The letter itself was not momentous: it simply carried on the friendship that they had so long and so gradually cultivated. They were discussing Frances's niece and grandniece, and Frances sadly related that her niece's husband could not leave an allowance for the family when he left for China on a two-year stint of work on the Navy ship, the *Caradoc*. Always attentive to the interests of her friends, Frances also advised O'Connor on a publishing contract for a book he had translated. She concluded by noting that there were some difficulties at her local parish. She looked forward to an upcoming trip to the United States so she could go to Notre Dame, where there would be many spiritual opportunities.

Once again, this was a trip long scheduled but more than once delayed. Frances's repeated illnesses always intervened. When asked why she did not just stay home, she said, "Gilbert gets so lonely without me."

Fr. Charles O'Donnell, president of Notre Dame, arranged this second trip to America, through a friend of Gilbert's, Robert Sencourt. Chesterton was scheduled to give two series of lectures in the spring of 1930. He would be paid $5,000, in addition to the fact that the university would cover all of his travel expenses. Gilbert agreed to the terms, with the exception that his wife and secretary were to accompany him. The initial plan backfired, though, when Gilbert became ill in early 1930. Dorothy Collins wrote to the priest informing him of the illness, and the lecture series was rescheduled for the fall. Such was the recurring pattern; Frances once said that her illnesses upset all their plans, but it was more of a combined effort at disruption. A considerable portion of their married life involved one nursing the other.

Eventually their good health aligned. Their England boat left on September 19, and they arrived in Canada on October

4, 1930. Visits and a series of well-attended lectures in Montreal and Toronto preceded their travel down to the United States. Many news agencies filmed Gilbert during this trip, and the film was probably shown in theaters on the newsreel.[1]

Crossing the border on their way to Notre Dame was a nerve-racking experience for Frances since they were carrying what she called "contraband". She was relieved when the border police failed to notice the flask of brandy hidden in her suitcase.

The two lecture series at Notre Dame were a great success, and students and faculty would long remember the visit. Gilbert, Frances, and Dorothy stayed in the home of a young family named Bixler; Frances befriended the children, as usual, and Gilbert got on well with the grandfather in the house. Gilbert lectured Monday through Friday evenings, and took side trips on the weekends to Chicago, Milwaukee, and Detroit. The University bestowed an honorary doctorate upon Gilbert on November 5, 1930.

They became "Domers" during this visit, and were present when the stadium opened for the first time. They attended a football game with head coach Knute Rockne. As Frances later wrote to Father O'Donnell (with whom she kept up a correspondence after their visit): "We often think and talk of Notre Dame and never forget the weeks we passed there."

After leaving Notre Dame, Gilbert lectured throughout America. Reports of his visit can be found in the archives of numerous newspapers. It was a time of some suffering for Frances, who felt hounded by the press:

---

[1] The tiny clips that exist show Gilbert and Frances standing on the boat; these are shown during the opening sequence of Eternal Word Television Network's *Apostle of Common Sense* show.

Since we arrived in New York our life has been a nightmare. Publicity men, reporters, interviewers, photographers even film producers dog our uneasy footsteps.[2]

Despite this frustration, Frances maintained her sense of humor. "While my husband is going on a lecture tour," she told one reporter, "I am organizing a campaign for the emancipation of the wives of famous men."

It is an interesting note that, among these crowds of eager media representatives, Frances lists "film producers"—alas, few film records of the trip exist. Holy Cross College in Worcester, Massachusetts offers one, where the students adopted Gilbert into the ranks of the "Holy Cross Crusaders." In the film, one can see Frances Chesterton standing on Gilbert's right, and Dorothy Collins standing on his left.[3]

In early December 1930, the *Albany Evening News* published a story specifically about Frances. "Mrs. Gilbert K. Chesterton Important Help to Husband, Making His Tour of Lectures; Couple Share Same Views" was the lengthy headline. The article described Frances as a quiet woman who was charming, small, and unassuming. She was marked with the same simplicity, the same sincerity, and the same kindness and earnestness as her husband. The reporter stated that as he listened to Gilbert and Frances talk to each other, he was impressed by what a tremendous influence they had on each other, and how inseparable they were.

The reporter went on to ask questions about current events in contemporary literature. Sinclair Lewis had recently won the Nobel Prize for Literature, so the reporter asked Frances what

---

[2] Letter to Mr. Charles Phillips, Nov. 25, 1930.

[3] http://www.youtube.com/watch?v=K4wUYTMcXBE.

she thought about it. She said she believed others were more deserving of the award, and that she personally admired the works of Willa Cather, Edith Wharton, and Thornton Wilder.

The Chestertons continued their travels, touring the northeastern United States—New York City and Worcester—before heading south. In Chattanooga, Tennessee, on January 6, 1931, Frances fell ill once more. Gilbert was obligated to fulfill his lecture regime, so he left Dorothy to take care of Frances, and continued on his tour. Frances's temperature then rose to 103 degrees, and a doctor was called. He immediately recommended she be admitted to a hospital. As her condition worsened, Dorothy became worried that Frances would not recover. She wrote to Gilbert, and he hurried back to his wife's side, canceling many lectures on short notice. Frances soon turned the corner on her illness, however, and as soon as she was even a little bit better she insisted that Dorothy accompany Gilbert on the remainder of the tour. Gilbert and Dorothy obediently traveled to the West Coast, and Gilbert delivered his scheduled lectures.

Frances slowly recovered, and took one of her nurses on the train to rendezvous with her husband and secretary. On February 17, she arrived in California, and a hotel was found where she would remain to convalesce, under the supervision of the nurse. Gilbert and Dorothy continued on the lecture tour to San Francisco, California; Portland, Oregon; Seattle, Washington; Vancouver and Victoria, British Columbia. Gilbert told a friend that Frances's illnesses usually came on very rapidly, but that her recovery was always very slow.

It was an anxious time for Gilbert, and he (and Frances) found great relief in being reunited. The Chestertons left California together on March 23, dropping off the nurse in Kansas City before traveling on to New York again. Gilbert had several more lectures scheduled in the northeast before they could return home.

At the end of March, they received word that Knute Rockne had died in a plane accident. Frances wrote O'Donnell to express her condolences to the president and the school. Then she continued:

> I feel somehow we have never thanked you properly for all your goodness to us at Notre Dame. It must have been a bit of a nuisance to you to think for a man's wife and his secretary— but you will have realized how impossible it would have been for him without us. No man was ever so dependent on his belongings—no man was ever more compelled to carry his home with him wherever he might go. But we all had a very happy time and for us there are nothing but loving memories of Notre Dame and all she stands for.[4]

Upon their return home, Frances would keep informed of Notre Dame's football games. She knew, having attended the stadium dedication during the first week of their trip, the importance of the football team to Notre Dame, and refers to it in her letters to O'Donnell. Nearly a year later, for instance, Frances sent a letter to O'Donnell when the team was defeated in an important game:

> We do not imagine that the defeat of the Notre Dame Football Team has depressed you unduly—though we felt quite sad when we saw the note in the "New York Times."[5]

The trip to America illustrates two important elements of the life of Frances Chesterton: her repeated illnesses and the overarching focus on Gilbert's popular public image and

---

[4] FAC letter to Fr. O'Donnell, Nov. 11, 1930, Notre Dame Collection.

[5] FAC letter to Fr. O'Donnell, Dec. 10, 1931, Notre Dame Collection.

performance. Nevertheless, her own individual work quietly continued to have an effect. Indeed, while she was still in America, Frances received a letter from the English poet Walter de la Mare regarding the publication of one of her poems in a collection:

20th April 1931

Dear Mrs. Chesterton,

I am so very sorry to hear that you have been ill, and particularly in Tennessee. I do hope now indeed that all is well. . . . Thank you very much indeed for letting me use the poem in the Collins collection. The title is "Children's Song of the Nativity," and it begins, "How far is it to Bethlehem?" The collections will probably also be published in America, so if I don't hear from you I will ask a similar fee from the publishers there as you have suggested for England, though I think it is far too little. So please let me know what you think when you re-consider this.

We shall look forward very much indeed to seeing you both when you are safe in England again. I saw in the *Daily Telegraph* this morning that you are on your way.

Yours Sincerely,
W.J. de la Mare

Her literary work, though she happily set it as secondary to her larger task of keeping Gilbert alive, happy, and effective, had yet life.

Later that year, Dorothy Collins went on vacation. While she was away, Frances wrote to her, revealing a development that would give joy to both the Chestertons—the conversion of their secretary:

My very dear,

I had your lovely letter this morning-time when I have seen Ella [Church] and heard about you and all your doings. Of course I am more happy than I can say that you are going to be of the Faith. I have prayed for you and longed for it. I can hardly believe it—it is going to come true. I will help you all I can over the difficult road you've got to tread. But I believe you will think any sacrifice worth while. You will make a better Catholic than I ever could be, because you have come to it by such a process of hacking your way through the jungle to the clear light. God bless you, Christ fill you, the Holy Spirit guide you, and Our Lady hold your dear hands.

Gilbert has been really ill, dull on the liver, but is ever so much better, but is still in bed. The rest is doing him good, and he is his most poetical and loving self. I am having a quiet time now I am no longer anxious and anyhow I got Nurse Clancy to stay the nights here. I look after him, and Pamela is here to spend the evenings with me. So far, I've not had any secretarial help as he is not working it has not been necessary. I've chucked everything except what <u>had</u> to be answered into your basket. You'll find heaps when you come back.

Darling, don't hurry back, please take an extra week any-how—we shall not get away for another week, perhaps later.

Catherine is waiting to post the letters for me, so I wind up rather hurriedly. All my love, all my sympathy, all my thoughts are with you.

The battle against illness continued for both Chestertons, but the triumph of the Faith remained ever more wondrous to them than physical health could be. Upon Dorothy's conversion in 1932, Gilbert and Frances stood as godparents.

At Christmas in 1931, Gilbert began a successful career as a radio personality with the BBC. His approach and his method were distinctly personal; he would prepare a talk, then press Frances, Dorothy, or both of them into service as his audience. They would sit across from the microphone so that Gilbert would have someone to whom he would speak. This method produced a radio show that sounded like Chesterton was chatting to the listener in a normal voice. Prior to that, radio announcers used an affected "announcer" voice. Sales of radios improved as so many people wanted to be addressed so personally and accessibly by the great man.

These stories, as well as the interviews frequently granted by Gilbert, give an entertaining insight into the life of the Chestertons. In 1932, when a reporter came to interview Gilbert at Top Meadow, the reporter was introduced to the dog Quoodle. Gilbert explained that he had named the dog after a character in an earlier novel just so that he could always explain the name and thus advertise his forgotten work. Later, he was asked about a costume party given by a literary club where Gilbert had dressed as Doctor Samuel Johnson. The reporter asked if Mrs. Chesterton had likewise dressed as a character.

"My wife went dressed as one of the characters in a novel that I am going to write in the near future," Chesterton replied. "You see that I devise ways and means to advertise both my old novels and my new ones!"[6]

Gilbert, ever busy, that year wrote *The Surprise* for Patricia "Patsey" Burke,[7] an actress friend in Beaconsfield. The script was laid aside and never produced during Gilbert's lifetime.

---

[6] *Chesterton as Seen by His Contemporaries*, 134.

[7] Frances's will stated that Olga Burke was Patricia's mother, and according to Gilbert, she was an old friend from Bedford Park. *The Incredulity of Fr. Brown* was dedicated to

In April, the seesaw of sickness took a new angle—Dorothy fell ill. Frances wrote to her, full of sympathy and tenderness:

Dearest,

I was glad to get your letter this morning, and to feel you are on the mend and our plans will really [?] at last.

I am having a very worrying time, and shall be thankful when it is over and I've fled the country!

I didn't realize, my very dear, how terribly I depend on you. I don't mean only for ordinary help, but for understanding and sympathy. I am always afraid though, of involving you in too much, and making life harder for you. But when I know you are <u>there</u>, and I can call on you, I am thankful indeed.

I have lots to tell you. I am just off to town, but I've been kept hanging about all the morning, and now I shan't have time to do what I want there.

God bless you. . . .

Dorothy would not long be ill; that burden would quickly return to the Chestertons. When Dorothy traveled to Europe on vacation, it was Gilbert's turn. One of Dorothy's letters at the time contains this illuminative passage: "It seems almost inevitable that he should have these attacks at stated intervals. I suppose it is nature's warning to him that he is not made of cast iron and that he must be careful. . . . Is he fairly cheerful or has he got one of his bad fits of depression?" Such a suggestion, while illustrating the very humanity of the great man (whose energy and vigor might easily lend itself to occasional bouts of depression), shows something even more vital regarding the character of his wife: Frances never recorded or alluded to any such tendency in her husband.

Patricia. "To Patricia Burke, Who Acted," *The Collected Works* Vol. 10-A, 334.

Through the next year, Gilbert battled sickness almost continually—it was the beginning of his decline years. 1933 would be challenging because of this, with the additional distress of the death of both of their mothers. Frances had continued to visit her mother every day that she could. Blanche was in St. Joseph nursing home, within walking distance of Top Meadow, and died of old age that year. She was buried next to her husband and three daughters at Highgate. Marie Louise's death brought one benefit—Gilbert's inheritance from her took away all financial pressures.[8]

At around this time, the women's poetry circle of which Frances was a member decided to collect poems and publish their own book. Titled *The Writer's Club Anthology*, it was edited by Margaret Woods and included three poems written by Frances.[9]

Even repeated illness could never stifle the ambition and drive of the Chestertons. As Frances wrote to O'Donnell in December 1933: "If it is anyway possible we hope to go to Rome after Christmas—to get there before the Holy Year ends—and then our dream is to go on to Palestine."[10]

It was an important trip for Gilbert; Pope Pius XI granted both he and Hilaire Belloc the Knighthood of the Order of St. Gregory.[11] The Knighthood would be officially conferred upon them by Cardinal Bourne in 1934. Gilbert was now officially allowed physically to carry the sword he so loved and had so long

---

[8] Bentley. Her estate had over £9,000, which was a lot of money back then, the equivalent of about $265,000 in today's dollars. Marie Louise divided her estate between Gilbert and Ada, which would include the sale of her former home.

[9] "Sonnet," first line, "Why did you call beloved in the night?" and "Cradle of the Winds" and "Sed ex Deo Nati Sunt".

[10] FAC letter to Fr. O'Donnell, December 8th, 1933, Notre Dame Collection.

[11] http://www.knightsofchristsmercy.com/st_gregory.html.

wielded metaphysically. Their trip to Rome for this honor took place during the summer of 1934. Their ambition to continue on to the Holy Land was sadly dashed, by the same heartless culprit: illness. Gilbert's poor condition required a five-week layover in Rome. They returned home after visiting Malta.

Probably because of illness, the only books that came out in 1934 were compilations: a selection of *Illustrated London News* columns titled *Avowals and Denials* and an anthology to celebrate the 10th year and 500th issue of *Chesterton's newspaper*: *GK's: A Miscellany of the First 500 Issues of G.K.'s Weekly* (published by Rich & Cowan).

In December of 1934, a year and a half before his death, Chesterton may have had a heightened sense (brought about by his continued illness) of his own mortality. In any case, he wrote as if he knew he was coming to the end of his career, if not his life. In *G.K.'s Weekly* he wrote at length about his view of life, how he believed in the beginning in the miracle of all existence, and the wonder of all experience, and continued to believe it "at the end."

Meanwhile, his legacy, already well-established, received a new and special honor. In February of 1935, Frances received a letter from R.N. Green-Armytage, who was putting on an exhibition of some sort, and had asked her for one of Gilbert's handwritten manuscripts to display. Frances wrote back and said she doubted she could find anything, as Gilbert now dictated directly to a secretary who was typing, and even his corrections were typewritten. However, Green-Armytage pressed her for something, so in April, Frances searched the house and found two manuscripts: one was a section from *The Ballad of the White Horse*, and the second was a Father Brown story. (Frances warned Green-Armytage that the manuscripts were worn and had probably been in Gilbert's pockets for ages.

She asked Green-Armytage to return the manuscripts, but not until the couple returned from their travels, and mentioned Gilbert would be lecturing in Florence.)

In March 1935, Gilbert satisfied his detective fiction fans by releasing another collection of Father Brown stories, *The Scandal of Father Brown*. Frances was preparing the home, garden, and pets so that they could be away for several months. She scheduled home maintenance and a spring cleaning for while they traveled.

Dorothy Collins drove Gilbert and Frances to Spain via France. The trip was a working vacation, not a lecture tour; Gilbert dictated and Dorothy typed. Additionally, they were able to enjoy themselves. Gilbert and Frances were especially delighted in Barcelona, where Gilbert purchased a cardboard toy theater with electric lights and cherished the souvenir.[12]

They arrived in Florence in time for Gilbert to deliver a lecture on English literature at the International Festival. This lecture was in honor of Luigi Pirandello, who had recently received the Nobel Prize in Literature. Afterward, they traveled back through Switzerland and Belgium. They had traveled over two thousand seven hundred miles—an exhausting ordeal, but a welcome respite from winter in cold, damp England.

Upon their return, Gilbert resumed the work of the *Weekly*, and debated Bertrand Russell on the BBC. In June of 1935, Gilbert was asked by the BBC to contribute to a series of radio shows on the subject of liberty. Gilbert's talk prompted a huge stack of mail—some positive, some critical.

The following month, Green-Armytage's exhibition concluded. Frances wrote and said he could keep the Father Brown manuscript if he liked. She informed him they were back from Florence, adding that she wished she and Gilbert could get

---

[12] The Spanish toy theater is at the Oxford Oratory in the G.K. Chesterton Library.

away to a desert island to be far from proofs, telephones, and Americans.

In addition to the public efforts for the Church of which they were now members, the Chestertons continued to influence many regarding the faith. On All Saints' Day in 1935, Hugh Paynter—the serviceman Gilbert and Frances had first met when they visited him in the hospital back in 1916, with whom they had kept up a friendship—became Catholic, along with his wife; Gilbert and Frances were their godparents.

Their joy in the Paynter conversion helped bring the year to a happy ending. Christmas, however, was overshadowed. It would be Gilbert's last, and he was already visibly unwell. They celebrated the feast with the Nicholl family at Christmas Cottage, down the road from Top Meadow. The girls had become very close to Auntlet and Unclet over the last years, and also noticed Gilbert's decline.

In early 1936, Dr. George G. Coulton,[13] a fierce anti-Catholic who had debated both Belloc and Knox, chose Chesterton as his new opponent. The Coulton controversy was not unlike the Blatchford controversies, the long debate which began Chesterton's career.[14] Gilbert was not up to the challenge, though he tried; his health was too uncertain for him to have the energy for the combat. It was a grief to him and thus to his wife, as is shown in a February 1936 letter to O'Connor:

> I wish you were here that we might talk. Poor Gilbert gets so overwhelmed with all the questions and letters he is sup-posed to answer and (though I think it useless) immersed in

---

[13] See: http://archive.thetablet.co.uk/article/1st-october-1921/18/dr-g-g-coulton-and-catholics-to-the-editor-of-the- and http://en.wikipedia.org/wiki/G._G._Coulton.

[14] See http://www.chesterton.org/miracles-and-modern-civilisation/ and "The Blatchford Controversies" in *The Collected Works* Vol. 1.

controversy with Coulton. I never feel he has a chance to do his own job properly.... We've kept fairly well in spite of cold G. had his usual bronchial catarrh but seems better and I've got to have teeth out and be made generally uncomfortable before the doctor thinks me fit.

I've been very occupied with family affairs. My youngest niece Catherine broke off her engagement and has dashed off to a post in Australia—I am glad she should launch forth on her own account but we had a hard time with her mother who has been so desperately ill and only now, after nearly a year, is beginning to recover.

And I have the eternal problem of my nephew Peter, who either <u>can't</u> or <u>won't</u> manage to make a living. <u>Can't</u> I really think....

If the weather improves, I hope to go to town tomorrow to the Lourdes service at Westminster Cathedral and incidentally if I can fit it in to Cruft's Dog Show. I want a new dog and I had to part with Dolfuss—a heart-breaking affair....[15]

"I never feel he has a chance to do his own job properly." This was a shared cause of distress to both Frances and O'Connor. They both believed Chesterton had great books yet to write, but sacrificed his time for the less-important enterprise of his newspaper work and letter writing with antagonists like Coulton. His articles, of course, have remained accessible and alive through reprinting. Nevertheless, many planned books—on Shakespeare, Napoleon, George Meredith, and Savonarola—were never written. O'Connor would later respond empathetically to Frances: "To hell with Coulton."

---

[15] British Library Folder 73196.

In February and March, Gilbert brought his *Autobiography* to completion. By this time, he was sick constantly, as was Frances. Gilbert had a cough he could not shake, and suffered fevers repeatedly. He was weak and tired, his breathing labored.

Gilbert's final radio lecture took place that March. In his last talk, he answered T.S. Eliot's "This is the way the world ends . . ." and his voice sounds very tired.[16] His last poem appeared in *G.K.'s Weekly* that month as well. The couple planned a trip, hopeful that it would bring about some improvement in Gilbert's health. In May they went to Lisieux and Lourdes, driven by Dorothy. Gilbert had grown to admire the "Little Flower," St. Thérèse of Lisieux, who had been canonized in 1925. She was geographically close to them in one way—the Catholic Church in Beaconsfield was named for her. She was born in 1873, and thus was a contemporary of both Gilbert and Frances. Gilbert was sick throughout the trip, but seemed to improve on the long drive home, singing songs to Frances and Dorothy.

Back home, his health declined, and worsened. He would lose his concentration and fall asleep at his desk. Frances was terribly worried—he'd never fallen asleep while dictating before. She called a doctor. The diagnosis was not promising; the doctor recommended Gilbert go to bed. Frightened, Frances dropped everything. She wrote to Coulton, to whom Gilbert had been in the middle of responding, and said that Gilbert would need several months to recuperate from this illness before he could answer back properly. Then she left everything—the house, business, correspondence—all to Dorothy, so that she could sit with her beloved Gilbert.

Her letter to Fr. Vincent McNabb, one day before Gilbert's death, expresses her hope and her intense suffering at this time:

---

[16] Aidan Mackey recollection. Mr. Mackey has this last BBC talk recorded.

June 13, 1936

Dear Fr. Vincent,

The news will probably reach you sooner or later, that my dear "G.K." is very seriously ill—mainly heart and kidney trouble. Will you of your charity pray for him and for me. He had Extreme Unction this morning & received Holy Communion.

Though very ill, the specialist thinks he has a fighting chance & I have the best doctors and the best nurses in the world to help.

Yours always,

Frances Chesterton.

The last thing he read & delighted in was your pamphlet of Cardinal Pole's Address—He read it to me.[17]

She held onto this "fighting chance" with passionate hope. After all, he had been at death's door before, and had returned. But this time there would be no rally.

The day before he died, Frances kept vigil.

For one moment, he regained consciousness and looked up to see her sitting, faithfully beside him.

"Hello, my darling," he said.

Those were his last words to his loving wife. The next day, June 14, 1936, he died at ten in the morning.

Frances was bereaved, lost, shocked, and overwhelmed. At some point during the day, she wandered over to the calendar on the desk, the calendar that had kept all their appointments, and crossed out two visitors for the 14th. Then she wrote, "The Lights went out at 10:15am."

---

[17] Wade Center folder 308. "Cardinal Pole's Eirenikon," *Dublin Review*, trans. Fr. Vincent McNabb, O.P. (1936): 149-60.

That evening, Edmund C. Bentley, Gilbert's friend since boyhood, announced on the BBC that Gilbert had died. Family, friends, and fans alike grieved the news. The love and esteem of so many combined to dash Frances's last hope for a quiet, private funeral. Gilbert was hers—her lover and friend—but he also belonged to the world. A public funeral was unavoidable.

The funeral Mass for Gilbert Keith Chesterton took place at St. Teresa's[18] in Beaconsfield on Wednesday, June 17. The church of St. Teresa was still incomplete and people overflowed into the temporary wooden narthex; the rest stood outside. Following Frances's instructions, a cross of dark red roses adorned the casket. "Red roses full of rain—" read a note on the flowers: "for you—as you would wish."

The local priest from St. Teresa's, Monsignor Smith, celebrated the Mass, with Father McNabb, Father Rice, Father Fulton Sheen, the Archbishop of Westminster, the Bishop of Northampton, along with many other clergy.[19] O'Connor's absence must have been an additional sorrow to Frances; he was sick in bed that week, and was unable to attend.

The mournful crowd drove or walked slowly behind the mile-long funeral procession to the cemetery. The policemen redirected the path of the hearse to take a longer route so the procession could pass by the old center of town, where Gilbert had spent so much time with the local proprietors.

It was a day of overwhelming and shared grief. The people of Beaconsfield came flooding out to say goodbye to the great man, who had known them all personally. One policeman was

---

[18] Although St. Thérèse's name had the usual French spelling, when the people of Beaconsfield chose her for their patron, they used an anglicized version of her name.

[19] Information provided by Canon John Udris, former parish priest at St. Teresa, Beaconsfield, see also, http://archive.thetablet.co.uk/article/20th-june-1936/6/gilbert-chesterton.

found in tears. Another apologized that the constables were unable to attend the funeral because unfortunately, they had to work. Hilaire Belloc was found weeping disconsolately at the Railway Hotel, the place of Gilbert's 1922 conversion.

After the burial, a small reception took place at Top Meadow. It was a solemn, challenging day. Gilbert's looming, electric personality was gone, and the house felt eerily empty without him. Guests stood on tiptoe, as if expecting he might come around the corner at any moment and say hello once again.

Ada Chesterton later criticized Frances for "hiding" (adding that there wasn't enough food). In fact, the heartbroken widow, for once overwhelmed with the task of serving as hostess to Gilbert's friends and followers, eventually took refuge in another room.

On Saturday, June 27, two thousand people, including, of course, Frances Chesterton and Dorothy Collins, attended a requiem Mass at Westminster Cathedral, in London. Fathers John O'Connor, Vincent McNabb, and Ignatius Rice, all so instrumental in Gilbert's conversion, assisted. Ronald Knox delivered the sermon, which was later printed in *G.K.'s Weekly*. Immediately after the Mass, Frances lunched with Eric Gill[20] and O'Connor. Afterwards, O'Connor returned with Dorothy and Frances to stay a few days at Top Meadow.

Across the Atlantic, a requiem Mass was said at St. Patrick's Cathedral in New York City on June 20, Monsignor Michael J. Lavelle was the main celebrant. The Rann-Kennedys, the Chestertons' old flat neighbors, as well as 1,500 others, including members of many literary societies, attended.

---

[20] Gill was an artist and friend of the Chestertons. He was commissioned to create the gravestone for Gilbert's grave in Beaconsfield.

Letters and telegrams of condolence poured in. In response to a widespread desire to contribute money in Gilbert's memory, Frances set up a G.K. Chesterton Memorial fund, which would help the parish church of St. Teresa retire its debt and complete the building of the English Martyrs chapel.[21]

In the wake of the death of Chesterton, as his overwhelming legacy continued to influence an admiring world, few voices remained to speak of the woman behind the man who was Chesterton. And yet, the loyal O'Connor knew well what Frances had meant to and for Gilbert:

June 18, 1936:

Dear Frances . . . Notices are all nice and reasonable . . . but no one tells the secret—must it remain secret?—of how much of him and his best might have been lost to the world only for you.[22]

On December 17, 1938, an article appeared in the *Tablet* with a contribution from O'Connor, in which he made these thoughts public:

. . . it was her steady care and encouragement that kept him faithful for two years to a task [writing *The Ballad of the White Horse*] so often broken by alien interest. She kept him to the height of it by always taking advantage of a lull or a holiday, in just the same way, with the same happy knack, she used towards children. In another place I think I have indicated that we owe much of his best and highest work to her never-failing enthusiasm.

---

[21] *Catholic Herald* (September 25, 1936): 1.

[22] British Library Folder 73196-0278.

I expect the life of her husband will tell us more at length what the burden was of administering such an unruly inheritance as Gilbert. Yet she was so tactful, understanding, and patient not only with him, but with his besiegers, let us call them, that he was saved much waste and wear, and they were saved as to face, if not to soul.[23]

O'Connor would remain a devoted Chesterton apologist. Soon after Gilbert's death, he visited Stanbrook Abbey, the Abbess of which was Dame Laurentia McLachlan, a Scottish Benedictine nun, correspondent and sometime friend of George Bernard Shaw. O'Connor's report of the visit shows his enthusiasm (centered on a "BIG KNIFE" which belonged to Chesterton):

July 20, 1936

Dear Frances,
I am home again this week past and only just recovering from the journey. People keep telling me to be careful! I'm careful. Wish they took half the care.

If you have any memorial cards left, send me a few. I deal them carefully to good and prayerful persons who remember the blessed dead.

There is a Lady Doc. doing locum[24] in Beaconsfield. But shy of calling. She is very anxious to see at least the empty husk of Gilbert's surroundings. I received her into the Church last year. Alison Hamilton 5 Highway Court in the village.

I had several talks with the Abbess of Stanbrook and her nuns, and passed the BIG KNIFE to them through the bars of their cage. They say I made Gilbert live to them. At least for two hours. I've been re-reading St. Francis. Amazing. Fr.

---

[23] "Requiescant: Mrs. G.K. Chesterton," *The Tablet* (December 17, 1938): 26.

[24] Substituting for another doctor.

Rice at Douai has an album of *Daily News* and other cuttings. One letter of the *Times* on the Jewish question could be cut in marble. Must not be lost. Even I have a lot of Daily Newses. Her chaplain at Stanbrook is a Son of Sir William Butler, the sort of man Gilbert would love.

Mother Laurentia showed me her three relics and gave me an autograph. Shawtograph, I should have said. She says Our Lady will not let him go. He wrote her sixteen pages from Palestine, with a photograph entitled "Temptation and the Devil," and lo it was Barney[25] and Dean Inge. I send two letters if you are not blind with reading such—from priests who say Mass for him. One I have mislaid came punctual from Newfoundland, from a Father Sheehan. Do not return.

Many things remain to be said if I could recall. Love to Dorothy. To hell with that Coulton.

Yours affectionately,
John O'Connor.

Gilbert had carried the knife around for twenty-four years, even taking it with him when he traveled. Frances frequently had to retrieve it from under the pillow at the hotels when he forgot it.[26]

Frances's response to O'Connor contains, as always, insight into her mind and heart. This is perhaps the most challenging letter for the devoted followers of her husband—and Frances herself—to accept:

July 21, 1936

Dear Padre,

---

[25] Bishop Barnes.

[26] *Gilbert Keith Chesterton*, 253.

I return the letters because I have so many—and eventually I suppose I shall have to destroy them.

A. Hamilton is coming to see us this evening. It will be very nice to make her acquaintance. I am sorry her locum here ends so soon. She wrote me a very charming letter.

I find it increasingly difficult to keep going. The feeling that he needs me no longer is almost unbearable.

How do lovers love without each other? We were always lovers.

I have a Mass said here for him every Tuesday—but I feel it is more for the repose of my soul than for his.

Take care of yourself,

Yours ever,

Frances

Her suffering is clear and understandable. "How do lovers love without each other?" She was devastated, grieving, and lonely. How could she *not* struggle, missing her Gilbert so terribly?

Nevertheless, the question remains: *why* would Frances eventually destroy the letters? What was the compelling need that would dictate this cruel blow to posterity? It was not uncharacteristic; Frances and her sister Ethel, like their mother Blanche before them, were pyromaniacs with regards to letters.[27]

Perhaps they were a sore reminder of Gilbert's absence; keeping the letters would not bring him back to her.

Perhaps they were overwhelming; indeed, Gilbert was prolific in all things, especially with the support and assistance of Frances.

Most likely, an old-fashioned sense of privacy combined with pragmatism; for all she cherished every word her husband had ever scribbled, she "could not" keep everything.

---

[27] However, this was not unusual. When George Washington died, Martha burned all of their personal correspondence, as was the custom of the time.

The correspondence with O'Connor continued to be a primary means of solace and guidance:

July 23, 1936

Dear Frances,

No more use expecting you not to grieve and take it hard than commanding you not to feel pain. Only time will dull the edge, and you will realize more the value of the work in which you took so good a hand. Thy Maker is thy Husband now. Widows were very early associates of the Hierarchy at least as honorary members. The husband who came back to ask for more prayers said: *We cannot hold intercourse with one another, but no words of mine can describe to you the comfort we all feel when anyone on earth does any good deed on our behalf, especially having Mass but most of all receiving Holy Communion.* There, that's the first I've ever written down of the best and truest of all the ghost stories I have heard.[28] Vex not his ghost: is an old Catholic tradition. Let him comfort you by praying quietly for him. Indeed it is the repose of your soul now that is in demand, I am certain Gilbert will do all he can to help. Have you any memorial cards left?

I enclose a Carol[29] of yesterday's Prize Day. Did you do it first or did he steal it??? Or is it just a lark?

Thank you on behalf of Alison. She'll tell me all about it I'm certain.

Yours affectionately in J.C.,
John O'Connor.

---

[28] O'Connor collected ghost stories.

[29] One wonders what carol Fr. O'Connor is referring to, which must have been a "Gilbert" but sounded like a "Frances" poem.

Frances received many other beautiful letters of sympathy from friends and strangers after Gilbert's death, and many of these she did not destroy. They flooded in, including from Maurice Baring:

> My dear Frances,
>
> . . . There is nothing to be said, is there, except that our loss, and especially yours, is his gain.
>
> I wish I could come down to-morrow. . . .
>
> O Frances! I feel as if a tower of shelter had tumbled and my crutch in life had gone.[30]

And from Knox:

> Dear Mrs. Chesterton,
>
> This is only to assure you of my prayers, for you as well as for his soul. The world, I feel, can console itself for the loss of what he might have written, by having all that he wrote; your loss is irreplaceable—here. I won't write you with praise of him; he has been my idol since I read *Napoleon of Notting Hill* as a schoolboy; I'll only hope that you, who knew as no one else does what we have lost, will find it easy to imagine as well as believe that he is alive, and unchanged. Thank God for that faith, that I have it when so many of my friends lost it. . . . God comfort you.[31]

From McNabb:

> Dear Frances,
>
> I feel I must write to you.
>
> But what to write I do not know.
>
> I have wept—and yet Gilbert's death is not just for tears, but for pride.

---

[30] Wade Center folder 17—June 16, 1936.

[31] Wade Center folder 185—June 15, 1936.

God gave him to England—and England gave him to the world—as one of God's best gifts to England for three centuries.

His mind alone would have been gift enough for any land to make its boast.

But we who knew his heart—and you who knew it best—felt that it almost dwarfed his mind by its greatness.

To-day we are listening to our Blessed Lord telling us about His Heart—in the room of His Sacred Heart. He tells us how He could not rest until all the poor of the village and the roadside shared his "good cheer." That was Gilbert's heart; and also Christ's.

Another of God's best gifts to us was the one whom Gilbert thought God's best gift to him. Today when God has summoned him first and left her in tears, her prayers of accustomed self-forgetfulness have been answered.

The England, the Church that feels an unpayable gratitude to Gilbert, counts you amongst its creditors.

And from G.B. Shaw:

It seems the most ridiculous thing in the world that I, eighteen years older than Gilbert, should be heartlessly surviving him. However, this is only to say that if you have any temporal bothers that I can remove, a line on a postcard (or three figures) will be sufficient. The trumpets are sounding for him; and the slightest interruption must be intolerable.

From Rome came a most remarkable telegram—Cardinal Secretary of State Eugenio Pacelli (the future Pope Pius XII) writing to tell Frances of the Holy Father's grief at hearing of Gilbert's death. The message was read out loud at the memorial service in Westminster Cathedral:

HOLY FATHER DEEPLY GRIEVED DEATH MR. GILBERT
KEITH CHESTERTON DEVOTED SON HOLY CHURCH
GIFTED DEFENDER OF THE CATHOLIC FAITH STOP
HIS HOLINESS OFFERS PATERNAL SYMPATHY PEOPLE
OF ENGLAND ASSURES PRAYERS DEAR DEPARTED
BESTOWS APOSTOLIC BENEDICTION = CARDINAL
PACELLI

From J. M. Barrie:

21 June 1936

Dear Mrs. Chesterton,
It would ill become me to intrude upon you at this time, but
I hope I may just send you my deep sympathy. He was a
glorious man, loveable beyond words and I think the greatest
literary figure left to us. One aspect of him that I have not
seen mentioned but that is clear to me is that he was such
a gentleman. Chaucer's perfect gentle knight. He was this
beyond compare. I feel very, very sorry for you, left without
him. A bit of yourself dies with him, and in a way that perhaps
makes it less hard to bear.
    With my affectionate sympathy.
    Yours,
    J. M. Barrie.

Each of these letters, and so many others, express the love, appreciation, and dedication of the friends, all of whom were inspired
by the greatest and goodness of Gilbert Chesterton and of his
wife. The sense, seemingly universally shared, was that Frances,
without Gilbert, was at a loss. Her cross had altered; no longer
was she the woman with a keen mother's heart, burdened with
tragic infertility. She had found a unique fulfillment in being
the wife of Gilbert Chesterton. Now she was alone and bearing

that cross. In that loneliness she could turn only, in faith, to God. "Thy Maker is thy Husband now." O'Connor's comment would be well-received; Frances, ever faithful and patient, would be faithful and patient now, in her darkest hour.

She later wrote a poem as a tribute to Gilbert, titled, "In Memory of G.K.C.,"[32] and it includes these beautiful lines:

> Your hand was stretched to all who knocked, "Hail, friend!"
> And which of those who hungered was not fed
> With wine of your warm mirth, with wisdom's bread
> The door stood wide, the hearth glowed to the end.

And the last guest entered, says Frances, and it was death. Even there, strengthened always by his own faith, the welcome had been certain.

---

[32] *How Far Is It To Bethlehem*, 301.

Chapter Nine

AFTER THIS OUR EXILE (1936–1938)

I stumble on down the unending slope. I am alone.

What is there left to do when the purpose and focus of your life is gone? Frances Chesterton, robbed of her lover, her friend, her primary occupation, descended into deep sorrow and suffering.

On October 19, 1936, Frances composed a poem in her poetry notebook titled "Question." In it she spoke of the bitter longing of her restless soul, which no balm could restore or make whole. She spoke of an aching wound. She said she felt she was playing a sorry part, struggling to appear pleased and proud that Gilbert was free of all the world's indelicacies, and pretending her heart was not wounded through.

> Death took you, and left me with a broken wing
> To trail upon the ground, no more to fly
> As we two flew, ah love, so high, so high
> I could not follow, you would call and sing
> And woo me ever upwards, to the heights
> Of boundless space, now space is yours alone.
> I am confined and caged, my mate has flown.
> Draw to the curtains. Put out all the lights.

The poem concludes heartrendingly—when her longing was greatest, she liked to imagine that they were holding each other close, but, because of the veil between life and death, they could not see each other face to face.

Her letters are full of suffering:

October 25, 1936

Dear Padre,

I get so tired and confused these days I don't know if I wrote and thanked you for your article on Gilbert. I loved it so much—there was so much of him in it. I seem to feel his loss more and more. It does not get easier to bear as time goes on. I am glad about the Memorial here and hope it will really be accomplished at any rate before I go to join him.

It is good of you to subscribe and I don't feel you ought to, but I shall love to think you had a finger in <u>that</u> pie as well as in so many others.

Dorothy is well—starting in on Mr. Garvin's work. I hope she is going to like it.

I am so glad you are better for Lourdes. Our Lady's answer to any prayer for him here is not what is expected—but right. I know however hard.

Yours always,
Frances Chesterton.

In addition to the interesting and perhaps surprising tidbit that Dorothy was already working for someone else,[1] we find here Frances's quiet acceptance and belief: "Our Lady's answer to any prayer for him [Gilbert] here is not what is expected—but right." Frances had prayed, had hoped for a miracle. Her heart is broken, but though the truth is "hard", she knows and accepts it.

---

[1] James Louis Garvin, see http://en.wikipedia.org/wiki/James_Louis_Garvin.

Frances was "emotionally unstrung" after Gilbert died.[2] Her grief was possibly made all the more intense by the fact that she had no one intimately bound to her—like a child or a grandchild—with whom she could speak of Gilbert. Her only sister was still married, with her own children and grandchildren to occupy her time. Her cousin Margaret came to stay with her for a while with her daughter, but she could only temporarily keep loneliness at bay. Although Frances had family company, and family was important to her, the long, lonely nights were a heavy burden.

During the remainder of 1936, Frances was kept somewhat busy organizing the memorial fund (which was to help fund the remainder of the building of St. Teresa's in Beaconsfield), collecting Gilbert's works, and visiting and being visited by friends and relatives. Neighbors dropped in to tea every day. O'Connor notes that one thing that made Frances happy after Gilbert's death was being asked by Monsignor Smith at St. Teresa's to teach Sunday school.[3]

The legacy of her husband was already prompting biographical interest. Late that year, Gilbert's friend and fellow journalist William Richard Titterton published the first posthumous biography of Gilbert. Titterton stated that Frances had become known as a writer of strength and delicacy, but that her best claim to fame was as the better half of GKC.[4]

Perhaps inspired by this example of the endurance of the public's interest in Gilbert, Frances started thinking about her own death, and requested that Dorothy Collins destroy certain

---

[2] Maisie Ward, *Gilbert Keith Chesterton*, viii.

[3] *The Tablet* (December 17, 1938): 27.

[4] Titterton, 38. Note: he mentions an incorrect wedding date, June 1900—they were actually married in 1901.

personal correspondence after she died, particularly the love letters. Dorothy would faithfully carry this out.[5] In addition to burning, some of the papers that Dorothy lent to Maisie Ward for her biography of Gilbert were destroyed in an air raid during World War II.[6] Both Frances and Dorothy Collins also freely gave away papers as a sort of souvenir to visitors to Top Meadow.[7] Undoubtedly, the letters that do remain are treasures.

In December, Frances visited Gilbert's grave, and planted a dandelion over it. She later wrote a poem describing the experience. In "The Dandelion", she spoke of how she kept thinking she heard him calling in the house. She kept expecting to see him leaning on the gate. She walked through the house: here was where he loved to stand, this was his room, there his chair and a book he treasured. It was his kingdom, and death took him away from home.

> Beloved, oh beloved, hold my hands
> Fast in your own
> Mine tremble, are cold, they grope and grope
> Cold as a stone
> There is no answering touch; there is no hope
> I stumble on down the unending slope.
> I am alone.

And yet, she clung to the real source of her hope; she composed a poem for the annual Christmas greeting in 1936, "After This

---

[5] Ian Ker, *G.K. Chesterton: A Biography*, ix. As discussed earlier, letter burning was common. Gilbert's mother Marie Louise destroyed her personal letters. Ethel Oldershaw burned letters. Blanche Blogg burned letters. So many of the letters and papers that might have told us the most about Frances are lost to us.

[6] *Ibid.*

[7] *Ibid.*

Our Exile",[8] comparing earth to heaven, and finding a true home in the Stable at the End of the World. *How far is it to Bethlehem?* Not very far.

1937 was largely uneventful; a continuation of the same life without Gilbert. Frances continued to write letters, as always. She watched as the GKC memorial helped finish up a side chapel in St. Teresa's. She requested any letters Gilbert wrote to be collected and sent back to her. She went to daily Mass. She was made honorary president for life of the Chesterton Club. She wrote poetry, received visits from neighbors, and continued to tend her garden and her pets and love her nieces and nephews—who were now getting married and starting families of their own. Time had not necessarily softened her grief, but she had so far progressed in her grieving that now it had greater voice. Her output of poetry at this time was considerable.

She happened to read the newspaper one day, and discovered the tram car in London was to be discontinued. It must have reminded her of Gilbert's description of the tram car;[9] she submitted a poem to the paper about its demise[10], along with the line of Gilbert's. Both were published.

In June 1937, she composed a poem called "First Communion: From the German." Frances wrote poetry in German, a language she loved, and then translated her own work into English.

---

[8] *How Far Is It To Bethlehem*, 229-32.

[9] "Basil Grant and I were talking one day in what is perhaps the most perfect place for talking on earth–the top of a tolerably deserted tram car. To talk on the top of a hill is superb, but to talk on the top of a flying hill is a fairy tale." From *The Club of Queer Trades*.

[10] "Must We Forever Say a Long Goodbye."

It all comes back like some white dream of spring
So blessed a memory in the darkening streets
When the bright flame of youth has died quite down
And my tired heart now only faintly beats.

A soft white dress, the first one made full long
The little wreath they fastened in my hair
The golden cross about my childish neck
And in my hands an ivory book of prayer.

If all the silver bells have sung for naught
And the spring flowers of my heart are dust
I feel the dress, the chain, the ivory cool
And with that child find God, because I must.

In February of 1937, she wrote a new poem, "To G.K.C. For
Any Birthday," anticipating his birthday in May, a month he had
loved. She felt as though her youth were a thousand miles away.
She said they made a vow that they would never part, but Gilbert
could not stay; death took him away. She laid roses on his grave.

To the strong day-light, adamant and bright
I have no glimpse to ease my straining sight
My lover gone, I have no power to fight
Only when darkness comes and no one cares
Is that a whisper, a footstep on the stairs?
You—sword in hand, a single shaft of light
Oh treacherous day, oh faithful, faithful night.

June of 1937 saw the one-year anniversary of his death. Frances
remembered the day with another poem: "Comfort Ye—Comfort
Ye." She remembered his footsteps, and when she used to pass
him on the stairs, how he would grasp her hand. Now he can
no longer hold her hand or stroke her hair. She could always

pick out his laughter in a crowded room—but there is no more laughter now.

> Ah night, when all was still, the encroaching world asleep
> I said, "Pray for me," and from the unconscious deep
> You would faintly murmur, "Now, and at the hour of death,"
> And now I never hear the words without a catching
>   of the breath.

She goes on to say that she no longer anticipates the spring, in fact, spring and summer are already passing, and autumn and winter are coming and she knows she must leave this place, her home. She cannot endure the bare trees, the quiet air with no birds singing, no dandelions growing.

> Forgive me, oh forgive me, if loved voices are all stilled
> If the hearth place is empty, and the wine cup unfilled
> If laughter comes not easily and footsteps are but slow
> Dear love, I've been so long alone, the flame is burning low.

In October of 1937, she wrote another poem expressing her loneliness without Gilbert:

> Last night you came and took my hand in yours
> I knew it was your hand, I felt the glow
> Of your warm fingers, but my spirit shrank
> At the cold touch of the ring I gave you, long ago.
>
> I moved your hand my love that it might rest
> Upon my head in blessing as of old
> You let it lie until the midnight air
> Turned the full pulsing warmth to death's remembered cold.
>
> Cold as a stone, I laid it against my heart
> To hold it there in that warm secret place
> Whether I triumphed, love, I do not know

Last night it was so dark, I could not see your face.

Were your hands warm oh loved one, were they cold?
My heart within me beat with wild affright
That they were cold. But throbbing strong with life
For your dear hands were warm, beloved in the night.

1937 momentously marked the publication of O'Connor's biography of G.K. Chesterton, *Father Brown on Chesterton*. His representation was, of course, faithful, and subject to her approval. In fact, as O'Connor was completing his biography, he gave it to Frances to read over. She took her time with it, and O'Connor, confident she would approve, gave the manuscript to his publisher, Frederick Muller, to prepare for publication. When Frances objected to something O'Connor had written, O'Connor immediately changed it (to the great irritation of his publisher).[11]

Frances could not bear Christmas alone at Top Meadow in 1937, and went to visit her cousin Margaret Heaton Arndt in Germany for several months. Her visit initially brought some consolation, but tragedy struck, suddenly and ruthlessly, when Margaret died from a stroke while Frances was present. Frances's letter to O'Connor expresses the torrent of emotions to which she was prey:

21 Hindenburg Strasse
Bad Wildungen

---

[11] This is clearly shown in Muller's letter (British Library 73196-0310):

> My dear very Rev. Father,
>   Your letter is rather a blow, but I have sent word to the printer to remove the passage to which Mrs. Chesterton objects. I can't see much wrong with it really, for everybody knows that G.K. shared the feelings of many people. . . .

Germany

Quinquagesima[12]

Dear Padre,

Bad Homburg turned out tragically indeed. I have not yet got over the shock. My cousin Frau Prof. Arndt had a sudden stroke and died in a few days, never regaining consciousness.

It happened in the middle of the night and I was with her and did all I could before a doctor arrived. I hardly felt fit to cope with such a situation and it took all I had of courage and endurance to face it. I am now at Bad Wildungen with her daughter for a few days, before returning home. I don't know how to leave them, there never was such a time of difficulty and complexity in my life before. . . .

The "in Memoriam" aspect of everything has me beat. I can't think of things like that. I dread going back more than words can say—but I'm pretty much of a coward though I hope a deceptive one. . . .

    Yours ever,

    Frances

Frances did not know how to cope with such a thing, except that she did. *I dread going back more than words can say—but I'm pretty much of a coward though I hope a deceptive one . . . it took all I had of courage and endurance to face it . . .* She dreaded going back to the home she loved because the one she loved best was missing. Her pets, her garden, even her nieces and nephews could not take the place of Gilbert. She missed him terribly. In addition, this statement shows her humility about herself—she calls herself a coward—but she heroically and courageously overcame her feelings when she was called upon

---

[12] The Sunday before Ash Wednesday—February 7, 1937.

to do so. The courage and humility of Frances are characteristics worthy of imitation.

Late that year, she was diagnosed with cancer. She knew that it was a matter of time before she herself would die. She penned a poem, "A Rendering of Chaucer's Alphabet of the Letters F., G., & C." She was worried about the tempest, and she was full of dread for the future. She begged the Lord to stay near her. She begged forgiveness for past wrongs, and begged Our Lady to help.

> For thine enemy and mine, Lady give heed
> To waiting now to lead me to my death.

A poem written in March of 1938 is labeled "Rome," so it would seem that after Germany, Frances traveled to Rome. She would not have traveled alone, but whom she went with is unknown. The poem is called "Sun and Shade," and recalls memories of Gilbert:

> I who walked with you in the sun
> But now walk in the shade
> How can I feel the warmth and light?
> I am afraid.

> Afraid to enter in these holy doors
> Where once you prayed with me
> How can I see the glory of the Mass
> In poverty?

> Poor am I, lacking your tender love
> Not even the widow's mite
> To cast into the treasury heap
> With such delight

> That I could add to your vast store
> Of generosity?

That gave your mirth, your love, yourself
In boundless charity.

Frances returned to Beaconsfield, and composed another poem, also in March 1938. Called "Light and Warmth," she recalls how light and warm their home was with Gilbert in it, how it feels dark and cold now without him. She sees his chair, kneels beside it, and cries for his hand to hold hers. She was now anticipating meeting him again; she wanted to forget her pain and reach heaven so they could be reunited.

But when I come to die
Build me a fire, and light a candle wick
That presently, I see my love bathed in the vibrant air
Of fire and candlelight
And in those consuming powers I may know
The passing of the night.

This time of her life is quite a mystery. One could presume she was not living alone, but Dorothy Collins was not living with her either: the former secretary had an apartment and a job elsewhere. The most likely candidate for helper and companion was her sister, Ethel. However, there just is no evidence—so far—to help.

She suffered symptoms from her cancer, and had an operation to relieve the pain during the summer. After the operation, she was transferred to the St. Joseph Nursing Home run by the Sisters of Bon Secours—Frances had been influential in inviting them to come to Beaconsfield years before.

The last poem written in her poetry notebook is dated May 29, 1938, the second time Gilbert's birthday had come around since he died. The poem is titled, "You and I."

Did we sing our songs as spring passed by
Did we walk once in green fields, you and I
Did we have friends, and happiness, and trust
Though sorrow broke our hearts, as sorrow must
Under a waning moon in silver sky
Did we weep together, you and I?

Did we face life and never thought to die
Nothing could ever part us, you and I
We did not see the sword that would divide
The waters of our souls, at the ebb tide
The flaming sword across the morning sky
Could we not stay together, you and I?

Did we see the seasons fade and did we sigh
For Beauty, heavenly beauty, you and I
Beauty dwelt with us and we never knew
That beauty passes, as the evening dew
And leaves an empty, colourless grey sky
Did we once know Beauty, you and I?

And Death has come, surefooted, silently
And we are not together, you and I
I laugh and weep alone, you so far away
I in the night, you in splendour of the day.
You in the sun, I in the moon cold sky
When shall we be together, you and I?

In November of 1938, Dorothy must have written to O'Connor regarding Frances's condition. He wrote back on November 30:

Dear Dorothy,
It is sad and serious indeed that the dear Frances is in heavy trial. I have sent an S.O.S. for prayers to our schools. The

children's prayers have done wonders for her in the past, as she so well deserves. May they do greater things now. . . .[13]

A visitor who came to see Frances towards the end described her as lying on a bed next to a table filled with flowers. She was lying with her arms outstretched, as if on a cross. Her pain was great and her suffering could be seen on her face. Dorothy visited her, bringing the dog so Frances could see and pet him. Dorothy brought paperwork to the nursing home and sat and talked with Frances as she worked.[14] The sisters attended to Frances's physical needs. She remained lucid until the end.

As she was dying, she knew that her niece Catherine[15] was expecting her first baby, and Frances longed to live to see the infant.[16] She did not make it. Frances died on December 12, 1938, during her favorite season of Advent; and fifteen days later, her great-nephew, Geoffrey Neil Guinness, was born.

The biographer is tempted to imagine her passage from this life to the next in all of its joyful brilliance. At last together again with Gilbert, holding hands, gazing face to face. Reunited with her lover, her parents, her siblings, and all the angels and saints, with music and poetry and love and beauty, and standing in the presence of Light and Love.

When shall we be together, you and I?

How far is it to Bethlehem?

---

[13] Wade Center folder 234.

[14] *The Chesterton Review* Vol. 14, no. 4 (1988): 593.

[15] "Kate," the one who earlier broke her engagement but was now married to Brian Guinness. She was the youngest daughter of Frances's sister Ethel and Lucian Oldershaw.

[16] *Return To Chesterton*, 120.

In faith, Frances could tell us, the answer to these two questions is the same.

Chapter Ten

THE FATE OF MRS. CHESTERTON
(1938 AND BEYOND)

We are prepared and ready. Let us kneel here
And pray the saints to keep us safe from fear.[1]

Nary one of us can control our legacy. In some ways, Frances Chesterton might have approved of the way her memory was treated after death; her person was, by many, subsumed into that of her husband. She was the wife of Chesterton, remarkable for that fact only. Truly, this is the characteristic because of which many have come, even indirectly, to make her acquaintance. Her own contributions to faith and literature were not, of course, immediately forgotten. Many praised her both on her own merits and by linking her name with his. The obituary in the *Catholic Herald*, for example, reads as follows:

> *Mrs. G.K. Chesterton: English Author's Widow Had Large Influence on His Work.*
>
> Mrs. Frances Chesterton, widow of Gilbert K. Chesterton, the noted writer, died today at Beaconsfield. Her deeply religious nature was the most powerful influence in the intellectual and spiritual change so manifest in Chesterton between the writing of *The Wild Knight* and *Orthodoxy*. Mrs. Chesterton

---

[1] "The Children's Crusade," *How Far Is It To Bethlehem*, 25.

was regularly consulted by her husband on even the smallest decision, and one of his literary dedications was "To You who brought the cross to me." She was received into the Roman Catholic Church four years after her husband. Mrs. Chesterton, the former Frances Blogg, was a poet of note and once was described by her husband as "In all ways a kindred spirit."

There were other extraordinary obituaries, as well.[2] Friends of both Chestertons attended her funeral, held on Friday, December 16, 1938, at St. Teresa in Beaconsfield. She was buried, the papers said, in "his" grave.

They were both significant enough figures in English Catholicism to warrant attention after death. In Fr. John O'Connor's correspondence with Dorothy Collins, he encouraged her to write memoirs of her life with Gilbert and Frances. Although she did write some recollections of Gilbert,[3] the requested book never appeared.

Ada Chesterton published *The Chestertons* a few years after Frances's death. Frances's closest friends responded with outrage and horror. The correspondence between Fr. O'Connor and Dorothy Collins passionately addressed the topic:

August 21, 1941

Dear Dorothy,

I excuse your TPW[4] on condition that you excuse my bad writing. When two strong-minded women are at variance, strong-minded in such opposite ways, who shall dare and

---

[2] See Extras.

[3] *G.K. Chesterton: A Centenary Appraisal.*

[4] Typewritten letter.

come between or compose the variance? J.K.P.[5] is strong unto coarseness, hence her heavy hand in such delicate matters as marital rights. I think money is not her object. I saw the reviews which called her treatment of Frances "cattish."[6]

In the first part of the book I thought it was the RR[7] who were cattish then. Because Frances was never luxurious or luxuriant, and very frugal in the beginning, being so prudent. The 2/6 pocket money was very playfully regarded by both I know, since I witnessed. What could she do when Gilbert went out with £5.18.6 or words to that effect, and came back invariably without a copper, not knowing where his money had gone? Here the heavy hand is too evident. I can testify to the loving care with which Frances anticipated all his wishes—never was the cigar box out of date—you know this, and it was so long before you came. . . .

The Ballad of the White Horse . . . was never penned in Fleet Street. . . . Nor *The Everlasting Man*. He wrote verbosely there in the office. At Beaconsfield, he was pulled together, braced. She [Frances] knew who would make him drink too much and she discouraged them, even Cecil who was much more robust, and Belloc who was *le Cadet de Gascogne* in all things. She nursed H.B. through pneumonia at Battersea before I knew them.

When I got to the marital interchanges I woke up and said, 'behold the cat.' Only a strong, too strong-minded woman would have put in that. Who told her anyhow? In the second or third year of our acquaintance I walked from the Waterloo Place —the hospital in Chelsea where she was getting over her

---

[5] J.K. Prothero, a.k.a. Ada Chesterton.

[6] *Catholic Herald* (September 26, 1941): 6.

[7] Aidan Mackey believes this means "Rolling Rich."

first Amazonian op[eration]. She wrote and told me about the
second, years after. Her strength was not as that of Mrs. Cecil,
but entirely on a higher plane. She [Ada] reminds me of the
all but fabulous bridesmaid who went on the honeymoon.
(This happened in Ireland when I was a kid. Even then I
hardly approved.)

You see what a lot can be said. I wish it could be as St. John
prefers, not by pen and ink. . . .[8]

O'Connor and Collins were not the only ones. A review by "G.T."
in *The Guardian* of July 29, 1941, reads:

Mrs. Chesterton's discursive book contains many racy memories of her own career, and her portraits of her husband and
her brother-in-law are perhaps more an unconscious reflection
of her personal standards and values than a really objective
estimate of two brilliant yet vividly contrasted men. There is
no denying the interest or vivacity of these pages. But their
intimacy, as in certain revelations of Gilbert's married life, is
often in grossly bad taste.

The reviewer goes on. He suspects an underlying bitterness in
the attack on Frances and reveals the paradoxical nature of Ada
Chesterton's discussion of how much care Gilbert really needed,
being entirely unpractical with regard to day-to-day life; while at
the same time she criticizes Frances's careful attention to Gilbert.

London society was abuzz with the scandal. Among many
others, Lady Ettie Desborough, the famous heiress and socialite,
wrote a letter to her friend, Ethel Oldershaw, Frances's sister:

---

[8] O'Connor is here referring to 2 John 12: *Though I have much to write to you, I would
rather not use paper and ink, but I hope to come to see you and talk with you face to face.*

May 1944

Will is deep in the life of dear Gilbert Chesterton and will hand [the book] on to me directly he has finished it. Maurice Baring liked it so much.

That other book [*The Chestertons*] made me more angry than any book ever, and I simply longed to barge in and contradict those lies—but how right everyone was to ignore it and to leave all the absurdities and spite to reveal themselves. I thought it was a shocking revelation of what must be the writer's mind.

Aidan Mackey, a Chesterton follower who knew Ada personally later in her life, gave this added insight:

I met Mrs. Cecil Chesterton when she was in her 90s. She insisted on being called "Keith" since she was a teenager. In her days as a Fleet Street journalist, she could match anyone pint for pint at the pubs. She was uninhibited and had a penetrating voice. She still wore high heels and plucked her eyebrows . . . ludicrous results.

She liked me but I told her I did not approve of her book, *The Chestertons*. She said, 'I suppose I was a little harsh to Frances.'

I replied, 'No, you were damned unfair!'

She said sheepishly, 'Oh, all right.'

She was savagely untruthful [regarding Frances]. I think it was because Frances had no interest in fame for herself, but only in providing for G.K., that Ada was jealous and held a grudge.[9]

---

[9] Aidan Mackey, "Mrs. Cecil Chesterton," *Gilbert* Vol. 16, no. 4 (2013): 10-11.

What did Frances think of Ada Chesterton? There is no documentary evidence to help us answer that question. The only exchange Frances ever recorded between herself and Ada took place at Gilbert's funeral—Frances noted humbly to her sister-in-law that Ada's grief must have been so much more intense because she only had Cecil with her for such a short time. Frances, ever a gentle soul, is unlikely to have recorded uncharitable thoughts about anyone.[10]

There is, however, some evidence of Gilbert's attitude toward Ada. He referred to her as "Jones" or "Prothero" even long after she became his sister-in-law. A letter to Belloc, discussing the affairs of the *New Witness*, is particularly illuminative:

> The case of my sister-in-law cannot be for me even an ordinary case of treating an assistant well. Those nearest to our nearest may not happen to be the people who would have been our chief chosen friends, but they must be our friends; or memories are wounded and life made very ugly.[11]

In another letter he refers to her as "Miss Prothero . . . the most intransigent of New Witnessers".[12]

As editor, Gilbert was more than once occupied in the unhappy task of cleaning up difficulties brought on by Ada's distinctive attitude toward the laws against libel. H.G. Wells wrote to Chesterton letting him know he was cancelling his subscription to the *New Witness*—because of a book review written by J.K. Prothero—and that he was angry with Gilbert. Gilbert tried to placate Wells by telling him that,

---

[10] Aidan Mackey states that in the G.K. Chesterton Library at Oxford, there is a copy of Chesterton's autobiography signed by Frances to Ada with a very kind inscription.

[11] Chesterton/Belloc correspondence, Boston College Library, letter dated August 25, 1919.

[12] Chesterton/Belloc correspondence, Boston College Library, letter dated Feb. 2, no year.

I very often disagree with the criticisms of Prothero. . . . I cannot help being entertained by your vision of Prothero, who is not a priest, but a poor journalist, and I believe a Free Thinker. But whoever he may be, (and I hardly think the problem worth a row between you and me), he has a right to justice: and you must surely see that even if it were my paper, I could not either tell a man to find a book good when he found it bad, or sack him for a point of taste which has nothing in the world to do with the principles of the paper.[13]

The effect of Ada's semi-biographical book on the legacy of both Chestertons has, alas, been long-lasting. Dudley Barker's biography of Chesterton, for example, published in 1973, leaned heavily on Ada's. The response of Chesterton's closest friends was, once again, outrage. In the letters of Dorothy Collins to Father Brocard Sewell we see this observation:

Some of the remarks in the Dudley Barker book have angered me very much, they are so untrue, and I warned him of this before it went to press without any success. He is most unjust towards the happy marriage of Gilbert and Frances. He has taken far too much from Mrs. Cecil's libelous book. Lucian Oldershaw thought very seriously of bringing a case against it, but decided not to as it would have publicized the book too much.

Beyond the obvious inventive liberties Ada took with the truth, one of our primary sources is itself problematic: Maisie Ward.

Looking back to the difficult days preceding Gilbert's conversion, we are reminded of his poignant letter:

---

[13] Wade Center folder 307—GKC to Wells, about 1917.

> For deeper reasons that I could ever explain, my mind has
> to turn especially on the thought of my wife, whose life has
> been in many ways a very heroic tragedy; and to whom I am
> so much in debt of honour that I cannot bear to leave her,
> even psychologically, if it be possible by tact and sympathy
> to take her with me.

To an extent, Ward dismissed this notion of Frances's life as a
"very heroic tragedy". This was not at all malicious; Ward was
fond of the couple, and felt an intimate friendship with them,
both through her parents, Wilfrid and Josephine Ward, and
in her own right. There is, however, an important distinction:
Gilbert's biographer was twenty years younger than Frances.[14]
The generational difference was monumental, especially when
added to the quiet, retired, humility of Frances. In addition,
Ward was angry with Ada's biography, and finished her work as
a means of contradicting what she viewed as Ada's inaccuracies,
if not lies; leading Ward, at times, to swing too far the other
way. Neither biographer could be said to be impartial; neither
was objective.

Ward, even as a dedicated biographer and an intuitive historian, was not likely to be able to break through the self-deprecating
smile of an unwilling subject—who was not, after all, Ward's
primary focus. For instance, Ward admitted that she never even
knew until after Frances died that Mrs. Chesterton suffered
from arthritis in her back. Ward's work, rightly treasured as
the only authorized biography of G.K. Chesterton, is a vital
source for Frances, of course; it is simply that, when it comes
down to a question of accurate, intimate knowledge, we ought

---

[14] Frances was friends with Maisie's mother, Josephine Ward, a novelist, and wife of
Wilfrid Ward, one of the most influential Catholic converts and writers of the preceding
generation.

to trust Frances's own accounts (in her few remaining letters) and Gilbert, who knew her best, over anyone else.

Thus, when Ward says that Frances did not view herself as anything other than happy,[15] we can unite this with Gilbert's descriptions of Frances and all that we have read about her, to determine through inductive reasoning: first, that such was the face Frances presented to the world; and second, that in her humility and patience she could very well have been truly joyful; accepting, as best she could, the crosses in her life. Indeed, interior sadness and suffering does not make overall contentment—in appearance or reality—impossible. Such is the case of the soul who is truly abandoned to the will of God.

We consequently find the true direction for our attitude to Frances by looking once again to her obituary:

> Mrs. Frances Chesterton, widow of Gilbert K. Chesterton, the noted writer, died today at Beaconsfield. Her deeply religious nature was the most powerful influence in the intellectual and spiritual change so manifest in Chesterton between the writing of *The Wild Knight* and *Orthodoxy*. Mrs. Chesterton was regularly consulted by her husband on even the smallest decision, and one of his literary dedications was "To You who brought the cross to me." She was received into the Roman Catholic Church four years after her husband. Mrs. Chesterton, the former Frances Blogg, was a poet of note and once was described by her husband as "In all ways a kindred spirit."

---

[15] *Gilbert Keith Chesterton*, 537.

EPILOGUE

Therefore I bring these rhymes to you
Who brought the cross to me.

During the writing of this book, the Bishop of Northampton announced that he was assigning a cleric to explore the possibility of a sainthood cause for G.K. Chesterton. This was met with pleasure and hope. Gilbert Chesterton has certainly written plenty, has numerous biographies, and has left a trail of witnesses as to his likely sainthood.

The news gave pleasure to Chesterton's many admirers, even as it provoked outburst from his critics (who, unlike those who disagreed with him in life, have no opportunity of entering into open debate with the gracious, charitable, undaunted defender of the Faith).

Is G.K. Chesterton a saint? (Incidentally, this is not a question Frances herself asked; she had an assurance that Gilbert was with God, and that she could rely on his intercession on her behalf.)

While leaving this question to the wisdom of Mother Church, it is useful and instructive to explore what this entire question means for us as readers and (it is hoped) admirers of his work. What purpose might it serve to investigate such a cause? Does our admiration of him require this recognition?

For our answer, we look to the source. Who are the saints? *The Catechism of the Catholic Church* provides a concise answer:

828 By canonizing some of the faithful, i.e., by solemnly pro-
claiming that they practiced heroic virtue and lived in fidelity
to God's grace, the Church recognizes the power of the Spirit
of holiness within her and sustains the hope of believers by
proposing the saints to them as models and intercessors....[16]

"The saints have always been the source and origin of renewal
in the most difficult moments in the Church's history."[17]

Indeed, "holiness is the hidden source and infallible measure of
her apostolic activity and missionary zeal."[18] The purpose of the
saints, the faithful witness and heroic virtue that brings renewal
to the Church, is a purpose to which all souls are called to aspire.

But did Gilbert thus aspire?

We have the answer, from his own lips. As he wrote to
Maurice Baring, describing that tenuous time between his
decision to convert and its actualization: "I am concerned most,
however, about somebody I value more than the Archbishop
of Canterbury; Frances, to whom I owe much of my own faith."
Here is the woman who first inspired in him respect for sacramental Christianity.[19]

Imagine for a moment Gilbert Keith Chesterton without
Frances. Gilbert alone could have been a famous author, but he
would have failed to arrive at most of his speaking engagements.
He might have indulged his appetites disproportionately. He
might have died in 1915, failing to write *The Everlasting Man,
Eugenics and Other Evils, St. Francis of Assisi, The Outline of*

---

[16] Vatican Council. *Lumen Gentium* (Dogmatic Constitution on Church), November
21, 1964, §40; 48-51.

[17] John Paul II, *Christifideles Laici* §16, 3.

[18] *Ibid.*, §17, 3.

[19] *Gilbert Keith Chesterton*, 460.

Sanity, many Father Brown stories, *St. Thomas Aquinas,* all issues of *G.K.'s Weekly*, and a host of other articles and books. He might never have converted to the Catholic faith. Without Frances, he simply would not have been able to do all he did. As O'Connor wrote to Frances after Gilbert's death: "How much of him and his best might have been lost to the world only for you."

Like most married women, Frances did not know what to expect out of her married life or her husband. We have seen that her dream, particularly as regards those "seven beautiful children", never reached fulfilment. Some things she *did* know, of course. After almost five years of knowing Gilbert, she was well aware of his wonderful, exuberant ways, as well as his quirky eccentricity. (Like most wives, she perhaps thought she would change his habits; like some wives, she was wise enough, in practice, merely to seek to amend and work with them.)

Gilbert was not famous when they met and married. Frances could have had no idea he would become *so* famous, so well-known, such a public figure. She could not have known how much he would depend on her—or how much she would depend on him. It was a struggle for each of them to be so needed by the other, and yet their bond was tightly bound by this mutual need: it caused them to cling tightly to each other.

Of all people in the world, Frances knew Gilbert best—knew him, and loved him. She helped him become the person he was, write all he wrote, and see the world in the way he did. Theirs was a truly deep, truly divine, truly loving love story, and, because of this, well worth knowing.

Frances's life was indeed courageous. She had many tragedies to overcome, and yet, left a lingering memory of a woman who was unwavering in her unselfishness, charitable without limit, devoting every thought and action to others—with that gift for "self-forgetfulness", as Fr. Vincent McNabb put it. Her life was one of service: listening to young people; taking care of and visiting the sick; creating plays for entertainment and pleasure and moral edification; taking care of Gilbert in every way, always thinking of him and what he needed before thinking of herself. Because of Frances, Gilbert could write what he wrote. Because she took good care of him, he lived past the illness of 1914-15. Because she encouraged him, he sought and found success through publishing in the first place. Because she supported him emotionally, he was able to love one woman, be beloved by that woman, and give himself to England. Because she loved him, he belonged to her; because she helped him, he belonged to the world.

Looking once again to Gilbert, he shows us how to value her:

Therefore I bring these rhymes to you
Who brought the cross to me.

This dedication of *The Ballad of the White Horse* says everything.

In my introduction to this book, I suggested Frances as the forerunner of her husband; a sometime John the Baptist, who might have said: "He must increase, but I must decrease." This is only an earthly reflection on his success; there is a supernatural angle to be considered as well. Frances's true witness is as a forerunner to Jesus Christ. She who quietly carried the cross within the context of her own life, through the duties of the married state and the extra duties of marriage to Gilbert Keith Chesterton, was thereby able to bring it to another. This is an authentic apostolate, a bringing of Christ to a fallen world. And, as an enduring example to married women, she did so through the very basic, repetitive duties of her state in life (duties that might be monotonous, even married to G.K.).

She brought Christ to Gilbert. She brought Christ to everyone she met. We see this clearly in numerous letters, and perhaps none so poignantly as this letter of sympathy written by a stranger after the death of Gilbert:

Dear Mrs. Chesterton,

I am loathe to intrude on you in these sad hours of bereavement, and pray that God may give you strength to bear your loss bravely; but I wanted you to feel the sympathy of one of the many millions to whom G.K.C. was an inspiration and delight through his works.

Our family are converts, and to such he was, no is especially dear because of his brave self-sacrificing fight in defence of the Faith.

Personally I cannot put into words my regard for the great minded gentleman to whom the world owes an inestimable debt.

Genius, the same world declares him, yet I often wondered if he could have done so much without your able help and unstinting love. It is you who must be thanked for fostering and allowing that genius full play. God bless you. . . .

The family and all my friends send messages of deep sympathy. Though we are strangers yet you shared the biggest blessing of your life with the world and them and so made them your friends.

Maude McKendry[20]

The facets of her example are numberless: acceptance of infertility; acceptance of financial struggles; patience in and out of adversity; heroic endurance in sickness; loving care as an aunt and godmother; gracious, enthusiastic hospitality, especially

---

[20] British Library folder 73455 A-D.

to children; the kindness of a listening ear; docile following of Christ, even in the midst of intense doubts or spiritual aridity.

As Chestertonian scholar Peter Floriani, Ph.D., remarked about Frances: "I just know it makes sense, for a saint like him needed a saint like her, and we indeed learn much from that—maybe more than from GKC's most profound writings!"[21]

Together they lived holy lives, dedicated to one another, to their faith, to the poor and the sick, and to all the children they knew. And because of that faith, they lived the way they did, generously sharing their lives with family, friends and strangers. Without lapsing into too much hagiographic enthusiasm, I think we can truly say: if Gilbert is to be considered a saint, we must look to his wife, for she was, if not the "saint-maker" *per se*, the saint beside the saint. May she, as she did for Gilbert, bring yet the cross to us.

---

[21] Private correspondence with author.

EXTRAS

The funeral card of Frances Chesterton:

OF YOUR CHARITY
Pray for the repose of the Soul
Of
Frances Chesterton
Who, fortified by the Rites of the Church,
Died on
December 12, 1938

+

Behold, the Lord cometh, the Prince of the
Kings of the earth: blessed are they that are
ready to go forth and meet Him.
Advent Antiphon

Eternal rest give unto her, O Lord, and let
Perpetual light shine upon her.
May she Rest in Peace.   Amen.

Obituaries:

The London Catholic Herald
Frances, Wife of G.K. Chesterton
By Maisie Ward (Mrs. F. J. Sheed)

Mrs. Chesterton died at Beaconsfield on Monday, December 12, 1938

Frances Chesterton was the eldest daughter of the late George William Blogg, a diamond merchant, of Albemarle

Street. Douglas Jerrold, the famous editor of *Punch*, was her great-great-uncle.[1]

She was educated at the first kindergarten in England, started on German lines, then at Notting Hill High School; finally at St. Stephen's College, Windsor, the school of an Anglo-Catholic Convent.

G.K. Chesterton speaks in his autobiography of her being sent to this last school as an accident. It was one of those human accidents that God seems to take delight in designing. For the atmosphere and the ideas in the convent were utterly congenial to this girl, coming from agnostic surroundings, and became the ideas and the atmosphere of her life.

Chesterton confesses his amazement when they first met at discovering that she not only professed, but also practiced a religion. Clearly enough this constituted part of the charm and force of personality, which he was not alone in recognizing, and which he has conveyed in his autobiography as could no other.

"A QUEER CARD"

"She was a queer card," he says, when talking of their first meeting in the "fantastic suburb" of Bedford Park, where the couple talked about art and talked about religion and followed crazes and intellectual lectures.

> She wore a green velvet dress barred with grey fur, which I should have called artistic, but that she hated all the talk about art; and she had an attractive face, which I should have called elvish, but that she hated all the talk about elves. But what was arresting and almost blood-curdling about her in that social

---

[1] This is not accurate. Samuel Laman Blanchard was Frances's Great-Uncle. Jerrold was his best friend. Jerrold's daughter married Blanchard's son.

atmosphere, was not so much that she hated it, as that she was entirely unaffected by it.

She never knew what was meant by being "under the influence" of Yeats or Shaw or Tolstoy or anybody else. She was intelligent, with a great love of literature, and especially of Stevenson. But if Stevenson had come into the room and explained his personal doubts about personal immortality, she would have regretted that he should be wrong upon the point, but would otherwise have been utterly unaffected. She was not at all like Robespierre, except in a taste for neatness in dress, and yet it is only in Mr. Belloc's book on Robespierre that I have ever found any words that describe the unique quality that cut her off from the current culture and saved her from it. "God had given him to his mind a stone tabernacle in which certain great truths were preserved imperishable.

"G.K." WROTE TO HIS LADY

When "G.K." was writing his autobiography, Frances Chesterton's one request to Gilbert was to keep her out of it. But indeed from the year 1901, when this most happy married life began, down to his death two years ago, it was impossible that he should ever keep her out of his work, for she was ever in his thought.

Let anyone take down the volume of his collected poetry and scan the lyrics, and they will find that no poet since Browning has ever written more perfectly to his lady, or more deeply appreciated all that is meant by the great sacrament of marriage. It was ever in both their thoughts. The grief of those years of perfect companionship was the absence of the children that they longed for.

But unlike many childless couples that are embittered by disappointment and dislike the children of others, Gilbert and Frances loved their nieces and nephews and innumerable godchildren, and established with them an intensely personal relationship.

No mother could have discussed the future of an only child with more affection and understanding than I heard Frances show as she talked of some niece or nephew. They delighted in preparing parties and surprises for their young neighbors, and even went so far as to select by preference a railway carriage full of children.

To Beaconsfield

In 1908[2] they moved from Battersea, where they had lived in a flat, to their first little house at Beaconsfield—Overroads.

Mrs. Frances Chesterton found some satisfaction for what Gilbert has called her "hungry appetite for all the fruitful things like fields and gardens."

It was surely from his wife's attitude to life that Gilbert Chesterton drew the theory of woman's powers and position which he expressed so eloquently.

Woman was queen, and being queen, she had no use for a vote. This certainly was the view of Frances Chesterton.[3] She kept deliberately away from publicity. She wrote poetry which her friends loved, but she wrote it for her friends, not for the public. She was pleased when Walter de la Mare praised it,[4] but probably equally pleased that it had given joy to a Beaconsfield neighbor.

---

[2] Actually, 1909.

[3] This last was not true, and again proves Maisie Ward was not an intimate of Frances. Frances did want the vote, and was friends with many suffragettes.

[4] See "Walter de la Mare and Chesterton" in *Chesterton Review* Vol. 10, no. 1 (February 1984): 36. It is, then, a little surprising to find some evidence that Chesterton was definitely not de la Mare's literary cup of tea; in the over three thousand pages of his six

"Therefore I bring these rhymes to you,
Who brought the cross to me."

Says the dedication to Frances Chesterton of the *Ballad of the White Horse*, and I think it was largely this fact that made "G.K.C." linger so long in what was for him a half-way house between his youthful agnosticism and the logical outcome of his philosophy, the Catholic Church. But in fact, Gilbert Chesterton was received into the Church in 1922, and Frances only in 1926. Henceforward the little Catholic Church at Beaconsfield became central in both their lives. It was Frances Chesterton who brought to Candlemas Lane, Beaconsfield, the nursing sisters of the Bon Secours, and in her last illness she was under their loving care.

In our last talk together she told me that Candlemas Lane was a relic of the old Catholic titles of medieval Beaconsfield, and she sent me to visit the little Chapel in the hospital, so close to her own flower-filled room. The church of St. Teresa is the memorial of both Gilbert and Frances Chesterton. They rest together under Eric Gill's fine monument.[5]

⚘   ⚘   ⚘

---

anthologies of prose and verse, de la Mare quotes Chesterton only once, and even then the choice falls upon a passage from his study of Chaucer. But in his charming children's anthology, *Tom Tiddler's Ground* (1931, reprinted New York, 1961, 176) de la Mare gives pride of place to a poem by Frances Chesterton. Mrs. Chesterton's poem, "Children's Song of the Nativity" is set beside the exquisite fourteenth-century lyric "I sing of a Maiden." Frances and Walter, says Gilbert, discovered a shared passion for "collecting minute objects, of the nature of ornaments, but hardly to be seen with the naked eye."

[5] *Catholic Herald* (December 16, 1938): 9.

The London Times
December 14, 1938
Page 18

Mrs. G.K. Chesterton
A friend[6] writes: —
Frances Chesterton has died at the Hospital of Saint Joseph
in Beaconsfield. It is little more than two years ago on a
June night when the sky was like a thrush's egg with a single
star on it, that she followed G.K.'s bare coffin to the "decent
inn of death." Writing of her one writes of both: they seem
inseparable. Both of them were eternally secure in an armour
that protected them against the vulgarities of the world, the
squalors of life, and, at the end, this integrity was utterly
preserved and they passed quietly without noise, drama, or
impertinent observation. A few months ago, I took a small
boy to call upon her. "I think," he asked with great tact, "it
would be better not to mention Him to Her?" I agreed. I did
not know how little it was going to matter; how short the
parting was going to be. There was a toy cupboard there. It
was opened and denuded, that toy cupboard with the smallest
rabbit, the smallest candlestick, the smallest doll in the world,
and the youthful visitor departed with the smallest something
in the warm walnut of a hand that lay in mine.

When I first knew her she still lingered in the cool cloisters
of Anglo-Catholicism, and later I saw her pass to the warmer
earth of the Roman Church. For her, faith must always colour
existence, and I do not think she had very much sympathy
with anything that did not reflect it. "Anemones," G.K. had
said, "are the most Christian of flowers—they are the colours
of stained glass." She also would have found her Chartres in

---

[6] Mrs. J. L. Garvin.

a bunch of spring flowers. The last flowers I saw beside her bed were gentians in a bowl and, doubtless, watching them, she remembered that holy coat whose colour was better than good news. It will be some time before the inhabitants of Beaconsfield, passing by her house, without the daily bread of dropping in, will be able to console themselves with the thought that she is almost certainly more at home where she has gone.

❦   ❦   ❦

Mrs. Frances Chesterton
By E.C. Bentley

If Frances Chesterton is best remembered as the wife of Gilbert Chesterton, it is certainly not in the sense of her having sunk her individuality in that of her renowned husband. It is because theirs was so close and natural a union that those who knew them both could hardly think of them apart; and so it was for their thirty-five years of married life.

She was from the first a woman of firm personality and definite habits of mind, masked by gentleness and quietude of manner due, perhaps, to her serenity of religious conviction. G.K.C. met her first in a circle in which a loose culture and a vague soulfulness were the fashion; and what interested him in her was her active dislike of all such laxity and aimlessness.

She was practical, she was an organizer, she was, above all, a devout Anglo-Catholic, and her unparaded literary gift came out in the simple devotional poetry known only to her friends, and treasured by them. G.K.C., when he first met her, was a creedless pantheist; he became her convert: as he wrote in the dedication to the *Ballad of the White Horse*, "I bring these rhymes to you, who brought the Cross to me."

After he was received into the Church of Rome many years later, it was at her own time and by her own way of thought that she followed him.

The basis of what he called his "indefensibly fortunate and happy life" were the devotion of his mother and the devotion of his wife. He passed directly from the care of the one to the care of the other. Frances Chesterton made his household and home, shared his every interest, was his right-hand in all his dealings with the world. They had in common that goodness which, as he wrote, "is God's last word." Limitless charity, steady pursuit of the Christian ideal: they had humour, the love of friends, delight in letters and art. It was a perfect companionship.[7]

Geoffrey Shaw wrote on December 13, 1938, of Frances:

What a lovely spirit! Whenever I met her, I always felt I was in the presence of absolute goodness. She reflected this in her poetry quite simply and naturally. She was a heavenward mortal.

The following interesting tidbit was published just after Frances died. It is included here as a sort of proof of how little we know about Frances Chesterton's personal connections. These people who attended her funeral we can presume knew her well, loved her, respected her—these were her friends. And yet, many of

---

[7] "Mrs. Frances Chesterton: G.K.C. and His Wife," *The Observer* (December 18, 1938): 9. E. C. Bentley met GKC at St. Paul's when they were but boys, and one of the original members of the Junior Debating Club, and author of the well-known work *Trent's Last Case*. He married Violet Boileau, of whom Chesterton wrote many teasing poems.

the names are unfamiliar, unknown and likely unknowable. However, to probe even further into her life, it would be interesting to look these unknown folks up and see what their connection was to Frances and/or Gilbert. The following has been transcribed verbatim.

The Funeral of Mrs. G.K. Chesterton
The Catholic Herald
December 23, 1938
Page 12

The funeral of Mrs. G.K. Chesterton took place at Beaconsfield on Friday. The Requiem Mass was sung by Mgr. C.W. Smith, parish priest of St. Teresa's Church, assisted by Fr. Vincent McNabb, O.P.

Among those present were:
Mr. and Mrs. Luchian (*sic*) Oldershaw (brother-in-law and sister), Mrs. Cecil Chesterton (sister-in-law), Mr. Oliver Chesterton, Mr. Charles Johnson, Mr. and Mrs. Maurice Chesterton, Commander and Mrs. Smith (nephew and niece), Miss R.K. Bastable, Mr. Charles Bastable, Miss Dorothy Collins (secretary), and Mr. C. Child (staff).

Dr. V.G. Bakewell, Miss Phyllis Brandon, Mrs. R. Bedding, Miss Patsy Burke, Mr. and Mrs. Patrick Braybrooke, Dr. M. K. Braybrooke, Lady Bennett, Mr. Hilaire Belloc, Mr. E.C. Bentley, Rev. Fr. A. Brennan, Miss Buckland, Count and Countess Michael de la Bedoyere, Mrs. Bowley, Mr. and Mrs. Hugh Clerk, Mrs. G.N. Church, Miss M. Church, Mrs. Edred Corner, Mme. De Montaner, Mr. and Mrs. De Ayaia (representing Mr. and Mrs. P. Franklin), Mrs. R. Deeves, Mr. Eugene Dutton, Mr. Eastman, Major K. Fasken, Dr. P.J. Flood,

Captain and Mrs. Fairholm, Mr. and Mrs. J. Bally Gibson, Mr. B.C. Guiness (*sic*), Mr. and Mrs. Eric Gill, Mrs. B.J. Grey.

Mrs. J.L. Garvin, Miss Graham, Miss Garry, Mrs. S. T. Greenwood, Mrs. E. M. Henderson, Lady Heal, Mrs. M. Halford, Mrs. F.M. Harvey, Mr. and Mrs. Harvey, Mr. Maurice Healy, K.C., Miss Hickey, Mr. and Mrs. R. Jebb, Mrs. Hugh King, Mr. J.V.A. Kelley, Miss E. Lambert, Mr. and Mrs. R. Oswald Lamigeon, Mrs. De Luzy, Miss M.E. Langton, Fr. Lockyer, Miss McDonnell, Fr. F.G. Murphy, Miss K. Meates. Mr. G. Macdonald, Mr. S.S. Macdonald, Miss M. Maloney, Mrs. F. Mackrell, Fr. Maunsell, Mrs. Saxon-Mills, Miss Joan Saxon-Mills, Miss Grace Saxon-Mills, Mr. Gregor Macdonald, Mr. E.J. Macdonald (representing Westminster Catholic Inquiry Bureau), Mrs. Nicholl, Miss C. Nicholl, Mr. Richard O'Sullivan, K.C.

Mrs. Gordon Phillips (North Provincial Cross, Gerrard's Cross), Mr. and Mrs. H. S. Paynter, Mrs. Charles Preston, Mrs. Pepyat-Evans, Mrs. M. Ryan, Mr. Gerald Ryan, Mrs. Cecil Roscoe (representing Writers' Club Poetry Circle), Mrs. And Miss Rushton, the Rev. J. Rigby, the Rev. W.I. Rice, Mrs. Malcolm Smith, sisters from St. Joseph Nursing Home, Mr. and Mrs. Shee, Mr. F.G. Salter, Mr. Lawrence Soloman, Miss G. Shaw, the Rev. Hy Thompson (hon. Sec. Fellowship of the Philosophical Society of England), Miss R. Townsen (representing Miss Bore), Mr. J. Walsh, Miss L. Watts, Miss M. Wace, Mr. and Mrs. Hanzard Watt, and Mr. and the Hon. Mrs. Douglas Woodruff.

❧   ❧   ❧

Frances Chesterton's Bequests
Published in the *U.K. Guardian*
April 26, 1939, page 8

> Mrs. Frances Alice Chesterton, of Top Meadow, Beaconsfield, Buckinghamshire, widow of Gilbert Keith Chesterton, the well-known writer, and daughter of the late George William Blogg, the diamond merchant, died on December 12 last, leaving estate of the gross value of £30,752 with net personally £25,060 (estate duty £2,917). She gives:

> £1,500 and a piece of land to Miss Dorothy Edith Collins, and the use of her residence Top Meadow for one year and £500 towards its upkeep.

> And subject therein her property Top Meadow to the Roman Catholic Church, Beaconsfield.

> £2,000 to the Chesterton Memorial Fund if not already given.

> Any literary assets accruing from the sale of her husband's books to the Royal Literary Fund.

> Her personal papers and letters to Dorothy Edith Collins, to be dealt with at her discretion.

> £500 each to the Converts' Aid Society, the Catholic Relief Fund for Homeless and Destitute Men, St. Joseph's Hospital, Beaconsfield, the Crusade of Rescue.

> £250 to the convalescent home for journalists run by the Institute of Journalists.

> £250 to the Babies Convalescent Home, Beaconsfield.

> £500 to the Cecil Houses (Inc.) for Homeless Women.

And subject to the disposal of her effects, the residue of the property to Miss Dorothy Edith Collins for the Benefit of the Roman Catholic or other public objects, but desiring her to put aside £3,000 for the benefit of her nephew Peter Oldershaw for life.

❧   ❧   ❧

Here we can see the causes Gilbert and Frances cared about and contributed to, and in particular to note her willing money to Ada Chesterton's cause, the Cecil Houses, a cause which Frances and Gilbert fully supported.

❧   ❧   ❧

Just for curiosity's sake, let us for a moment look at G.K. Chesterton's will:

THIS IS THE LAST WILL AND TESTAMENT of me, Gilbert Keith Chesterton of Top Meadow Beaconsfield in the County of Buckinghamshire.

Executrix: I appoint my Wife, Frances Alice Chesterton Sole Executrix and Trustee of this my will. I give and bequeath the following legacies free of duty to:

Grace Gilbert
Winifred Gilbert
Kathleen Sandys
Dorothy Gilbert, two hundred pounds each.

To:
Patricia Burke, one thousand pounds.

To:

The parish priest of the Catholic Church of Beaconsfield, five hundred pounds.

To:

Dorothy Edith Collins, two thousand pounds and I DECLARE that Dorothy Edith Collins shall have the sole custody of all my papers, letters, manuscripts at Top Meadow and I request her to use them as may be most advantageous for the benefit of my Wife during her life and after her death for her own benefit but with full power to suppress or destroy any of them as she may in her absolute discretion deem well.

I GIVE and BEQUEATH all my books to my Wife for her life and after her death I direct that Dorothy Edith Collins shall be at liberty to choose any she may wish to have for herself and also to give any to any of my friends and that the remainder shall be sold and the proceeds given to the Royal Literary Fund.

I GIVE and BEQUEATH unto my Trustee and Dorothy Edith Collins jointly all my literary works published and unpublished and the copyrights therein and all my literary property of every kind (except my before mentioned papers, letters, and manuscripts) subject to and with the benefit of all contracts and licenses affecting the same with full power to deal with the same as in their absolute discretion they may think best as fully and effectually as I myself if living could to PROVIDED ALWAYS that such power shall be exercised only upon the advice and with the approval of A.P. Watt and Son of Hastings House Norfolk Street London . . . who shall be employed as Literary Agents and advisers in all matters relating to my literary property for as long as they are willing to act in that capacity and paid their usual commission and charges for all work done.

And as to the remainder of my estate of whatever kind I GIVE DEVISE and BEQUEATH the same unto my wife absolutely and lastly I revoke all former wills . . . signed G.K. Chesterton.

A Codicil was added on Feb 17, 1934:
In the event of my wife Frances predeceasing me:

1. I GIVE my property known as Top Meadow Beaconsfield to the Roman Catholic Church at Beaconsfield to be sold or used as may be determined for the welfare of the parish it being my wish that the property should if possible be used for Educational purposes such as a Convent School or Seminary

2. I GIVE AND BEQUEATH the following legacies free of duty namely to:

Edward Macdonald, two thousand pounds.

Ada Elizabeth Chesterton, one thousand pounds.

Lucian Oldershaw, one thousand pounds.

Rhoda Bastable, five hundred pounds.

Cecil Houses (Inc.) for Homeless Women, five hundred pounds.

Converts' Aid Society, five hundred pounds.

Catholic Fund for the Homeless and Destitute Men, five hundred.

Saint Joseph's Hospital, Beaconsfield, five hundred.

The Convalescent Home for Journalists, run by the Institute of Journalists, two hundred and fifty.

The Babies' Convalescent Home, Beaconsfield, two hundred fifty Mary Rushton, one hundred.

I GIVE and BEQUEATH the residue of my estate to Dorothy Edith Collins to be used at her absolute discretion for the benefit of Catholic or other public objects AND in all other respects I confirm my will, etc. Signed G.K.C.

The estate left by Gilbert to Frances was worth about \$141,945 in US dollars. The equivalent in today's dollars would be about \$2.3 million dollars.[8]

At the same time, Frances Chesterton made out a will, too. Her bequests are listed above, but here I will list the more personal items.

To my sister, Ethel Oldershaw, one thousand pounds.
To my three nieces: Gertrude Smith, Pamela Oldershaw and Catherine Oldershaw, one thousand pounds each.
One thousand pounds to be used for the education of Sheila. Smith (daughter of my niece Gertrude Smith).
To my nephew Basil Oldershaw, five hundred pounds.
To Michael Braybrooke, five hundred pounds.[9]
To my cousin Rhoda Bastable, one thousand pounds.
To Olga Burke, nine hundred pounds (or if not living, to her daughter, Patricia Burke).
To Madeline Hamilton Watts, one hundred pounds.

---

[8] "G.K. Chesterton Estate of \$141,945 Goes to Wife," *Chicago Daily Tribune* (September 10, 1936).

[9] Semi-adopted by Gilbert and Frances, from 1907-1917 he lived with them on all school holidays, served in the Royal Army as a Medical Corps; full name Michael Knollys Braybrooke.

To Edward MacDonald in trust for the education of his children in equal shares, one thousand five hundred pounds.
To Mary Rushton, one hundred pounds.
And to Dorothy Edith Collins, my furniture silver place china ornaments and other household effects, also all my jewelry, watches, trinkets and ornaments to be dealt with by her in accordance with my wishes of which she is fully aware.

There was a codicil dated October 12, 1938—exactly two months before she died—stating that she revokes the one thousand five hundred pounds given to Edward MacDonald for the education of his children.

❧   ❧   ❧

CHRONOLOGY OF FRANCES ALICE BLOGG CHESTERTON

1869	Birth of Frances Alice Blogg
1871	George Alfred Knollys born
1872	Ethel Laura born
1873	Helen Colborne born
1874	Gilbert Keith Chesterton born
1875	Helen died
1875	Gertrude Colborne born
1876	Unnamed brother stillborn
1878	Rachel Margaret born
1879	Cecil Chesterton born
1881	Rachel died
1875-83	German Kindergarten and elementary School in London
1883	Father's death
1886-87	Notting Hill High School (age 17-18)
1888-91	St. Stephen's College (age 19-21)

1891	Employed variously as teacher/tutor/governess
1894	I.D.K. Debating Society started
1895	Begins work at P.N.E.U. as secretary
1896	Meets Gilbert Keith Chesterton
1898	Midsummer—Becomes engaged
1899	Gertrude's accidental death
1900	GKC's first two books published, *The Wild Knight* and *Greybeards at Play*
1901	Marriage to G.K. Chesterton, set up house in Kensington for a few months
1901	Move to 48 Overstrand Mansions, Battersea, London
1902	Operation
1904	Gilbert and Frances meet Fr. John O'Connor
1906	Operation
1908	George Knollys commits suicide
1908	Operation to improve fertility
1909	Move to Beaconsfield—Overroads
1909	Accepts the fact that she cannot bear children
1911	*Ballad of the White Horse* published— dedicated to Frances
1911	Chesterton quote book published, selections made by Frances
1912-1913	Marconi Scandal
1914-1915	GKC's major illness, almost dies
1915	"Poems" by Frances Chesterton published privately and given to friends
1917	GKC's brother Cecil marries Ada Eliza Jones— a.k.a John Keith Prothero
1918	Cecil dies
1919	Palestine tour
1920	Italy tour

1921	United States tour
1922	Edward Chesterton dies
1922	GKC converts to Roman Catholicism—move to Top Meadow
1922	Writes the play *The Children's Crusade* and Geoffrey Shaw sets "Crusader's Carol," a.k.a "The Shepherds Found Thee by Night" to music
1922	"How Far is it To Bethlehem?" published by Novello & Co as musical score
1923	"The Shepherds Found Thee by Night"—lyrics by Frances Chesterton published by Novello & Co.
1924	*The Children's Crusade, Sir Cleges, The Christmas Gift: Three Plays for Children* published by Samuel French
1925	*Piers Plowman's Pilgrimage* published by Samuel French
1926	25th wedding anniversary
1926	Frances converts to Roman Catholicism
1926	Dorothy Collins hired as GKC's secretary
1927	Poland trip, *Faith and Fable* performed in Bath
1928	*How Far Is It To Bethlehem and Other Carols* published by Sheed and Ward
1929	Italy trip, Rome, audience with Pope Pius XI, meets Mussolini
1930/31	United States again, Canada—Frances ill in Tennessee
1931	GKC began radio talks on the BBC
1932	Dorothy Collins converts to Roman Catholicism
1932	Trip to Dublin

1933	Marie Louise Chesterton dies. Blanche Blogg dies
1934	Rome again
1935	Spain, France, Italy, Switzerland, and Belgium
1935	GKC nominated for the Nobel Prize for Literature[10]
1936	Reviews *I Lived In a Slum* by Ada Chesterton in *G.K.'s Weekly*
1936	Lourdes and Lisieux, France
1936	GKC dies
1938	Frances diagnosed with cancer
1938	Frances dies

THE CHILDREN OF GEORGE AND BLANCHE BLOGG

Frances Alice Blogg, June 28, 1869
George Alfred Knollys, April 10, 1871[11]
Ethel Laura, May 2, 1872[12]
Helen Colborne, November 22, 1873[13]
Gertrude Colborne, May 14, 1875[14]

---

[10] Chris Chan, "Why Didn't G.K. Chesterton Ever Win the Nobel Prize for Literature?" *Gilbert* Vol. 7, no. 6 (2004): 28.

[11] Godfathers were William Wilson and Ben Nattali (The Library, Windsor Castle), godmother was Emma Heaton.

[12] Godfather Uncle Wm. Cosmo Monkhouse, noted poet and art critic. Godmothers Alice Martin, daughter of Charles Martin, diamond merchant, and Mary Braybrooke, cousin of Blanche Blogg.

[13] Godfather, her uncle, the Honourable Edmund Colborne, godmothers, Aunt Julia Marsden Blogg and Blanche Blogg, her mother; died January 24, 1875, at about fifteen months, cause of death—gastric fever and bronchitis.

[14] Godfather, her uncle, the Honourable Edmund Colborne, godmothers, Aunt Julia Marsden Blogg and Lilly Ivan Muller.

A son, December 11, 1876, stillborn[15]

Rachel Margaret, August 15, 1878[16]

KNOWN ADDRESSES WHERE FRANCES
LIVED PRIOR TO HER MARRIAGE:

1869	No. 22 Hart Street
1870-71	No. 20 Baker Street
1875-78	No. 37, Upper Bedford Place
1881	17 Tavistock Square
1881	1 Oxford Villas Brown Road
1882-84	Spencer House, No. 22, Woodstock Road, Bedford Park, Chiswick
1885-86	1 Thames Place, Putney
1886-1901	No. 8 Bath Road

LIST OF KNOWN PUBLISHED WORKS &
MUSIC OF FRANCES CHESTERTON

1897	*L'Umile Pianta*	July, Conference Write-up for P.N.E.U.
1898	*L'Umile Pianta*	July, Conference Write-up for P.N.E.U.
1900	*L'Umile Pianta*	July, "The Suggestiveness of a Conference"
1900	*Parents' Review*	Volume XI, "The Open Road"

---

[15] The Blogg family Bible, as shown to me by Frances's grand nephews.

[16] Godfather, Alfred B. Keymer and godmothers, Sonya Keymer and Emma Blogg, and died Feb 6, 1881, cause of death—bronchitis and pneumonia at two and a half years of age.

1901	*Parents' Review*	Volume XII P.N.E.U. <u>Natural History Clubs</u>
1908	*Westminster Gazette*	March 25, "Lady Day"
1908	*Westminster Gazette*	June 24th, "Midsummer Day"
1909	*Westminster Gazette*	March 2nd, "Winter's Prisoners"
1909	*Westminster Gazette*	August 10, "The Unforgotten Feet"
1909	*Westminster Gazette*	December 19th, "Mater Invicta"
1910	*Westminster Gazette*	April 12th, "An Unknown April"
1910	*Westminster Gazette*	June 26th, "The Longest Day"
1910	*Westminster Gazette*	November 1st, "All Saints' Day"
1912	*Westminster Gazette*	February 21st, "To Gertrude Monica"
1912	*The New Witness*	Nov. 7th, "All Souls Day (Of Your Charity)"
1913	*Westminster Gazette*	January 7th, "The Small Dreams"
1913	*Westminster Gazette*	March 25th, "Une Nuit Blanche"
1913	*Ashburton Guardian*	March 27, "The Small Dreams"
1913	*The New Witness*	March 27, "Our Lady's Day"
1913	*The Living Age*	March 29, "The Small Dreams"
1913	*Westminster Gazette*	October 25th, "So Must It Be"

1913	Thomas Bird Mosher	*The Mosher Books*, "The Small Dreams"
19??	*Westminster Gazette*	Nov. 13, "London Leaves"
1914	*The New Witness*	May 21, "The Vale of Avalon"
1914	*The New Witness*	Sept. 10, "To A Rich Man"
1914	*The Daily Chronicle*	November 2nd, "Le Jour Des Morts"
1915	Jarrold & Sons	"Le Jour Des Morts" reprinted in the anthology, *Lest We Forget*
1915	*The Daily Chronicle*	November 2nd, "All Saints & All Souls"
1915	*The Daily Chronicle*	June 12, "Is There Freedom Left in England?"
1915	Beaconsfield	*Poems* Privately published
1917	*The Daily Chronicle*	November 1st, "Hurt Not the Earth"
1918	Stainer & Bell	"Here Is the Little Door" (Lyrics)
1920	*The New Witness*	July 2, "A Ballade of Fulfillment of Craving"
1921	MacMilliam & Co.	"To Felicity Who Calls Me Mary" in *A Book of English Verse on Infancy & Childhood*
1922	*Daily News*	December 25th, "How Far Is It To Bethlehem," won prize in the carol competition

1922	Novello & Co.	"How Far Is It To Bethlehem?" (Lyrics)
1922	*The New Witness*	Dec. 8, book review of *On the Road in Holland* by Charles Harper
1923	*The New Witness*	Jan 5, book reviews of *Georgian Poetry 1920-1922, edited by E. Marsh, and Shakespeare and Hardy: an Anthology of Lyrics* by Sir A. Methuen
1923	*The New Witness*	Jan 26, book review of *The Anchorhold*, by Enid Dinnis
1923	*The New Witness*	Feb 16, book review of *Short Stories,* by R. Ellis Roberts
1923	*The New Witness*	Feb 23, book review of *As You See It,* by F.L. Garvin; and poem, "For an Eighteenth Century Air"
1923	*The New Witness*	Mar 23, book review of *Next of Kin*, by E. Norris
1923	Novello & Co.	"The Shepherds Found Thee by Night" (a.k.a. "The Crusader's Carol") (Lyrics), in *The Musical Times* (Vol. 64, No. 970)
1923	*The Observer*	August 26th, "A Sonnet"
1924	Samuel French, Ltd.	*The Children's Crusade, Sir Cleges, The Christmas Gift: Three Plays for Children*

1924	Houghton Mifflin	"How Far Is It To Bethlehem? reprinted in *The Magic Carpet: Poems for Travelers*, selected by Mrs. Waldo Richards
1925	*Oakdene Magazine*	July, "June 21ˢᵗ"
1925	Samuel French, Ltd.	*Piers Plowman's Pilgrimage: A Morality Play*
1927	Beaconsfield	*Christmas Carols*, a book of poems
1927	Methuen & Co.	*Piers Plowman's Pilgrimage*, included in the collected book of plays, *The Curtain Rises*
1927	Oxford University Press	"How Far Is It To Bethlehem" (as "Nativity Song") in *Modern Verse for Little Children*, Michal Williams, ed.
1928	Oxford University Press	"How Far Is It To Bethlehem?" in *The Oxford Book of Carols*, Percy Dearmer, et al., eds.
1929	*Evening Post*	December 17, "A Nativity Song" (a.k.a. "How Far Is It to Bethlehem?" a.k.a. "Children's Song of the Nativity")

1931	Collins' Clear-Type Press	"How Far Is It to Bethlehem" in *Tom Tiddler's Ground: A Book of Poetry for the Junior and Middle Schools* (1931), Walter de la Mare (1873-1956), ed.
1932	*American Journal of Nursing*	December 1932, "Children's Song of the Nativity"
1932	*The Writer's Club Anthology*	Edited by Margaret L. Woods, "Sonnet" (a.k.a, "Why did you Call Beloved in the Night?") and "The Cradle of the Winds" and "Sed Ex Deo Nati Sunt"
1934	Sheed & Ward	"The Lowly Gifts" in *Gospel Rhymes*
1935	*The Observer*	June 12, 1935, "Alle Vogel Sind Shon Da"
1935	Harcourt Brace & Company	*Best Poems of 1935* "Alle Vogel Sind Shon Da"
1936	*Woman's Home Companion*	December 1936, "How Far Is It To Bethlehem"
1937	*The Observer*	October 3, "Must We Forever Say a Long Farewell"
1938	*UK Guardian/ Observer*	November 27, "Things to Think About"
1949	Oxford University Press	"Nativity Song," *Modern Verse for Little Children*

1954   Edwin Ashdown Ltd. "The Kings of Old," lyrics,
        music by Eva Fovargue

SOURCES:

Balfour, Ian. "The Agra Diamond," *Famous Diamonds*, http://famousdiamonds.tripod.com/agradiamond.html.

Balston, Jenny. *The Story of St. Stephen's College*, (Kent: The Old St. Stephenites Society, 1994).

Barker, Dudley. *G.K. Chesterton: A Biography* (New York: Stein & Day, 1973).

Basset, Bernard S.J. "Frances & Gilbert," *The Sacred Heart Messenger*, (June 1984), 16-18.

Blanchard, Edward Leman. *The Life and Reminiscences of E.L. Blanchard*, 1891. http://archive.org/details/lifeandreminisce02blanuoft.

Blanchard, Samuel Laman. http://en.wikipedia.org/wiki/Samuel_Laman_Blanchard

Blogg & Martin: http://www.archive.org/stream/galaxymag06newyrich/galaxymag06newyrich_djvu.txt.

Blogg & Martin: http://www.archive.org/stream/populartreatiseo-oofeucrich/populartreatiseooofeucrich_djvu.txt.

Boyd, Ian C.S.B. "Dorothy Collins, 1894-1988," *Chesterton Review* Vol. 14, no. 4 (November 1988).

Braybrooke, Patrick F.R.S.L. Fellowship of the Royal Society of Literature, *I Remember G.K. Chesterton* (Epsom: Dorling & Co.), April, 1938.

Brown, Nancy Carpentier. "Happy Evenings," *Gilbert* Vol. 15, no. 8 (July/August 2012): 27.

Brown, Nancy Carpentier. "Mrs. Cecil Chesterton," *Gilbert* Vol. 15, no. 3 (November/December 2012): 16.

Brown, Nancy Carpentier. "Frances Chesterton and Her Father," *Gilbert* Vol. 14, no. 5 (March/April 2011): 32.

Brown, Nancy Carpentier. "Brother-in-Law of G.K. Chesterton, George Alfred Knollys Blogg (1871-1908)," *Gilbert* Vol. 17, no. 2-3 (Nov./Dec. 2013): 8-10.

Brown, Nancy Carpentier. *How Far Is It To Bethlehem: The Plays and Poetry of Frances Chesterton* (Chesterton & Brown Publishing, 2012).

Central and Cecil Housing: http://www.ccht.org.uk/main.cfm.

Chesterton, Ada Eliza (Mrs. Cecil). *The Chestertons* (London: Chapman & Hall, 1941).

Chesterton, Ada Eliza (Mrs. Cecil). *In Darkest London* (London: Stanley Paul, 1926).

Chesterton, Ada Eliza (Mrs. Cecil): http://underworldarchaeology.wordpress.com/2012/04/12/ada-chesterton-slumming-it-in-1920s-london/.

Chesterton, Ada Eliza: http://www.oxforddnb.com/templates/article.jsp?articleid=39077&back=.

Chesterton, Frances. *The Children's Crusade, Sir Cleges, The Christmas Gift: Three Plays for Children,* (London: Samuel French, Ltd., 1924).

Chesterton, Frances. *How Far Is It To Bethlehem and Other Carols*, Sheed & Ward, year unknown.

Chesterton, Frances. *Piers Plowman's Pilgrimage: A Morality Play* (London: Samuel French, Ltd., 1925).

Chesterton, Frances. *Poems* (Beaconsfield: Excelsior Printing Works at 24, Aylesbury Street, 1915).

Chesterton, Frances. http://www.chesterton.org/discover-chesterton/other-resources/frances-chesterton/.

Brown, Nancy Carpentier. "The Woman Who Was Chesterton," talk given at the 29th Annual Meeting of the American Chesterton Society, http://www.chesterton.org/store/#!/~/product/category=704003&id=7492171.

Brown, Nancy Carpentier. "The Plays and Poetry of Frances Chesterton," talk given at the 31st Annual Meeting of the American Chesterton Society, http://www.chesterton.org/shop/the-plays-and-poetry-of-frances-chesterton/.

Brown, Nancy Carpentier. "The Marriage of Gilbert and Frances Chesterton," talk given at the 33rd Annual Meeting of the American Chesterton Society.

Chesterton, Gilbert Keith. *Autobiography* (San Francisco: Ignatius Press, 2006). And his poems (Ignatius Press, three volumes in *The Collected Works*, Vol. 10 A, B, and C) and everything else he wrote.

Chesterton, Lilian. "Further Chesterton Recollections," *Mark Twain Quarterly* Vol. 5, no. 4 (Spring 1943).

Clemens, Cyril. *Chesterton as Seen by His Contemporaries* (New York: Gordon Press, 1972).

The Collected Works of G.K. Chesterton, Ignatius Press, all volumes.

Conlon, Denis. *Basil Howe: A Story of Young Love* (London: New City, 2001).

Dale, Alzina Stone. *The Outline of Sanity: A Biography of G.K. Chesterton* (Grand Rapids, Mich.: Eerdmans, 1982).

Davenport-Hines, Richard. *Ettie: The Intimate Life and Dauntless Spirit of Lady Desborough* (London: Weidenfeld & Nicolson, 2008).

Evans, Tony. "Chesterton Around the World: News from London," *Gilbert* Vol. 1, no. 6 (February 1998), description of a walk through Bedford Park.

Greene, Dana. *The Living of Maisie Ward* (Notre Dame, Indiana: University of Notre Dame Press, 1997).

Hansen, Ron. *Gerard Manley Hopkins: Exiles* (New York: Farrar, Straus and Giroux, 2008).

Heaton, Mary Margaret: http://www.dictionaryofarthistorians. org/heatonm.htm.

Hood, Alban, O.S.B. "In Diebus Illis: Father Ignatius Rice, O.S.B., (1883-1955)," *The Chesterton Review* Vol. 15, no. 3 (August 1989): 354-363.

Howard, Montague. *Old London Silver, Its History, Its Makers and Its Marks* (London: C. Scribner's Sons, 1903).

Jerrold, Douglas. http://www.findagrave.com/cgi-bin/fg.cgi?page=gr&GSln=jerrold&GSiman=1&GS-cid=658403&GRid=12603206&.

Jerrold, Walter. *Douglas Jerrold and 'Punch'* (St. Martin's Street, London: Macmillan & Co., 1910).

Jessey, Cornelia, and Sussman, Irving. "Frances and Gilbert Chesterton," in *Spiritual Partners: Profiles in Creative Marriage* (New York: Crossroad, 1982): 20-30.

Johnson, Reginald Brinsley. *Minute Book*; London, 1894-1899, The I Don't Know Debating Society, Beinecke Rare Book and Manuscript Library, Yale University. http://orbis.library.yale.edu/vwebv/search?searchArg=chesterton&searchCode=GKEY^*&limitTo=TYPE%3Dp%3F&recCount=50&searchType=1&page.search.search.button=Search

Kent, J.J. "History of the Akbar Shah or Jena Ghir Shah Diamond," http://www.jjkent.com/articles/akbar-shah-diamond.htm.

Keymer, James. http://www.bodley.ox.ac.uk/johnson/exhibition/201.htm. http://collections.vam.ac.uk/item/O363660/handkerchief-unknown/

Kurin, Richard. *Hope Diamond: The Legendary History of a Cursed Gem* (New York: Harper Perennial, 2007).

Lawrence E., ed., P. Woodham-Smith. "History of the Froebel Movement in England," in *Friedrich Froebel and English Education* (1952).

Monkhouse, William Cosmo: https://en.wikipedia.org/wiki/William_Cosmo_Monkhouse

Murphy, William M. *Family Secrets: William Butler Yeats and His Relatives*, (Syracuse, N.Y.: Syracuse University Press, 1995).

Noel, Conrad. *Conrad Noel: An Autobiography* (London: J.M. Dent & Sons Ltd., 1945).

O'Connor, John. "The Fantastic Courtship," in *The Voice of St. Jude* (May 1948): 9, 24-26.

O'Connor, John. *Father Brown on Chesterton* (Burns Oates & Washbourne; 2nd edition, 1938).

Oddie, William. *Chesterton and the Romance of Orthodoxy: The Making of GKC 1874-1908*, (Oxford: Oxford University Press, 2008).

Old Bailey Proceedings Online: http://oldbaileyonline.org, version 7.0, 18 March 2013), April 1823 (18230409).

Parents' National Educational Union: http://www.redeemer.ca/charlotte-mason.

Parents' National Educational Union. *In Memoriam: Charlotte M. Mason*, London: PNEU, 1923).

Paynter, Hugh. "Gilbert and Frances Chesterton," *Catholic Truth* (Autumn 1961): 8-11.

Pearce, Joseph. *Wisdom and Innocence: A Life of G.K. Chesterton* (San Francisco: Ignatius Press, 1996).

Sewell, Brocard, "A Memorable Chesterton," *Catholic Herald* (February 13, 1976): 7.

Sheridan, Richard Brinsley: https://en.wikipedia.org/wiki/Richard_Brinsley_Sheridan.

Sieveking, Lancelot (Lance). *The Eye of the Beholder* (London: Hulton Press, 1957).

Sieveking, Lancelot (Lance): http://en.wikipedia.org/wiki/Lance_Sieveking.

Slater, Michael. *Douglas Jerrold 1803-1857* (London: Duckworth Press, 2002).

Smith, Julia. *The Elusive Father Brown: The Life of Mgr. John O'Connor* (Herefordshire: Gracewing, 2010).

Speaight, Robert. *The Life of Eric Gill*, (New York: P.J. Kennedy & Sons, 1966).

Stanton, Elizabeth Cady, Anthony, Susan B., Gordon, Ann D. *The Selected Papers of Elizabeth Cady Stanton and Susan B. Anthony* (New Jersey: New Brunswick, 1997-2013).

Stewart, W.A.C. "Henry Morley and Johannes and Bertha Ronge," in *Progressives and Radicals in English Education 1750–1970* (1972).

Sullivan, John. *G.K. Chesterton: A Centenary Appraisal* (Harper & Row, 1974).

Tibbetts, John C. "High Tea with Judith Lea," *Gilbert* Vol. 3, no. 6 (April/May 2000).

Titterton, W. R. *G. K. Chesterton: A Portrait* (London: Alexander Ouseley, Ltd., 1936).

Valentine, Ferdinand. *Father Vincent McNabb, O.P.: Portrait of a Great Dominican* (Maryland: Newman Press, 1955).

Ward, Maisie. "Frances, Wife of G.K. Chesterton," *Catholic Herald* (December 16, 1938): 9.

Ward, Maisie. *Gilbert Keith Chesterton* (New York: Sheed & Ward, 1943).

Ward, Maisie. *Return to Chesterton* (New York: Sheed & Ward, 1952).

Williams, Ralph Vaughan. http://www.rvwsociety.com/about-society.html. http://www.rvwsociety.com/journal_pdfs/rvw_journal_11.pdf.

Wilson, A.N. *Hilaire Belloc: A Biography* (New York: Atheneum Books, 1984).

Wojtczak, Helena. *Notable Sussex Women: 580 Biographical Sketches* (Padstow, England: The Hastings Press, 2008).

Wright, Elliott. Chapter Four, "Gilbert Chesterton and Frances Blogg Chesterton", in *Holy Company: Christian Heroes and Heroines* (New York: Macmillan Publishing Co. Inc., 1980), 126.

ABOUT THE AUTHOR

Nancy Carpentier Brown is the wife of artist Michael Brown, and mother of two amazing young women. She became interested in the life of Frances Chesterton as she read biographies of G.K. Chesterton, and recognized in Frances a kindred spirit. Brown wanted to know more about the woman who was Mrs. G.K. Chesterton, and found that there was a dearth of information about her life. And so she took it upon herself to remedy that, and this book was born.

Brown is the author of numerous Chestertonian titles, including: *The Father Brown Reader: Stories from Chesterton*, *The Father Brown Reader II: More Stories from Chesterton*, *Chesterton's The Blue Cross: Study Edition* and *A Study Guide for G. K. Chesterton's St. Francis of Assisi*; *The Mystery of Harry Potter: A Catholic Family Guide*; *How Far Is It To Bethlehem: The Plays and Poetry of Frances Chesterton*; *The Children's Crusade*; *Faith & Fable: A Masque*, *The Three Kings: A Play for Christmas*. Brown is the winner of the Kilby Research Grant for her work on Frances A. Chesterton. She is a regular contributor to *Gilbert*, and has had articles, chapters, and poems published in many other magazines and books.

INDEX

1914-15
major illness of G.K.C., 96

ALLPORT
Nellie, 88, 153

ARNDT
Margaret Heaton, 8, 11, 16, 18, 22, 34, 56, 204, 255
Paul, 22

BARING
Maurice, 114-15, 117, 125, 191, 215, 222

BASTABLE
Charles, 52, 253
Rhoda, 51, 67, 143, 153, 161, 235, 240-41

BEACONSFIELD, 37, 78-79, 82-85, 87, 90, 99, 114, 126, 131, 144-45, 152, 161, 165, 176, 183, 185-86, 188, 199, 207, 211-13, 219, 227, 230-33, 235, 237-41, 243, 248, 250, 254

BEDFORD PARK, 1-2, 15-16, 20, 22, 33, 62, 67, 75, 88, 176, 228, 246, 255

BEERBOHM
Max, 98

BELLOC
Elodie, 44, 67, 77, 95
Hilaire, 2, 44-45, 61-62, 69, 71, 77, 83, 95, 108-09, 113, 131, 157, 165, 178, 181, 186, 213, 216, 229, 235, 259

BENTLEY
E.C., iii, 20, 25-26, 178, 185, 233-35

BLANCHARD
Mary Margaret, 7-8
Samuel Laman, 7, 228, 252

BLOGG
Blanche, 4, 6-8, 11-14, 18, 21, 32, 42, 51, 159, 178, 190, 200, 245
Ethel, ix-x, iii, 3, 8, 13, 15-16, 18, 22, 32, 42, 45, 58, 61, 76, 82, 87, 114, 116, 153, 157, 190, 200, 207, 209, 214, 240-42, 245
George Frederick, 4-5
George William, 4-6, 227, 237

Gertrude, 8, 13-14, 20, 22-23, 40-41, 43, 61, 78, 84-85

Helen, 8, 242

Knollys, 7-8, 13-14, 16, 17, 22-23, 32, 42, 57, 65, 69-70, 71, 72-73, 74, 80, 83, 129, 133, 242-243, 245, 253

Rachel, 8, 12, 242

BOORE
William, 15, 56

BURKE
Edmund, 88

CHESSHIRE
Kathleen, 125, 151, 153, 155, 168

CHESTERTON
Ada. *See* Prothero, J.K.

Cecil, 7, 20, 33, 53, 54, 55, 60-61, 89-90, 96, 106-11, 113-15, 132, 213, 216

Edward, 44, 58-59, 126

Marie Louise, 15, 33, 93, 116, 126, 178, 200, 245

CHILD
Doris, 51

CHRISTIAN SOCIAL UNION, 60-61

CHRISTIAN SOCIALISM, 59-60

CHURCHILL
Winston, 106

COCKERELL
Douglas, 20

COLLINS
Dorothy, 68, 76, 151-57, 159-60, 167, 169, 171, 174, 180, 186, 199-200, 207, 212, 214, 217, 235, 237, 238-239, 241-42, 244, 252

CONVERSION
of Dorothy Collins, 175

of Cecil Chesterton, 54

of Frances Chesterton, 146

of G.K. Chesterton, 87

COULTON
George, 154, 181-83, 189

Crystal Palace, 5

D'AVIGDOR
Waldo, 20, 102

DEATH
of Frances Chesterton, 209

of G.K. Chesterton, 184

of George William Blogg (Frances's father), 12

of Gertrude Blogg, 40

of Knollys Blogg, 72

DEDICATION
of *Ballad of the White Horse* to Frances, 224

DICKENS
Charles, 7-8, 18, 56, 60, 83, 86, 97

DISTRIBUTISM, 61, 130, 142

DISTRIBUTIST LEAGUE, 142-43

DÜRER
Albrecht, 8

EBHART
Frances Catherine, 4

EMANCIPATION OF DOMESTICITY, 37

ENGAGEMENT, 31-33

FABIAN SOCIETY, 60

FAIRY TALES FROM THE GERMAN FORESTS, 22

FERMIN
Annie, 33, 52, 58

Fisher Unwin, 44

FROEBEL
Education, 13

G.K.'s WEEKLY, 142,-43, 151, 159, 179, 183, 186, 223

GIRL'S REALM MAGAZINE, 23, 73

GREYBEARDS AT PLAY, 44

HEATON
Margaret. *See* Arndt

Mary Margaret, 20, *See* Blanchard

HENLEY
William Ernest, 39, 42

Highgate Cemetery, 12

HINKSON
Katharine Tynan, 94

HONEYMOON, 52-56

HOW FAR IS IT TO BETHLEHEM POEM
Frances Chesterton, v, vii, 80, 83, 94, 100-04, 128, 136, 139, 156, 160, 162, 166, 174, 194, 201, 209, 211, 244, 248, 249, 250-51, 253

I.D.K. DEBATING SOCIETY, 2, 16-17, 19, 20, 22, 62, 88

INFERTILITY, 53, 55, 71, 76-78, 81, 194, 225

JARDINE
William, 9

JERROLD
Douglas, 7-8, 228

JOHNSON
Reginald "Rex" Brimley, 20, 22, 44, 59, 78

JONES
Ada. *See* Prothero, J.K.

JUNIOR DEBATING CLUB, 44, 99, 102, 234

KEYMER
Blanche. *See* Blogg

James, 5-6

Mary Margaret. *See* Blanchard

KIPLING
Rudyard, 22-23

KNOX
Father Ronald, 84, 117, 129,
130-32, 146, 158-59, 162-63,
181, 186, 192

L'UMILE PIANTA, 23, 38, 71

LADIES' SCHOOL, 13-14

LEA
Judith, 157-58

LEDGERS & LITERATURE,
23, 73

LLOYD GEORGE, 89

LLOYDS OF LONDON, 22

LONDON, 1, 2, 5, 7, 12, 18, 22,
69, 80, 86, 93, 108-09, 111,
139, 147, 159, 186, 201, 214,
239, 242-43

**LONDON SCHOOL OF
MEDICINE FOR WOMEN**, 22

MACGREGOR
Archie, 2, 20

MACKEY
Aidan, 54, 59, 68, 79, 110,
183, 213, 215-16

MAIDENHEAD, 76, 87, 114

MANALIVE, 18, 36, 86

MARCONI SCANDAL, 89

MARTIN
Charles, 4-5, 9

MASON
Charlotte, 23-24, 26

McNABB
Father Vincent, 110, 117,
132-33, 183-86, 192, 223, 235

MEYNELL
Alice, 26, 67

MONKHOUSE
Cosmo, 8, 59

MONTESSORI EDUCATION,
13

NESBIT
E., 2

NEWMAN
John Henry Cardinal, 147

NICHOLL
Family, 161, 181, 236

NOEL
Conrad, 44, 49, 53, 62, 165

NOTRE DAME, 143, 164, 169,
170, 173, 178

NOTTING HILL HIGH, 14,
228

O'CONNOR
Father John, 62-69, 74, 85, 88,
94-98, 117, 129-132, 136-38,
144-46, 148, 155, 159, 164,
167, 169, 181-82, 185-91, 194,
199, 204, 208, 212, 214, 223,
243

OAKDENE
School, 83, 139, 165

OLDERSHAW
Ethel. *See* Blogg, Ethel

Lucian, 3, 18, 20, 41, 52, 61, 74, 87, 114, 122, 153, 209, 217, 240

ORTHODOXY, 35, 73, 211, 219

OVERROADS, 79, 88, 90, 125, 230, 243

OXFORD BOOK OF CAROLS, vi, 250

P.N.E.U, 21-23, 31, 37, 42, 44, 46-47, 49, 57, 60, 71-72, 243

PANKHURST
Emmeline, 89

PARENTS' NATIONAL EDUCATIONAL UNION. *See* P.N.E.U.

PARENTS' REVIEW, 22-3, 34-35, 37, 46, 71, 246-47

PERCY
Herbert S., 20, 250

PHILLIMORE
Jack, 20

PINERO
Arthur, 2

PISSARRO
Camille, 2, 20

POWELL
Yorke, 2

PROTHERO
J.K., viii, x-xi, 7, 53-55, 69, 77, 79, 89, 92, 106-15, 127, 138, 143, 155, 159, 178, 186, 212-18, 238, 240, 243, 245, 253

RICE
Father Ignatius, 130-31, 185-86, 189, 236, 255

RICHARDS
Grant, 44

SHAW
George Bernard, 60, 86, 92-93, 109, 147, 188, 193, 229

SHEEN
Fulton, 185

SHERIDAN
Richard Brinsley, 107

SIEVEKING
Isabel, 26, 34, 39, 46, 57, 67, 71

Lance, 26, 34, 47, 73, 257-58

SLADE SCHOOL OF ART, 8, 75

SMITH
Adolphe, 20

SPENCER
Freda, 106, 153, 155

SPIRITUALISM, 16, 75

ST. FRANCIS OF ASSISI, 37, 135, 168, 222, 260

ST. PAUL'S SCHOOL, 14, 234

ST. STEPHEN'S COLLEGE, 14, 16, 21, 51, 59, 87, 228, 242, 252

STEVENSON
Robert Louis, 18, 35, 83, 229

TENNYSON
Alfred, Lord, 16

THE MAN WHO WAS THURSDAY, 1, 18, 110, 137, 143

THE WILD KNIGHT, 44, 45, 62, 211, 219

TODHUNTER
Dr. John, 2

TOP MEADOW, 37, 79, 88, 126, 128, 151, 157, 161, 176, 178, 181, 186, 200, 204

VERNEDE
Robert, 20

WAIN
Mildred, 3, 102

WARD
Maisie, ii, 6, 13-15, 18, 54-55, 68, 99, 145, 148, 155, 160, 164, 198, 200, 217-18, 227, 230

WATT, A.P., 44, 239

WEDDING, 46, 51-52, 54-55, 57, 77, 127

WELLS
H.G., 92, 136, 147, 216-17

WHAT'S WRONG WITH THE WORLD, 37

WHITMAN
Walt, 17

WORLD WAR ONE, vi

YEATS
John Butler, 52

Lily, 13, 52

Lollie, 13, 20, 52

William Butler, 2, 16, 20, 52, 189, 256

 TAN·BOOKS

TAN Books is the Publisher You Can Trust With Your Faith.

TAN Books was founded in 1967 to preserve the spiritual, intellectual, and liturgical traditions of the Catholic Church. At a critical moment in history TAN kept alive the great classics of the Faith and drew many to the Church. In 2008 TAN was acquired by Saint Benedict Press. Today TAN continues to teach and defend the Faith to a new generation of readers.

TAN publishes more than 600 booklets, Bibles, and books. Popular subject areas include theology and doctrine, prayer and the supernatural, history, biography, and the lives of the saints. TAN's line of educational and homeschooling resources is featured at TANHomeschool.com.

TAN publishes under several imprints, including TAN, Neumann Press, ACS Books, and the Confraternity of the Precious Blood. Sister imprints include Saint Benedict Press, Catholic Courses, and Catholic Scripture Study International.

For more information about TAN,
or to request a free catalog, visit
TANBooks.com

Or call us toll-free at
(800) 437-5876

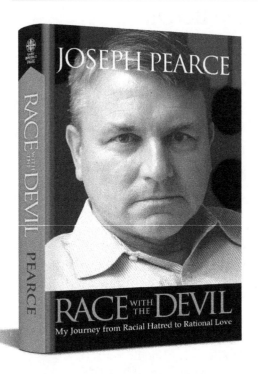

Spread the Faith with . . .

CPSIA information can be obtained
at www.ICGtesting.com
Printed in the USA
LVHW111631070619
620535LV00002B/313/P